D0852941

THE LOGIC OF PARTY DEMOCRACY

THE LOGIC OF PARTY DEMOCRACY

Alan Ware

University of Warwick

St. Martin's Press   New York

©1979 Alan Ware

All rights reserved. For information, write:
St. Martin's Press, Inc., 175 Fifth Avenue, New York, N.Y. 10010

Printed in Great Britain

First published in the United States of America in 1979

ISBN 0–312–49450–5

Library of Congress Cataloging in Publication Data

Ware, Alan.
   The logic of party democracy.
   Includes bibliographical references.
   1. Political parties. 2. Democracy.
I. Title.
JF2049.W28   1979   329'.02   79–1109
ISBN 0–312–49450–5

For Batperson

Contents

Tables and Figure

Preface

This book began as an attempt to show the relevance of conceptual analysis to empirical political research. I had become worried that students were often categorising very rigidly the issues of politics into those belonging in the domain of political theory, those relating to methodology and positive theory, and those that were the concern of the political sociologist or the specialist in 'institutions'. It did not surprise me that this was occurring. There were great pressures, particularly in America, for political scientists to become both more specialised and more interested in methodology than their predecessors of a generation earlier. In the 1970s the reason for this was not, as it had perhaps been ten years before, that behaviouralists had defined the problem areas for the political scientist to exclude the traditional interests of, for example, historians of political ideas. On the contrary, by the mid 1970s many of the leading exponents of behaviouralism, including Robert Dahl, were arguing that the analysis of political concepts was of direct relevance to their own analyses. Rather what has been leading to the compartmentalisation of the different areas of the discipline, each having its own 'language', is the career structure of university teachers, especially in the United States. With tenure increasingly difficult to obtain, many American political scientists have to take as their prime objective the maximisation of their published research. As a result, they specialise in one field only and have less time to devote to the writing of more general or more speculative essays on politics.

The final version of the book is rather different from my vision of it when I commenced work on it. As I proceeded there seemed less need to overtly emphasise the relevance of conceptual analysis and rational-choice theory to the study of democracy within political parties. My purpose did not change – I still hoped it might enable students to understand the relevance of the study of 'theory' to the 'real world' of politics – but I felt there was less need to explain in a detailed way throughout the book that this was what I was doing.

I imagine that this book is like many others: a large number of people have helped me to research and write it. The credit for whatever merits the book has is rightfully theirs, though of course the responsibility for any mistakes, and for the propagation of untenable opinions, is mine. For their helpful criticisms of earlier drafts of some of the chapters I wish to thank Alan Ryan, Jim Sharpe, Professor Wilfrid Harrison and Professor Jack Lively. I am particularly indebted to 'W. H.' who read and commented on the whole of the first draft. For the financial support that made possible the research in Denver I am very grateful to the Nuffield Foundation and the American Politics Group of the Political Studies Association. The typing of the various drafts was undertaken by Mrs. Susan Ridler and Mrs. Marlene Roberts, who typed two drafts including the final one, and I owe them thanks for the high level of skill, efficiency and good humour with which it was done. The research in Denver could never have been undertaken except with the cooperation, which was generously given, of the officials and activists of the Denver Democratic party. In addition to chairman Richard Young, I wish to thank particularly Ed Goldman, June Hurst, Bill Leavel, and Medill Barnes. I am also indebted to Ina Berzins and to the Political Science Department of the University of Denver who provided me with office facilities in the summer of 1976. Finally, I am especially grateful to Nora Ware for her continual encouragement.

ALAN WARE
August 1978

ABBREVIATIONS

In all relevant tables Denver Democratic Party Executive Committee Members is abbreviated to DDPECM.

1 Introduction

The subject of this book is intra-party democracy or, as it is often called, party democracy.[1] Although more attention has been given by political scientists and theorists to participatory democracy in the last decade than in the previous thirty years, party democracy is one of its aspects that has been least discussed. There would appear to be three main reasons for this.

First, there is the legacy of the arguments of Michels and Ostrogorski.[2] At least superficially, less of a challenge to the orthodoxy of minority control tendencies in organisations seems to be entailed in the case of industrial firms and units of local government, than with political parties. It was parties that Michels and Ostrogorski had dismissed as potential arenas for effective mass participation. By returning to local and industrial democracy, the respective concerns of J. S. Mill and G. D. H. Cole, participatory (or 'radical') democrats did not have to confront directly the arguments of a major tradition of political theory.

Second, in the years after the rise of totalitarian regimes in Europe, many democratic theorists emphasised both the dangers of mass participation and the virtues of the political stability produced by party competition. In part, democracy came to be identified with competition between parties. It was a piece of conventional wisdom in the 1950s that party democracy was at best irrelevant to, and at worst would destroy, the competitive mechanism. R. T. McKenzie, for example, claimed that intra-party democracy was 'incompatible with parliamentary government', while others maintained that it would weaken the strength of the centre in the political spectrum.[3]

Third, by the 1960s all the mass membership parties in the western democracies exhibited a disparity between the actual role of members and the control they had, in theory, over the party leadership. Even if, as the studies of Eldersveld and others indicated, there was no 'iron law of oligarchy', parties did not appear a possible forum for increasing citizen participation in the polity. In contrast to this, projects for participation in industry were developing in Britain, Sweden and in some other western European countries, whilst the experience of industrial democracy in Yugoslavia also attracted the attention of radical democrats.[4] Furthermore, in America some aspects of the Community Action Program suggested the feasibility of neighbourhood democracy. It is not surprising that these areas of citizen participation, rather than parties, should be examined by those advocating an increase in political participation. Mass activity in most parties was declining, and it was not until the late 1960s in America, and the mid 1970s in Britain, that activist control of parties became a major public issue. Both in the American Democratic party and in the British Labour party, demands increased in these periods for greater activist influence over the public policy objectives pursued by the party's public officials. The main difference between the two cases was that in the U.S. attempts to control or discipline public officials were brought about by a growth in the number of party activists; in Britain efforts to unseat Labour MPs were not the result of large increases in the number of active members in the affected constituencies.

The importance of now examining party democracy as a democratic device is twofold. In the first place, the limitations of competition for public office, as the main form of democracy, have become evident in many western states. Despite this competition, mass electorates have become increasingly distrustful of those seeking public office, and lack of confidence in, if not alienation from, western political systems appears to have increased. Moreover, as a complement to the electoral process, extensive pressure group activity no longer seems so benign an institution as pluralist democrats in the 1950s argued it was. Given this background of change in liberal democracies, it seems appropriate to pose two sets of questions:

(i)   Does the logic of electoral competition indicate that it may be an ineffective control mechanism for citizens? May electoral competition itself indirectly generate mass disenchantment with political leaders?

(ii) Would internal democracy in parties provide for more, or less, effective competition between them?

Secondly, the demands by activists in some parties for greater party democracy suggests that it is worthwhile considering some of the consequences of an increased activist role. It seems important for the political scientist to understand two possible effects that issue-oriented activists will have when they gain control of a party organisation. One is the establishment of, or failure to establish, accountability by public officials to activists; the other is the increase, or decline, in the scope of competition in which the parties engage in the electoral market. In this book we seek to provide such an analysis of party democracy. It comprises an outline of a justification for party democracy in terms of one major tradition of democratic theorising, and an examination of the results of one recent case of the democratisation of a party.

Obviously, a justification for party democracy cannot be derived from all strands of democratic theory. Thus, it is necessary to commence by explaining how the analysis presented here is related to what is now a large body of literature in political science. The starting point for this is the recognition that, as W. B. Gallie argued, democracy is an essentially contested concept.[5] William E. Connolly has classified such concepts as follows:

> When [a] disagreement does not simply reflect different readings of evidence within a fully shared system of concepts, we can say that a conceptual dispute has arisen. When the concept involved is *apprai-sive* in that the state it describes is a valued achievement, when the practice described is *internally complex* in that its characterisation involves reference to several dimensions, and when the agreed and contested rules of application are relatively *open*, enabling parties to interpret even those shared rules differently as new and unforeseen circumstances arise, then the concept in question is an 'essentially contested concept'.[6]

At the risk, perhaps, of over-simplification, disputes about the nature of democracy may be classified in terms of four overlapping areas of 'contest'. The principal issues raised in these four areas of dispute are described below. The focus of attention in this book is on the last of these four areas, one which, in comparison with the others, has been neglected in much recent comment on the concept of democracy.

MAJORITY RULE VERSUS MINORITIES (OR CONSENSUS) RULE

Whilst it might appear that there has been a major controversy about the relationship of 'the majority' to 'the people', the substantive issue of dispute has concerned the fairness of majority and consensus decision making rules.

Few democrats have claimed that democracy *is* rule by the majority, for few reasons can be advanced for identifying *a priori* the democratic objective with this procedure. Yet this characterisation of the 'majoritarian democrat' has served as a 'straw man' for many democratic theorists, particularly Americans, who advocate restrictions on the scope of government activity.[7] In support of consensus rule as a procedure, they have sought to discredit majority rule, by claiming both that majoritarian democrats advocate it as an objective, and that it is a dangerous objective. Superficially, rule by minorities would appear even less democratic, as an objective, than majority rule. Nevertheless, consensus democrats argue that it constitutes the best available procedure for protecting those rights of a minority that might otherwise be restricted by their fellow citizens.

Normally at issue between majority and consensus democrats are two sources of disagreement. The first concerns the proper end, or ends, of democracy. Unlike most majoritarians, many consensus democrats take as the main, and sometimes the only, objective the protection of particular kinds of freedom. The second source of dispute is the appropriate procedures for realising these objectives; given the former controversy, it is scarcely surprising that the latter should emerge. One of the most important developments in this respect in the last decade has been the growing acceptance of the arguments of majoritarians such as Brian Barry and Steven Brams.[8] They show that, if the democratic objective is conceived as being the promotion of the interests of all citizens (including their common interests), majority rule provides a more fair and efficient procedure for promoting interests. One effect of their arguments has been to expose different conceptions of the democratic objective. Whereas before, consensus democrats would not object to conceiving democracy in 'interest advancement' terms, more recent defences of this approach seek to undermine interests as 'a second-rate currency'.[9]

POLITICAL EQUALITY VERSUS THE MAXIMISATION OF LIBERTY

A second, fundamental, area of conceptual 'contest' has centred on the question of how political equality is to be reconciled with the maximisation of those freedoms regarded as central to the idea of democracy. Although political equality has traditionally been conceived as the defining principle of democracy, some democrats have argued that the end of democracy is the maintenance of the highest possible level of individual freedom.[10] Obviously, the two principles could conflict, and two distinct problems related to this conflict have emerged. One is the conception of freedom itself. This is an issue that necessarily links any analysis of democracy to the conceptual analysis of 'freedom' and 'autonomy'. An adequate account of, for example, even the alleged negative-positive freedom bifurcation requires a separate study from the one presented here. However, the concept of autonomy is central to the explication of the concept of interest in Chapter 2. For the purpose of this analysis, we assume that freedom and autonomy are conceptually related to each other in the way discussed by Connolly.[11]

The other problem is that of the nature of political equality and its relation to economic and social equality. Clearly, if the first is held to entail a high degree of equality of the second and third kinds, then, to make democracy possible, certain freedoms of some individuals might have to be restricted. This would occur when the economic and social relations of a polity were ones producing gross inequality of benefits. However, such issues cannot be discussed within the confines of the present study.

UTILITARIAN DEMOCRATIC THEORY VERSUS ITS OPPONENTS

The idea of a 'utilitarian' theory of democracy is an ambiguous one. On the one hand, it has been identified as a conception of democracy in which politics is seen as a 'market' activity, one which serves as an extension of the economic market. The purpose of such a market is to provide a mechanism by which conflicts are resolved and goods supplied, when this would not be brought about in the free market economy. On the other hand, a utilitarian democratic theory can be conceived, in a more general way, as one that postulates that the satisfaction of citizens' wants is at least one of the ends of democracy. Thus 'utilitarianism' would include theories in which it was assumed that the democratic government should only indirectly be concerned with the satisfaction of wants. Moreover, these wants might be made known to the government through procedures other than those akin to a market system. Opposition to both kinds of utilitarianism has come from conservative and radical writers. The former recognise that this approach seems to provide a plausible justification for an extensive, autonomous, role for government. The latter see it as linking the concept of democracy with the ethos of hedonistic individualism. The arguments we introduce are utilitarian in the more general sense identified above; for reasons of space, this book cannot be the forum in which to justify to its critics an 'economic' approach to democracy.

POPULISM VERSUS LIBERALISM

In part this controversy is a reflection of the long-standing debate about the desirable balance in a democracy between governmental responsiveness and accountability. That this is more fundamentally a dispute between what may be called a 'populist' and a 'liberal' view of democracy is suggested by L. J. Sharpe's distinction between two kinds of democratic theory. In examining the ideas and practice of American democracy, Sharpe introduces the notion of a 'populist' theory of democracy. The idea of a populist theory outlined in this book is derived from Sharpe's analysis, but differs from it in a fundamental respect. Sharpe sees the main problem of American democracy as that of how to make a government actually responsive to all demands. Populism is a deficient account of American democracy because America's political institutions cannot satisfy these demands. In contrast to this, it is argued here that populism is a deficient democratic theory, because some demands or wants should not be directly the proper concern of a democratic government.

As in Sharpe's article, an apology must be made for purloining the term populist when other social scientists have given it a rather different, specific meaning. Indeed, we owe an additional apology, for populism is contrasted with an approach to democratic theory which is here called liberalism, another term liable to produce confusion. Nevertheless, these seem to be the most appropriate labels to describe the two approaches.

Sharpe characterises the populist approach as:

> [reducing] democracy solely to the negative relationship between elector and elected: to how the former control the latter. How we are to control our leaders is assuredly a central problem in a democracy; but, if it is elevated to become the only problem, it is difficult to escape the conclusion that the incapacity of government is a positive good.[12]

Undoubtedly, populism has been the dominant kind of democratic theory in contemporary American political science, and Sharpe is correct in identifying Robert Dahl as the populist democratic theorist *par excellence*. Many populists, like Dahl, are 'pluralist' democrats but, neither in terms of Sharpe's definition of populism nor the one we propose, are populism and pluralism synonymous.[13]

Although it is not the main point emphasised by Sharpe, what underlies the views he calls populist is an assumption that government should be as responsive as possible to the wants of the citizens. Electors' control over elected has to be maximised, so that citizens can intervene in the policy making process whenever issues arise about which they have strongly-held opinions. The purpose of government is to translate wants, or opinions, into policies. Nevertheless this does not mean that all those we describe as populists (and they have formed the mainstream of American political science) would favour referendum democracy. In fact, many populists oppose the referendum as a democratic device. Yet populists do believe that in a democracy the wants of citizens should be responded to by public officials, even though they frequently require that wants should be channelled through a filtering device, such as a pressure group system.

Sharpe contrasts populists with those who value functional effectiveness in government. However, we draw a rather different distinction: one between populism and a liberal approach to democracy. As the term is used here, a liberal democrat is one who sees the object of democratic government as the advancement of the citizens' interests; their interests are assumed to be related to wants that the citizens have chosen autonomously. The liberal further values citizens having the highest possible degree of autonomy when making choices between wants. Liberalism, in this sense, has been a major strand in western democratic thought, though, perhaps, mainly a British, rather than an American, strand. The liberal does not deny that people's wants are of value. However, he recognises certain dangers in making governments responsive to the citizens' wants. Thus, he argues that the democratic objective is best conceived as the advancement of their interests, and that their interests are only indirectly related to their wants-for-policies.

If the populist sees the main problem of democratic government as that of how the bottom layer (citizens) can control the top layer (officials), the liberal sees it as being a more complex problem. For the liberal, popular control of government is essential if democracy is to exist. Nevertheless, he also demands that government should be free to be unresponsive to some kinds of demands that emanate from the citizenry, and the liberal also values a high degree of autonomy for citizens so that they can determine the nature of their own interests. That is, the liberal sees the central issue of democratic theory as being the question of how to make rulers responsible to (or accountable to) citizens. Naturally, this demands consideration of the question of the relation between responsiveness and accountability.

Government will be accountable to citizens when there are effective incentives for rulers to govern in the interests of all citizens. That is, there is accountability when appropriate sanctions can be imposed on those who are responsible *to* the citizens *for* the promotion of their interests, should they fail to exercise this responsibility. One limitation of Sharpe's analysis is that he appears to assume that accountability is not incompatible with a high degree of responsiveness by government to citizens' wants. What Sharpe requires is that government can actually respond to these demands. To accept this assumption is to ignore the fact that citizens in nation states can never be perfectly informed, autonomous agents; they may demand some policies that are against their interests. A responsive government can be put in the position of being unable to be responsible to the citizens. Moreover, a high degree of responsiveness on the part of government will mean responsiveness to only some groups and some demands. A political agenda could never be impartial between all demands, however equally most political resources were distributed. Access to the agenda will always be more available to those making claims regularly dealt with by government, than to new interests submitting demands. Of course, with unequally distributed political resources, other sources of bias are introduced into the public policy output of a responsive government.[14]

Responsiveness to all is impossible; responsibility to all is not, although it has proved difficult to devise institutional arrangements that provide a high degree of governmental accountability to citizens. One device that has been seen as an instrument for providing both responsiveness and accountability is the free electoral system. Populists see it as a means by which all major wants in the society can be 'weighted' one against the other. For the liberal, electoral competition provides the incentive for governors to take account of interests other than those currently attended to on the political agenda. In this book we examine two aspects of electoral competition. One is whether this mechanism introduces additional biases into a system of responsive government. The other aspect is how competition might provide for governmental responsibility to citizens. In regard to this latter, we discuss whether party democracy can supplement the electoral mechanism in providing accountability or whether, as some of its critics have argued, it destabilises competition.

The main objective of this book, then, is to contrast a liberal theory of democracy with populist theories and to show why party democracy is one of the prerequisites for the establishment of a liberal society. Consideration of the effects of party democracy on the accountability of political leaders through the electoral system necessitates an examination of party democratisation. As a recent example of this, the Democratic party in Denver was chosen for a case study.

This particular party was selected for two reasons. In the first place, unlike the European mass membership parties, from the mid 1960s onwards there was an influx of issue-oriented 'amateur' activists into the American Democratic party, particularly the party in Colorado. There the 'amateur' takeover of the formal party organisations was more complete than in most states. In comparison with the atrophy of party in western Europe, this is an example of activist mobilisation on a large scale in a period of only a few years. If the potential for party democracy is to be evaluated, it would seem that the Colorado Democratic party is an appropriate example, because a large body of party activists have attempted to expand the traditional functions of the party organisations. Secondly, it is argued in Chapter 5 that the system of nominating candidates in Colorado does not have the disadvantages of either the direct primary or the mass membership party in providing a bias in favour of public office-seekers *vis-à-vis* activists.

These two factors counteract the obvious objection to studying an American party: namely that the tradition of the American cadre parties runs counter to that of intra-party accountability. We should not expect full party democracy to be established in this kind of party, but the results of the study may indicate how effective partial democratisation can be, both in the American and other types of parties. For, whatever their dissimilarities, the large mass membership parties and American cadre parties are alike in that party democracy has rarely been practised. The main focus in this study of the Colorado Democratic party is on the party organisation in Denver. Not only has this been the main area of activist insurgence in the state, but Denver is also the primary source of Democratic voting strength and the city is the most important component of the state party organisation. In brief, Colorado seems at first glance to be fertile territory for party democracy, and this should provide a good case study of the potential for, and limitations of, party democracy.

Having outlined the general issues to be considered in the subsequent chapters, we can now summarise the organisation of the rest of the book. Its theoretical framework is developed in Chapters 2, 3, 4 and 5; the evidence from the Colorado Democrats' experience is related to the arguments of the earlier chapters in Chapters 6, 7 and 8. Some conclusions are drawn from this, and some more wide-ranging speculations made, in Chapter 9.

2 Interests

A utilitarian theory of democracy is one in which the object of government is taken as being connected with the satisfaction of the citizens' wants. Within the mainstream of western political science there have been two principal kinds of utilitarian democratic theory. The first, which may be called the populist approach, has been the dominant 'school' in America since the Second World War: the two best known populist theories being those of Robert A. Dahl and Anthony Downs.[1] The basic tenet of these theorists is that the object of government is to ensure the optimal satisfaction of the wants that the citizens happen to have: their wants are those goods that they are seen to choose now. In opposition to this is an approach that is more closely associated with the British political tradition; we refer to it as the 'liberal' doctrine, and it is best elucidated in the writings of E. E. Schattschneider and Brian Barry.[2] The liberal sees government as that social institution which can, and should, promote the interests of citizens, but he conceives their interests as being only indirectly related to their wants. As a preface to an outline of a liberal theory of democracy, this chapter commences with an account of why want satisfaction should not directly be the objective for a democratic government: from this an explication of the concept of interest is developed.

A. WHAT ARE WANTS?

It is appropriate to begin by observing an obvious feature of the concept of a want.[3] It appears that to say a person has a particular want x, is to say nothing about any other goods y; in fact, any statement about x being wanted by someone implies that a comparison has been made by that person between x and at least some of the goods constituting y.

On the one hand, it seems that to say 'A wants x' is to state no more than that A would prefer to have quantities of x rather than not to have

11

them, if he were offered them in circumstances in which he would incur no costs in having them. Of course, when identifying a person's wants, there is an important reason for eliminating from consideration the costs he might have to bear in acquiring (or keeping) x. We must avoid the fallacy that his wants are only those goods he could actually obtain with his current holding of social and economic resources. (It is perfectly correct to say of a pauper that his wants include a large mansion and fast cars, even if his expected lifetime earnings are lower than that required for him to either rent or own them.) For some purposes there may be good reasons for taking into account only those goods a person could obtain with his own resources, but this does not mean that these are the only things he can be said to want. Moreover, we cannot identify his wants with those goods that he actually buys: some demands may be completely frustrated because of constraints on the supply of the goods.

On the other hand, many goods can only be consumed at time t if the consumption of some other goods is postponed. It might be possible to listen to a recording of a Beethoven symphony whilst eating caviar without detracting from the satisfaction obtained from either. However, at the same time we could not also be mountaineering or water-skiing. If people were immortal and the world's resources were unlimited there would still be a limit to the number of wants that any individual could have satisfied at time t. To the extent that A prefers to consume x at time t rather than later, there is at least one cost he must bear in satisfying his want for x. This is the cost of delaying the consumption of other goods which he would otherwise prefer to consume at t. It makes no sense, therefore, to talk of someone being provided with goods that are free of *all* costs that have to be borne by him. To say that 'A wants x' is to imply at the very least that A is prepared to take the time to consume x, rather than consume other goods that he could reasonably expect to have as alternatives in that period. (Similarly wants for other people, as opposed to wants for oneself, will entail others making time available if the wants are to be satisfied.) In an important sense, then, wants are preferences. In theory, at least, for any given amount of those resources that secure goods, we could construct a matrix of a person's preferences. This is the starting point for a populist theory of democracy – a theory in which the function of political and economic institutions is to provide for the optimum satisfaction of all citizens' wants.

An obvious difficulty with such a theory is that of deciding what level of socio-economic resources each citizen is presumed to have for the purpose of optimising satisfaction. One solution to this – the one actually used by all populist theorists, is to assume that the distribution of resources has been determined autonomously. The wants of the citizens can then be taken to be those they happen to have at any given time. One objection to this last procedure is that unless socio-economic resources are equally distributed the requirement that citizens in a democracy must be politically equal does not seem to be met. With unequal distributions citizens are unlikely to have an equal say as to what government does. Even if this problem were overcome, the liberal theorist would still have two major criticisms to make of the populist conception of democracy as a high level of responsiveness to actual demands for want satisfaction. The first objection is that revealed preferences are not the only wants people have. A polity in which the institutions of government were designed to maximise the satisfaction of overt demands would ignore many important wants. A second criticism of populism is that the 'counting' of certain kinds of wants by a government could result in it upholding two kinds of tyranny. Before turning to examine the relationship between the concept of want and that of interest, therefore, we will consider these two problems.

Two reasons can be advanced in support of the argument that the government in a democracy should take account of wants other than those of which it is immediately aware. The first is derived from the 'rational' ignorance of the citizenry. Even the most intelligent and well-educated citizen cannot devote time and other resources to the discovery of which policies are most appropriate to the ends he wishes to pursue. Thus, even in a world in which all citizens sought to be perfect democrats, many of them would often claim to want policies that were inappropriate for the realisation of their objectives. To use Brian Barry's terminology, there is an incongruity between their wants for policies and their wants for results.[4] If the government has to be too responsive to the former it might be difficult, or impossible, for it to provide policies that would promote the results the citizens actually want. The more the citizens come to concern themselves with their individual affairs, rather than the affairs of the wider public, the more likely there is to be a gap between the opinions they have about public policies and the actual effects of the policies on their ability to get what they want.

The pursuit of self-interest, which is itself encouraged by a high degree of government responsiveness, is likely to develop citizen attitudes that, whilst 'reasonable' in one sense, are ultimately likely to make it more difficult for wants to be satisfied. In particular it should be noted that, in the case of certain public goods, the value of the goods to the individual is virtually impossible for him to calculate. It makes little sense for him to try to estimate the value of the benefits he receives from a given level of expenditure on either national defence or street lighting. Yet the taxes the individual citizen pays, particularly the direct taxes, are very obvious to him. Consequently citizens will normally tend to undervalue the less immediately apparent benefits.[5] However, even in a world with citizens who are perfectly informed about the connection between policies and results, there is still considerable potential for the introduction of a bias in the construction of a set of optimal public policies. This arises because, whatever the mechanism for making their preferences known in the public policy making process, there is an incentive for citizens to express 'strategic' rather than 'sincere' wants; the citizen who expresses his real wants may do less well in the policy process than if he lies about the nature of some of his priorities.[6] Most especially, in their public expressions of preference, there will be a tendency amongst 'rational' citizens to undervalue those wants they share with large numbers of other citizens. At the same time, for strategic reasons, they will tend to reveal an overvaluation of both those wants that only they have and those that they share with smaller, more cohesive groups of citizens. (Obviously there is another strategic consideration that may counteract the effect of this: no 'rational' citizen will expend resources on revealing a preference that he believes has no chance of being taken into account by the government.) This is the problem of the 'free-rider' – the person who reasons that, if he is going to receive a particular public good anyway, he may as well incur no costs in assisting in its procurement. When it is unlikely that he will make the difference between its provision and its non-provision, he will fail to bear the cost of a contribution, if he cannot be sure that others will contribute resources to ensure its provision.[7] This is the so-called 'Olson problem', and it exposes the lack of an incentive for rational, calculating citizens to show a preference for any good that is also wanted by large numbers of others. It is precisely this problem – the understating of support for many community-wide wants – that has been most evident in the United States, the country which has most exalted governmental responsiveness as a political value.[8]

The second objection to the direct translation of citizens' wants into public policies is the 'tyranny' argument. In fact, there are two rather separate phenomena that are tyrannical in their effects. The first, tyranny by small decisions, is best explained by outlining some of the arguments introduced in a seminal book by Fred Hirsch, *Social Limits to Growth*.[9] In part, Hirsch's concern is to rectify what he sees as a failure by economists in not making a distinction between different kinds of goods. In economics, goods are goods. 'Push-pin' has not only been treated as being no better or worse than 'poetry' by economists, but, as a good, it has been seen as qualitatively the same as, for example, open, unpopulated countryside or self-shaving products. Against this tradition, that economists should not make value judgements about the products, ends or goals that people demand, Hirsch introduces two important distinctions that serve to separate different types of good. In the first place, he recognises that some goods provide for the immediate satisfaction of wants. Poetry is an example of this. Other goods are wanted merely as intermediaries that make possible the satisfaction of ultimate wants. Unlike poetry, goods like self-shaving products are mainly wanted as regrettable necessities: in this case the need for time to consume other goods forces men to abandon the more leisurely service of the barber shop. (The 'consumer may lose satisfaction from his switch to self-shaving as such, but he may do so in order to use the extra time for tennis'.[10]) Of course, many goods provide both direct want satisfaction and are also regrettable necessities. For example, the car owner may get pleasure from driving on a Sunday afternoon, though he drives himself to the football match on Saturday only because there is no other way for him to get there. There is not a strict division between 'intermediate' (or 'defensive') goods and goods which satisfy wants directly; rather, there is a continuum of goods, the polar positions of which are the solely 'defensive' good and the solely 'end consumption' good. However, what Hirsch emphasises is that, in valuing economic output, the economist generates confusion if he treats defensive and end consumption or final goods as qualitatively the same.

In regard to this distinction between types of goods, one of Hirsch's main concerns is to draw attention to those 'defensive' goods which are wanted because they enable the person to 'protect the position of the individual in the social environment'.[11] And this leads to the second distinction Hirsch introduces: that between 'material' goods and 'positional' goods. Competition for positional goods, in contrast with that for material goods, is competition 'that is fundamentally for a higher place within some explicit or implicit hierarchy and that thereby yields gains for some only by dint of losses for other'.[12] Some positional goods are ones which necessarily involve a hierarchy of satisfaction (for example, positions of political leadership from the community to the national level). However, Hirsch sees the positional economy as also containing goods that give satisfaction partly through their intrinsic qualities but also because they are not extensively available. For example, the enjoyment of open countryside is diminished if everyone can choose to visit it at the same time and all do so. The crux of one of Hirsch's main arguments is that, in advanced economies experiencing continuous economic growth, the competition for positional goods amongst would-be 'purchasers' becomes increasingly intense. The richer everyone becomes, the more all will compete for those goods, previously only available to a tiny minority of the population, whose supply cannot be greatly increased. Thus, rather than leading to ever increasing satisfaction amongst consumer-citizens who are able to purchase more material goods, economic growth produces frustration (or dissatisfaction) for them. Even if Hirsch is incorrect in his argument about the increase in competition in the positional economy, he is clearly right to point out the limitations of political and economic theories that do not take account of the qualitative differences between respectively, defensive and final goods; and positional and material goods. The relevance of this distinction to the analysis presented here may now be explained.

Economists have long recognised the problem of identifying the actual demand for certain kinds of goods: these are public goods and those goods supplied in conditions which are such as to restrict the number and type of comparable alternatives available, i.e. goods supplied by monopolists or oligopolists. In such cases, traditional economic theory has acknowledged that the true structure of consumer preferences may not be reflected in the revealed demand for the goods. The government has often been seen by economists as the proper regulator of these weaknesses in the market system. It can arrange for the supply of many public goods (such as national defence) and can regulate the operation of monopolies and oligopolies. The logic of Hirsch's argument suggests that there is an equally important factor that may result in the failure of a market system to translate consumer-citizens' preferences into the provision of the most preferred set of goods. The problem is that of the conditions under which citizens, either as consumers or as sources of pressure on government, reveal their level of demand for defensive or positional goods. Of course, as with other goods supplied through a market system, choices involving regrettable necessities and goods that can only be enjoyed by a few people are made on a piecemeal basis. However, the multitude of unconnected choices as a whole affects the conditions under which these goods can be supplied in the future. Unlike final material goods, the future supply of these goods may be affected adversely by the piecemeal choices made now by individuals who cannot themselves, as individuals, safeguard that supply in the choices they make. In short, the grand alternatives open to the community are never available for choice, just as they are normally restricted for the individual consumer faced by an oligopolist's market. 'Everyone has a choice of living in the city as it is or in the suburb as it is, but not between living in the city and suburb as they *will be* when the consequences of such choices have been worked through.'[13] In consequence, thousands of small decisions can produce a result that is little wanted by any of those who took the decisions.

This point can be illuminated by an example. If there are no land use controls and all a suburban community's residents want cabins in the mountains, then a wilderness will rapidly become a suburb. It is rational for all to choose to build a cabin, rather than forego the opportunity, because individually they are unlikely to have much effect on the environment. Nevertheless, all may have preferred a world in which there were no mountain cabins and the area remained a wilderness to one in which the mountains have become as suburban as the flatlands. A common defensive good provides another example of the same point. By choosing to drive to football games, the spectators may force the bus companies to provide an ever-decreasing service, because the declining demand leads to losses for the companies on the 'football specials'. At the same time, the switch to cars creates increasingly severe traffic jams. It is worthwhile for all to choose to sit out the jams in their cars, rather than spend the time waiting for a bus, even though they would prefer that everyone went to the matches by bus, thereby eliminating the traffic congestion. By attempting to satisfy all *revealed* wants for positional or defensive goods, a government may make everyone worse off than if it could take account of wants for alternatives not available to the 'piecemeal' decision makers. And if all are made worse off in this way, all are tyrannised by the decisions they have independently made. When what everyone would most prefer is not the subject of immediate choice, each person reveals a preference for a less preferred state of the world, which a government responsive to public pressure would treat as a want that it should help to satisfy. Thus, it might be forced to remove subsidies to bus companies because car-driving football supporters can see no reason why the small number of bus-travelling spectators should receive a financial advantage not available to them. Consequently the traffic jams, both before and after games, get worse. However, if the government were responsible for promoting the citizens' interests, instead of merely being responsive to their demands, it would be possible for it to satisfy those wants that government as a market mechanism could not. This is an important assumption in the liberal view of democracy. One justification of government for the liberal is that it can correct the effects of small decision tyranny. Government is not merely a supplier of some essential public goods, nor is it simply a guarantor of extensive competition in the economy; it is a mechanism separate from the economy and one which can override market forces in the satisfaction of unrevealed wants. The main institutional problem, according to this view of democracy, is the discovery of which kinds of political arrangements will make it easier for small decision tyranny to be avoided. In this respect, particular attention has been given by writers such as Schattschneider and Barry to the role of centralising tendencies in government, especially that of highly unified political parties in a system of two-party competition. The main concern of this book is with an extension of their arguments, for the principal question being posed is: what incentive is there for parties to compete with each other in countering the effects of this kind of tyranny?

A second kind of tyranny that can be embraced by a policy in which both the government and economy are highly responsive to the wants of citizens is the tyranny of one man over another. Of course, it was the fear of majority rule, as the democratic method supposedly making it easiest for men to tyrannise one another, that underlay much of the debate at the Constitutional Convention in 1787. It has remained a dominant theme in American democratic theory since then. However, the problem for democratic theory is more extensive than Madison's worry about 'majority tyranny'. More generally the difficulty is that, if the government must be responsive to all wants, then it cannot avoid the fact that in being responsive to the wants of some citizens the welfare of other citizens might be damaged. One citizen's want for the extermination of Jews has to count the same as another's want for the maintenance of his family's welfare. Robert Dahl recognised that constitutional rules do not eliminate the problem. However, his reasoning away of it, by over-emphasising the beneficial effects of a plural society, was undermined by his own evidence that, even in pluralistic America, some groups were not considered legitimate. The groups he cites – Blacks in the 19th century and communists this century, were ones that had basic political rights removed from them by popularly elected officials.[14] The problem of the malevolent citizen is one which a populist theory of democracy cannot resolve. The liberal solution to it has been provided by Brian Barry. Barry sees the object of government as the promotion of citizens' interests and he argues that wants for other people do not constitute part of any citizen's interests. Thus governments need to be protected from demands that might force them to harm the interests of some citizens. Although this is the best way of removing the problem, Barry achieves it at the price of identifying a person's interest with his self-interest. In section B (E) of this chapter a modification of Barry's argument is presented that allows this difficulty to be circumvented.

B. THE CONCEPT OF INTEREST

Having outlined objections to a populist utilitarian theory of democracy, attention must now be focussed on three approaches to the concept that is central to a liberal theory – a person's interests. We may call them respectively populism, liberalism and authoritarianism.

In the first place, a person's interests might be identified with his revealed wants: if A wants x then it necessarily follows that x is one of his interests, and it is in his interest that x be provided. However some populists, including Dahl though not David Truman, allow elected public officials to initiate policies even when only the results are known to be wanted by the citizens. Yet this may only occur when there are no intensely held opinions in the community about the appropriate policies for an objective upon which there is general agreement, and to which there is little opposition.[15]

In contrast to the populist view, an authoritarian links a person's interests to a perceived desirable or inevitable condition of mankind. Thus, a Marxist claims that a person's interests are defined by his objectively identifiable class position.[16] As his wants may be the product of false consciousness, they are of no relevance in the definition of his interests. A rather different authoritarian viewpoint is the argument that a person's interests are related to his needs, which are determined not by the nature of his wants, but by the peculiarly human powers or potentials that are common to all people. Thus his interests reflect a particular interpretation of what people are or what they are capable of becoming. Clearly, the arguments for the validity of such an interpretation do not admit of proof in the same way that the nature of a man's wants can be demonstrated. A more 'moderate' version of the authoritarian approach to interests permits a democratic government to take account of the results citizens *will* accept after the relevant policies have been effected. For the government to be justified in implementing policies, it is not necessary at the time this happens for the citizens to want even the results they will produce. This 'moderate' authoritarianism is one with which William E. Connolly appears to flirt before he finally settles for the liberal position on the matter.[17] It is in this respect that the superiority of the liberal claim becomes apparent. For the liberal conception of interest is not incompatible with a belief in the desirability of a change in western man from being largely consumption-oriented, and partially self-interested into a very different kind of moral agent. However, the liberal can accept developmental goals only when the appropriate policies are compatible with the satisfaction of people's wants as they are. He cannot claim that it is in people's interest to be thus transformed, although like Rousseau he may also believe that the result of it would be a superior kind of society.[18] However, the liberal does argue that it is always in the interests of citizens to be informed about the potential for such a society, for without this knowledge they cannot have a high degree of autonomy in choosing their life-style, primary values or principal wants.

The liberal's concept of interest may now be outlined. Perhaps the most well-known, and arguably the best, recent analysis from this viewpoint is that of Brian Barry.[19] Barry rejects the assertions that '*x* is in *A*'s interest' means either '*A* wants *x*', or '*x* would be a justifiable claim on the part of *A*', or '*x* will give *A* more pleasure than any alternative open to him'.[20] His arguments are so clearly made that they need not be repeated here. In their place, Barry suggests that, as a first approximation in understanding interests, we may say that 'an action or policy is in a man's interest if it increases his opportunities to get what he wants'.[21] From this it follows that a person can be said to mistake his interest should he not want a policy when the results of it are ones which he does want. Although this is a largely correct analysis of the concept, there are several problems with the arguments Barry presents. An examination of three objections made by other political theorists and two further difficulties with the analysis, will show more clearly how interests are related to wants.

(A) In two recently published books William E. Connolly and Steven Lukes argue that a more 'radical' concept of interest than that of the liberal version can be expounded.[22] What is interesting about their claims is that they seem to believe that this would not be incompatible with the priority accorded by liberal theorists to want satisfaction in a democracy. That is, they suggest that a more radical concept of interest can be derived from essentially liberal premises. However, their analysis is ill-founded in two respects. In the first place, many of the situations which they seem to believe involve a conflict of interest between actors that cannot be analysed as such by the liberal are also cases of interest conflict for the liberal theorist. In particular, to the extent that a person's choice of wants has been constrained by the manipulation of others, it is not appropriate to identify his interests in terms of his wants. Secondly, it may be suggested that the radical can either be an authoritarian or a liberal in the way he conceives interests, but he cannot be both; Lukes, in particular, appears to want to be both.

Connolly's initial formulation of the radical concept, which he calls real interests is as follows:

Policy x is more in A's real interest than policy y if A, were he to experience the *results* of both x and y would *choose* x as the result he would rather have for himself.[23]

That is, a person's interests are related not to what he happens to want now, but to the policies and results he would want after he had experienced the alternatives available. In one major respect this does suggest a legitimate modification to the Barry analysis, for Barry incorrectly assumes that a person's wants should always be taken to be the ones he has now. Of course, Barry does admit that, when a person is not capable of making a rational choice about the best way to promote his interests, the decision can be taken by others on his behalf.[24] An irrational person – for example, an alcoholic or a compulsive gambler – is not capable of determining what is in his interest, because of a defect in his decision-making faculties. However, this does not provide a justification for refusing to treat as 'real' or 'genuine' the wants a person has acquired as a result of manipulation by others. Usually manipulation does not make a person irrational, but, in restricting the choices he can know about, it does undermine the validity of his choice.[25]

This point can be illustrated by considering a hypothetical case of a contented, relatively affluent, and well-educated slave. After a long period of manipulation by the owner, he believes that freedom is of little value in itself; he might 'rationally' claim to prefer slavery to freedom because he is materially better off as a slave then he would be as a free man. If, as in this example, there is evidence that manipulation has occurred, it is legitimate for the policy-maker to discount the person's wants when assessing his interests, because he was not an autonomous agent in the choice of his life-style. It is then necessary to consider a person's interests as if he did not have the wants he happens to have. Obviously manipulation is normally less complete than this. However, even in respect of specific issues, when a want has been manipulated, the policy maker is entitled to act in the 'real' interests of the citizen, rather than take account of his want. A liberal and a radical would be in accord on such cases.

However, the radical theorist may wish to go further than this. Lukes argues that for the radical:

> men's wants may themselves be the product of a system which works against their interests, and, in such cases, he relates the latter to what they would want and prefer, were they able to make the choice.[26]

In effect, this ends the restriction that the liberal places on the identification of interests in counting men's wants as they are. It extends the manipulation exemption to all cases in which an institutional bias in society, or simply an 'unfairness' in his social circumstances, has affected a person's choice. Whenever policy-makers believe people have wants that they would not have chosen in different circumstances, Lukes permits them to be dictators of other people's wants. It thus becomes possible for a government, or one of its agencies, to justify the imposition of its choices on others, when the latter are entitled to have their wants treated as being autonomously chosen ones. At this point Lukes's analysis departs from, and is incompatible with, the liberal assumptions upon which it originally appears to be founded.

(B) Theodore M. Benditt has argued against Barry that the concept of interest is directly connected with that of happiness, and only indirectly related to that of want satisfaction.[27] His argument may be summarised in the following way:

(i) The concept of a person's interest is very much like that of his good;

(ii) the good of a person consists in his being sufficiently satisfied in as many departments of his life as are necessary to make him happy;

(iii) people are not always made happy by increases in the resources
that permit more want satisfaction.

The contented-slave example is also relevant to an understanding of
the objections to this argument. Even if continued bondage would
make the slave happy, we might object to it on two grounds: that it is
not for his good, and that it is not in his interest. But these grounds are
not the same. The case for the first objection rests on the argument that
slaves are not independent moral beings and that it is not for anyone's
good to be lacking in independence in this way. We could argue that it
is not in his interest to be a slave because we could show that others had
manipulated him and had consequently affected his 'choice' of continued slavery.

Of course, it is not inconceivable that someone might want to
abrogate all responsibility in his life and, unmanipulated, freely choose
to do so. Given this goal, slavery might be thought to be in his interest,
even if it did not promote his good. The objection to this argument is
that the idea of interest is inapplicable to anyone who *will* not choose
autonomously now or in the future. To want to become an object,
rather than act as a human being, is against the interest of anyone
because only people, and not objects, have interests.

Once it was apparent that the slave had been manipulated, then
impartial observers would identify his interests with an increase in his
awareness of his position and with the maximisation of his socio-
economic resources such as wealth, power and status. These resources
are required for the satisfaction of the most common wants, although it
is the case that they are not necessary for, and are sometimes incompatible with, some life-styles. Certainly, the statement that a person's
interest consists in the accumulation of wealth, power and prestige and
similar goods is not an analytic truth, and this is a false assumption that
Barry seems to make. (This point is examined further in Section (E).)

To conclude. Against Benditt it can be argued that interests are not
directly related to happiness. His mistaken analysis stems from a valid
objection to Barry – namely that it is not necessarily in a man's interest
to have more wealth, power and status. Nevertheless, there is a link
between interests and these goods. This arises because of the large
number of wants in the most common types of lifestyle that can be
satisfied by them.

(C) Benditt does introduce one important modification to Barry's
analysis of interests. He argues that the latter incorrectly tied state-

ments about interests to comparisons *between* policies. Barry had contended that 'all statements about "interest" carry a "secret comparison" between one policy and another'.[28] However, Benditt suggests that, when all the alternative policies under consideration would have a net harmful effect on the person concerned, it is not appropriate to describe the least harmful as being in his interest. Instead it would be described as the policy which least harmed his interests. Moreover, Benditt is further justified in arguing that there is a comparison entailed by 'interest' statements. It is not one between policies, but between the effects of a policy and a (net) neutral effect on the person's interests. A policy is in *A*'s interest if it produces more benefit than harm for *A*, and against his interest if it produces more harm than benefit for him. Thus, if several policies provide a net benefit to *A*, they are all in his interest, but when they are compared with each other some may be more in his interest than others.

(D) Barry claims that a reference to interests entails an evaluation of policies or actions. He believes that a distinction should be drawn between statements about interests and those about 'being affected' by something:

> One can ask: 'Were you adversely affected by the cold weather?' (or some other natural phenomenon) but hardly 'Was the cold weather in your interests?' or 'Was it in your interests for us to have cold weather?'[29]

Two main criticisms can be advanced against this contention. First, it restricts the use of statements in a way that everyday language does not. Second, and as a consequence of this, it introduces an unwarranted conservative bias into the concept.

It is not always the case that the question, 'Was the cold weather in your interests?' is an absurd one: it depends on the context in which it is asked. If the question is directed at a manufacturer of central heating systems it is not an absurd one, nor is it an unusual (or strained) use of language. He may well reply: 'obviously cold weather is in our interest because it encourages people to buy our equipment. However, it is against our interest for there to be too many cold winters in succession, for this would encourage new firms to enter the market. In the long term there would then be too many suppliers for the normal size of the industry's market, and we should be left with excess capacity in our plants.' Nevertheless, Barry is right to suggest that *A* being affected by something is not synonymous with it being in his interest. The terms differ in that statements about interests are normally only appropriate when a person's longer term welfare is considerably affected. Thus, no one would speak of the cold weather as being harmful to his interests if he merely lost a day's pay because he could not travel to his place of work. He would have been affected by it, but its effects on his future want satisfaction would be sufficiently small as to make a claim about his interests an inapposite one. On the other hand, if it is believed that the central heating manufacturer may substantially increase his sales during and after the cold weather, it is correct to describe how he is affected in terms of 'interests'.

Barry's analysis produces a conservative bias in the concept of interest in that it permits the political scientist to ask of immediate alternatives (that is, policies or actions) only whether they are in someone's interest. However, the conditions under which a choice is made can favour, or be harmful to, a person's interests even when it is recognised that these are not really an object of choice now. For example, the American constitution is a fixed condition of public decision making in America; yet it is possible to ask whether federalism and the separation of powers works against the interests of some American groups. If Barry were correct, we could not ask whether particular institutional structures or practices adversely affected some people's interests whilst benefiting the interests of others. We would be prevented from arguing that certain institutions are harmful to the interests of some groups, for only the policies emanating from those institutions could be discussed in terms of interests. Attention is thereby directed away from the problem of institutional bias as an explanation of how values have come to be distributed in a given way, and is directed towards explanations of the alleged power of those responsible for the decisions.[30] It is ironic that one effect of Barry's analysis is to 'overload' the concept of power in this way, because his subsequent account of centralised and diffused decision making systems (see *Political Argument*) is itself an important contribution to the study of institutional bias.

(E) Barry argues that in considering what is in a person's interest the observer examines what it is that he wants. Nevertheless, the observer should exclude any wants that person has for other people to have opportunities for want satisfaction or be denied opportunities for want satisfaction.[31] That is, a person's interests are conceptually related only to those wants he has for himself or his family. This makes it a necessary truth that his interests are always self-interested ones. However, this is to conflate two of the three separate ways in which the term 'interest' is used in common language. The following example exposes the differences between these three uses.

The police take to hospital a man A who has just attempted to commit suicide. Subsequently they are approached by another man B, who asks for information about the incident. The police ask B 'Do you have an interest in this case?', and B provides one of the following answers:

(i) 'Yes, I live round here and I'm interested in all the gossip in the neighbourhood.'

(ii) 'Yes, I'm a committed Christian, and therefore I have an interest in assisting A.'

(iii) 'Yes, I'm his brother, and my interest is that if he dies I inherit his fortune.'

From the knowledge that B has an interest in the case, in the sense of being interested in or attending to something (i), we cannot infer anything about his ultimate values or his position with regard to personal gain. People can be interested in, and hence give attention to, subjects which they may regard as trivial in terms of any ultimate values and which do not increase their own opportunities for want satisfaction. Yet the analytic pluralists, such as Dahl and Truman, assumed that a person's interests, in the senses of statements (ii) and (iii), were the same as whatever it was that he devoted his attention to (i). Thus, according to them, a person's interests could be determined by an examination of his revealed preferences and the 'causes' to which he contributed: anything he was interested in (that is, concerned about) he also had an interest in.

In the case of answer (ii), B is not a beneficiary from the suicide, but he has an interest in it by virtue of his religious beliefs. Charity is the main value espoused by the Christian religion, and it is in B's interest that he assists A. That is, the assistance he renders A will promote his major goal in life, the greater glorification of God. (As with self-interest, the Christian could mistake his interests. For example, as a new convert, he might fail to assist A in the false belief that charity should not be extended to would-be suicides.) As with any primary value or chosen life-style, the Christian will normally take an interest in (that is, attend to) what he perceives to be his interests.[32] It would be either nonsensical or hypocritical of B to claim: 'I'm indifferent as to what happens to *A*, even though as a committed Christian I have an interest in the promotion of charity.' In one respect, then, the Christian is necessarily concerned about his interests: if he were not he could not claim they were his interests. Nevertheless, if he believes that the expenditure of time and other resources that is entailed by 'taking an interest' in particular cases is either completely futile or counter-productive, he may rationally choose not to concern himself with these interests. It is partly for this reason, and partly because a person can mistake his interests, that the analytic pluralist account of interest is incorrect.

In some respects answer (iii) is similar to (ii), although there is one important difference between them. This is that with (iii) *B* can be said to have an interest, in the sense of self-interest, in *A*'s death even if in terms of his own chosen life-style, or primary values, his inheritance of a fortune is irrelevant. That is, a person does not have to be self-interested for it to be correctly stated of him that he has an interest in outcomes that will increase his wealth, power, status or other social resources. In this sense a person's interests are necessarily those goods that provide opportunities for the satisfaction of the most common wants in western societies. It is this notion of interest as self-interest that Barry adopts. He assimilates this with 'interests' as related to chosen lifestyle and primary values. He then maintains that those 'interests' that a non-self-interested man has by virtue of his chosen lifestyle should not be counted as interests.

Now there are two related issues that need to be mentioned in connection with this concept of interest. In the first place, it would appear that to refuse to count as interests certain kinds of interest is to embrace an illiberal position. If a person wants to be a hermit or an altruist then what is in his interest is policies and institutional arrangements that enable him to lead this kind of life. The autonomy of citizen choice valued by the liberal is worthless, if his interests may be falsely construed by the policy maker according to a preconceived set of values or a hypothetical social norm. Such an approach is essentially authoritarian, and indistinguishable from the procedure by which Marxists identify a person's interests.

The second issue is that Barry's retreat into the claim that only 'self-interested' interests are to count as interests results from his recognition of the danger for a polity if public policy makers weight all interests equally. The danger is that when people have publicly-oriented wants, or social aims, the policy makers may have to initiate policies that lead to the tyranny of some groups in the polity. For example, religious groups may demand the subjugation of other religious groups or the imposition of certain tastes on others. The religious zealot might be as disturbed that others read pornographic books or go to theatres on Sundays, as he would be if he were forced to engage in these activities. Indeed on altruistic grounds he might regard it as more important that others, rather than himself, should not become depraved in this way. Whatever the decision-making procedure in a polity, when there are large numbers of such citizens, they might succeed in dictating to others the wants that they are allowed to satisfy.[33] Barry argues that the liberal government may reject wants to affect the want satisfaction of others as not being wants at all: they are not to be included in determining what interests the citizens have. We have already suggested that this solution to the tyranny problem is an illiberal one, and it can be shown that within the framework provided by Barry a more satisfactory alternative can be found.

One preliminary point must be emphasised about groups with life-styles or primary values radically different from those dominant in western societies. They usually coexist in the same territory as, rather than being fully integrated into, the polity. For some purposes, Amish and other religious groups in America are treated as not being constituent members of the State in the way that other citizens are. But the main thrust of the argument presented here is that, rather than restricting what is to count as an interest, the same result desired by Barry could be attained if the government is restricted in terms of the kinds of wants it can take account of. Thus, along with privately-oriented wants, a government would be allowed to take account of wants for others if three conditions relating to the type of benefit sought are met. First, the benefit must either be similar for everyone in the polity or must be made available to unassignable individuals. This provides a guarantee that some groups will not be excluded from the other-regarding wants of the altruist. Second, that which is wanted for others must be a benefit, and the total benefit must exceed any net losses that any specific individuals might incur. This would exclude the demands of the vengeful. Third, the benefit must be of a readily determinable kind. The government should not attend to the wants of others when, for example, the benefit is the 'improvement of the moral welfare of the citizenry' or 'an increase in the opportunity for eternal salvation'.

These last two examples may be contrasted with the case of the public-regarding suburban dweller who argues that cleaner air in the whole metropolis is in his interest. He claims this, not because he is particularly affected by air pollution in his outer suburb, but because his altruism leads him to want policy results from which all can benefit. He campaigns for stronger pollution laws to promote the interests of others, particularly central city dwellers, rather than to improve his own neighbourhood. Presumably this benefit is a general one for anyone who wishes to go to the city; let us also suppose that the total benefit shared by all exceeds the specific costs to motorists, workers in pollution-creating industries, and others. In this case whether the benefits are realisable could quite easily be established, so that there would seem no reason why it should not count as part of the suburbanite's interests in the public-policy process. It is only when social aims impose indeterminable objectives on others, or are likely to disadvantage a few yet provide no common benefits, that their inclusion as part of someone's interests will lead to tyranny.[34]

We have now outlined the liberal concept of interest. We have argued that a central component of this concept is the idea of citizens autonomously choosing their life-styles and their main values. Although the liberal values the highest possible autonomy for all citizens in making these choices, he only allows certain kinds of wants to be ignored by public-policy makers. These are wants acquired when the citizen could make no autonomous choices in their selection; they are the ones he acquires as a result of manipulation by others. But how is the polity to be organised so that the interests of all can be best promoted by the government?

In general, two main conditions have been thought to be necessary. First, socio-economic resources in the polity should not be so unequally distributed that they provide for inequality in the results of the public-policy making process. However, this has remained an implicit assumption in democratic theorising rather than being a starting point for research. There has been neither systematic analysis of the permissible limits of such inequalities nor systematic evaluation of whether the western democracies fall inside or outside these limits. In common with this tradition, these major issues are also ignored by the present study.

Second, liberal theorists have argued that majority rule decision making, in the form of government by single, cohesive parties competing regularly in a two party system, with the parties free from the demands of pressure groups, is essential.

The maximisation of governmental accountability is held by a liberal to be incompatible with a high degree of responsiveness by government to pressure outside the framework of party in the period between elections. There are four reasons for this. The first is that a pressure group system would always tend to exclude some groups, at least partially, however equally most socio-economic resources were divided in the community. Political agendas cannot be completely open when each one of a multitude of groups demands priority. Secondly, strategic considerations in the mobilisation of citizens would lead to the under-representation of groups promoting collective benefits. Thirdly, a government might be forced to concede to the demands of groups that sought to restrict its policies in providing for the autonomy of citizen choice. Finally, in one particular respect it will certainly reduce this autonomy. The political leadership has an educative function, in that it should seek to make coherent for the citizens both the alternative ways in which conflicts of interest in the society can be fairly resolved and the common interests of citizens that need to be promoted. However, if those seeking public office are primarily responsive to pressure group demands, they may seek to use their role as arbiters in a bargaining process to extract resources with which to compete in other ways for the popular vote. This problem is examined in Chapter 3. Furthermore, they will have an incentive to compete for those votes that can be influenced by pressure group affiliation, and this will entail competition between office seekers over the payment of specific benefits. In both these ways the educative aspect of electoral competition is reduced.

The superiority of the simple majority procedure as the means of generating the General Will was recognised by Rousseau, and a contemporary defence of this position has been provided by Brian Barry.[35] The disadvantage of the qualified majority system is that it makes it more likely that organised minorities can intervene decisively in the policy making process to obtain benefits for themselves. In particular, Barry identifies the threat of the offensive veto as a weapon available to such minorities. Majority rule will be most nearly approached if there are as few stages as possible at which those proposing policy have to compile different coalitions to support it. In turn this necessitates the existence of tightly knit political parties as intermediaries between citizens and government. Parties are the most effective institution for bringing about the sort of binding agreements between elected representatives that can prevent minorities from practising the most common feature of minorities rule – the politics of log-rolling through vote trading. The practical effects of this have been well illustrated by Schattschneider in his analysis of the legislation of the Smoot-Hawley tariff. Of this study Steven Brams has written:

Each member who joined the tariff combination for a price on some issue (usually a tariff on something manufactured in his district) gained an advantage for himself and his constituents. Such a large number joined, however, that protection was made indiscriminate – nearly everybody got something. Thereby, international trade was discouraged and disrupted – to the disadvantage of everybody in the society. To the extent that the Smoot-Hawley tariff deepened and extended the Great Depression in the 1930s, even the gainers probably suffered more than they gained.[36]

To be effective in countering minorities, parties must not only have strong internal discipline, they must be able to govern as a majority party without having to strike post-election bargains with other parties. If they have to do this, the resulting coalition government (or 'arrangement') will more easily allow minorities into the policy-making process. In addition, the electorate will have had removed effective means for imposing accountability on the leaders.

The problem that is being addressed in this book is: are centralised parties likely to provide for the genuine competition that liberal theorists see as the central component of democratic accountability? We will suggest in Chapter 3 that competition between parties is a restricted form of competition; as well as being centralised, competitive parties in a 'liberal' democracy would have to be internally democratic. In this respect we are revising a major part of the democratic theory of writers such as Barry and Schattschneider.

3 Competition, Oligopoly and Electoral Markets

In this chapter we argue that, by itself, the electoral mechanism does not provide the autonomy of citizens' choice that is necessary for the existence of a liberal society. On the contrary, given the oligopolistic nature of party competition, the mechanism introduces a bias into the procedures by which interests are identified. This is because there is an incentive for the parties to compete with one another mainly in the provision of what we refer to as 'disinformation'. First, however, it is necessary to examine a central problem for any 'liberal' theory of popular government. It may be outlined as follows.

The government in a liberal society is indirectly concerned with the wants that citizens happen to have, and therefore has to be responsive to new demands and to new social movements. Unless it is known that their wants are 'irrational' or they have been manipulated by others, the government's policies must enable citizens to maximise their opportunities for satisfying these wants. Thus political institutions must be designed to ensure that the parties are ultimately responsive to the citizenry. However, unlike the populist, the liberal theorist recognises two difficulties. First, because of a shortage of time and other resources, no citizen can autonomously select all his wants. As it is not worthwhile for citizens to independently acquire information about public policies, their opinions (wants for policies) will be taken largely from those sources, to which access involves little or no trouble or expense. Students of political socialisation have clearly demonstrated that this has resulted in the acquisition of political values and opinions primarily from the family, but also from the workplace and from social groups with which the citizen interacts.[1] Nevertheless, there is an important respect in which public leaders are able to affect directly the citizens' wants, and to affect also the extent of their autonomy of choice. For political leaders, particularly when organised in parties, can indirectly influence many wants through the alternative views of political reality they present to the electorate, both between and

32

during election periods. Because they are in a position to offer the citizens interpretations of the political universe, political leaders in part determine the nature of the socialisation process itself.[2]

Obviously the advent of television has increased the access of politicians to the public. Nevertheless, it could be argued that if television lowers the cost of political information to the citizen, it also makes it more difficult for party leaders to organise some issues out of politics. For example, the televising of the Vietnam war hardened opinions about it amongst supporters and opponents alike, thus reducing the policy options open to the Johnson administration. Yet perhaps the notable effect of television on post-war politics in America has been to erode the institutional constraints on politicians. Rather than being used to portray to the public alternative objectives for the polity, it has enabled politicians to circumvent the processes through which they are made accountable to the public. This point has been illustrated effectively by Theodore H. White:

> In the twenty-two years between 1952 and 1974 [the men of television's] electronic magic would change American politics. Television would free national candidates more and more from dependence on, or discipline by, their parties; the tube could sway more swing votes than any party organisation. A candidate's hopes could be destroyed by television in a single unguarded moment, as George Romney's were to be in 1967. Or a man could use it to appeal over his party, over its managers, even over the head of the ticket. One must mark 1952 as the date that Richard Nixon discovered how spectacular the influence of television could be, when, with his masterful and era-making 'Checkers speech', he reached for the first time, nationally, to stir the emotions of Middle America and override the decision of the party masters for his dismissal.[3]

To the extent that the alternatives that elected public officials present to the public are substantive, realisable and comprehensible, the autonomy of citizen choice is increased. By identifying what is both the possible and the desirable scope of government policy, they will either reinforce existing lifestyles or make possible the emergence of new ones. Particularly at times of economic and social transition, the parties are in a position to redefine the lines of political cleavage, thus affecting the sorts of wants citizens will have. Whether the parties have an incentive to do this is a question that will be examined in the course of this chapter.

The second problem recognised by the liberal, but not by the populist, is that some policies – namely those that provide for the conditions of autonomous choice, are in the citizens' interests irrespective of whatever wants they happen to have. For the liberal, *the* governmental problem has been that of devising institutional arrangements that will provide both a high degree of responsiveness to citizens and a high degree of responsibility to them by political leaders.

One of the best known 20th-century solutions to this dilemma is that of Joseph Schumpeter. Schumpeter argues that governmental responsiveness to the citizenry is dangerous for the polity. An electorate, that is of necessity ill-informed, will make demands of government that might well be counter to the interests of the groups making them and the interests of the community as a whole. These latter interests are best promoted when the government is freed as much as possible from pressure from the electorate. It will then be able to evaluate policy alternatives purely in terms of their 'technical' merit, and will subsequently implement those ones that further a wide range of interests. Although governments are freed from direct and continuous popular control, they are accountable to the citizens at elections. Perhaps more than any political theorist before him, Schumpeter relies on the electoral mechanism to ensure that governments are responsible to citizens. What should be at issue in an election is whether the ruling party is a more technically competent set of rulers than their opponents claim to be. Competition is not primarily centred, as it is in the later analysis of Anthony Downs, on the relative position of the parties on issues. It is because of this that Schumpeter can be regarded as being more like a liberal theorist of democracy, while Downs like Dahl propounds a populist theory.[4] It is this important distinction between the two that is confused by those who insist that the fundamental bifurcation in modern democratic theory is that between 'elitist' and 'participatory' theories.

Nevertheless, Schumpeter is not simply arguing that the leadership should remain unresponsive to demands from the electorate. Like Mosca in his later writing, Schumpeter recognises that not all popular demands can or should be ignored by the government.[5] However, if in one respect Schumpeter presents a non-populist face of democracy, his analysis is also based on an assumption that has been central to populist democratic theory. He believes, like many others before and after him, that the electoral mechanism serves a similar function to that of the price mechanism in an economy. Like most advocates of representative government, he assumes that one of its main advantages over non-representative forms is that it places some constraints on the policies pursued by elected representatives. Why electoral competition is likely to achieve this has never been fully explained. In the first section of this chapter we examine the logic of the competitive mechanism, and it is suggested that its performance is likely to be of less benefit to the electorate than is normally assumed.

A. THE LIMITATIONS OF ELECTORAL COMPETITION

It should first be noted that behind most theories of electoral competition lies an analogy that is drawn from perfect competition in economics. In the latter, the consumer is sovereign. Since the consumer will always purchase from the cheapest supplier, there is no incentive for any supplier to offer goods for sale other than at the price that provides him with a 'normal' profit. The supplier who attempts to sell goods well above this price will make no sales, whilst one who sells below it will make no profits. Given that the amount offered for sale at any particular price is determined by the schedule of costs, the price is determined by the level of consumer demand. Thus although they act individually, the consumers *en masse*, will directly affect the behaviour of the suppliers. In representative government the voter is supposedly the consumer and the candidate for public office the supplier.

Even before the complicating factor of political parties is introduced, it should be apparent that the analogy between perfect economic competition and electoral competition is not a complete one. Assuming that he is above the poverty line, the consumer in an economy is a purchaser of many goods, not just one. He is free to choose how many types of goods he will purchase, and in what quantities. However, the citizen can normally only express a preference for a fixed number of candidates, and cannot in voting show how much more he favours one candidate over another. In single-member districts he can only give a first choice vote to one candidate, and when this is combined with a plurality voting system, he can only choose to vote for one candidate and not for any of the others. No voting system used in the western democracies provides the voter with the opportunity to determine how many votes in the legislature a particular representative will have. (There is no equivalent to the consumer's choice of 'quantity' he purchases, for even in multi-member districts he cannot help to determine the number of votes the representative will have in the legislature.)[6] Furthermore, there is no incentive, in terms of his self interest, for the voter to participate or become informed about the political market. On the other hand, it is in the interest of the consumer to be informed about shifts in relative prices in some markets because he benefits individually from such information.[7] It is worthwhile for him to bear a higher cost in acquiring information about the supply conditions of private goods, than the voter would consider reasonable for information about public goods.

Two consequences might be expected to follow from this last problem, and there is evidence of their existence in real world polities. The first is that with completely uninformed 'consumers' (voters) there is no incentive for the 'suppliers' (representatives) to provide what the public wants over a long period of time. With an uninformed electorate, the representative who does attempt to do so may still lose to a candidate whose line on policies is little related to results which the public wants, and who only sees himself remaining in public life a short time. These 'non-market' candidates may offer themselves for election because they conceive it a public duty to do so, or because there are specific policies they wish to see implemented, after which they do not seek re-election. They are volunteers rather than career-oriented politicians.[8] Evidence from the United States suggests that such men are prevalent at the local council level, and indeed the democratic ethos seems to encourage such candidates. From the viewpoint of this ethos, public 'service' is seen as a duty and one which will impose 'costs' on the participants rather than providing them with 'profits'. The political perspective of the volunteer is likely to differ from that of the careerist, and he will less readily take account of his electorate when deciding how to vote on public policy matters.[9] The more local the level of politics, the easier it is for volunteers to flourish. Voter information and turnout decline sharply at these lower levels of politics. This makes it easier for a determined candidate to mobilise votes without attracting large-scale opposition. Volunteerism tends to prosper, and its effects are likely to be most serious, in polities with dispersed decision-making institutions that provide for a high degree of local autonomy.

The second effect that could be predicted from the absence of a 'consumer-type' incentive for the voter to acquire political information is that candidates for public office will not compete on similar terms with each other. Because they have no reason for acquiring political 'information', the citizens will rely on that which is cost-free. Anthony Downs, for example, argued that the rational voter would tend to use ideologies as a first resort in deciding how to vote: he would examine the ideological differences between the parties and vote for that which was nearest his position.[10] For Downs, ideologies were the least costly form of political information. In fact ideologies, or generalised issue stances are possessed by relatively few voters, as their acquisition is expensive. Nevertheless, the citizenry can, and do, perceive in a simplified form some issues as defined by the political leadership. These issues are ones which have had intense coverage over a relatively long period of time. This was probably the case with the controversy over British membership of the Common Market from the election of February 1974 until the referendum on the issue in June 1975. Surveys revealed that many electors reiterated as *their* position a view that many political leaders (especially those in the Labour government) had continually put forward. This was that a decision to leave the EEC had to be evaluated differently from the original decision to join, and that on balance the 'cost' of leaving was too great. (By a cynic it might be thought that this supports the line taken by the Labour M.P., John Mackintosh, to the effect that the people always do as they are told.)

In defining the issues of an election, and in supplying information about them, the incumbent office holder is clearly in a better position than other candidates. The electorate is more likely to be familiar with his name than any other candidate, and providing he has not taken an extremely unpopular stance on a matter of immediate concern to his electorate, this will normally ensure his re-election. It is not unreasonable to expect an electorate to use the little information it has, that of the incumbent's apparently adequate performance, as the decisive factor in determining their vote. This problem of the incumbent's advantage has been particularly remarkable in the U.S., where 85% of congressmen who actively seek re-election obtain it.[11] This particular example also exposes two more factors that may insulate the incumbent from electoral competition. First, if his length of tenure increases his influence in the representative body, he may attract the electoral support of specific-interest groups who wish to make use of this. Second, if there is no effective control of electoral campaign expenditure, such groups are more likely to give financial assistance to the incumbent than to his opponents.[12] Both these factors have been of major significance in American congressional elections.

Until now we have examined electoral competition without taking account of political parties. We have seen that, even excluding them, the analogy between electoral competition and economic competition in the free market has several weaknesses. Yet in most elections in western democracies, the political party is the most important factor determining electoral choice. In the remainder of this chapter it is argued that the introduction of parties further weakens the analogy with economic competition. Curiously, until quite recently, many political scientists have retained such an analogy even though econom- ists have developed theories of oligopolistic behaviour that are quite different from those of perfect competition.[13] These interpretations of oligopoly have serious implications for the conception of representa- tive government as free electoral competition.

A major part of the theory of free elections is that if the existing parties do not reflect political divisions that are significant for a large part of the electorate, then new parties will form. Certainly there are instances when it may appear that this has happened, as for example with the rise of the British Labour party at the beginning of this century. However, alleged examples of its occurrence do not prove that there will always be a tendency for it to happen whenever the existing major parties are out of line with socio-political divisions in the community. It can be argued that, rather than being a major constraint on the existing parties, the threat of new competitors is a fairly small one for them. In some countries, such as the U.S., the rise of more parties has been conceived by governments as being against the public interest. In 1968 the state of Ohio contended before the U.S. Supreme Court that the public interest was served by laws which discriminated against third parties, on the ground that such parties increased the chance that a candidate would win with less than a majority of the votes cast.[14]

Legal constraints on new parties, however, are uncommon and there are greater problems than this in founding a new major political party. The resources required to run a national party are enormous, and unlike competitive economic firms the small party cannot continuously expand until it becomes a large one. The small party usually stays small. There is a limit to its expansion, for, without electoral success, its resources are confined to those supplied by a membership attracted by its ideology. As few citizens want to bear the various costs involved in participation and in acquiring an ideology, the potential membership of such parties is small. To become a major party, an emergent one must attract financial and organisational resources that will be em- ployed to provide cost-free information to the voters. Indeed, given the advantage of 'free' publicity that the major parties have, the emergent party will probably require more resources than they do, and will certainly have to meet the cost of these resources over a period of several national elections. Even a party which was formerly large and could draw on its tradition, the British Liberal party, could not overcome these problems in the 1950s and 1960s. Even if the problem of organisational resources is ignored, the difficulty of acquiring adequate financing is usually insuperable. Both commercial firms and labour unions (the only possessors of sufficiently large funds) will regard the investment required in the emergent party as wasted. A new party that concentrates on a question of regional identity, or issues specific to a particular region, is more likely to succeed. It can ignore much of the electorate without at the same time appearing to be incapable of gaining major electoral victories in doing so.

This approach to the formation of major parties runs contrary to the conventional wisdom of the free electoral system. According to this, the failure to organise a new political movement indicates merely that it had little support: if the support existed then those who accepted its goals would contribute to the cost of their realisation. However, the difficulty in forming a new major party is that, whilst it is in the interest of all its 'supporters' that the movement is organised, as individuals it is almost certainly not worth the while of any of them to contribute to it. Once again, returning to the assumptions of self-interest and rationality, the logic of Olson's arguments is pertinent.[15] The individual decides whether to sustain part of the cost of the movement by comparing his share of the cost with the value he places on its success, discounted by the likelihood of his contribution making the difference between success and failure. He will only contribute if the former is smaller than the latter. Almost certainly it will not be. The likelihood in a large organisation that his contribution will make the difference is so small that, however much he values its success, its discounted value will be much less than the cost. (For if it succeeds why should he share part of the cost of providing it when he can have the benefits free of charge? If it fails he has wasted his resources.) The rational man therefore chooses not to contribute.

Olson has argued that all movements designed to realise a public good are likely to have fewer resources than if one individual could supply all those needed; political parties are a good example of this. He has further claimed that the only way a would-be multi-member movement can obtain resources is to offer selective incentives to its membership; that is, ones which are not available to non-members. In the case of a labour union such an incentive would be the requirement that union membership is a condition of obtaining a job in a particular firm or industry. However, there are few such incentives available to a party, and consequently new parties are unlikely to develop even if there is widespread support for them. They cannot attract resources until they obtain a large share of the popular vote. But they cannot do that until (i) a large section of the electorate is aware of their definition of political reality and accepts it; and (ii) it appears that they have a chance of winning the election, or affecting the composition of the government. The former requires them to have resources and the latter requires them to appear to be a major party for few voters will support a hopeless cause. Again, this latter in part necessitates them having the resources. The circle is complete; small parties rarely escape the ghetto of smallness. Equally the larger parties are protected from new competitors, so that unlike the perfect economic market there are only a few potential 'suppliers'.

B. OLIGOPOLY AND ELECTORAL COMPETITION

Those who see free elections as the defining characteristic of representative government would not argue that the threat from new parties is the main constraint on the policies of the existing parties.[16] Rather, they claim that it is the competition between these major parties which is the more important mechanism. At this point their argument departs from economic orthodoxy. Economists have long argued that the behaviour of a few suppliers – oligopolists – will be very different from that of perfectly competitive suppliers. For the political scientist, an interesting analysis of oligopolistic behaviour is that of Albert O. Hirschman. Hirschman's concern is with the reaction of consumers to a decline in the standard of a product from an oligopolist, although Barry has argued that the analysis is equally applicable to all forms of consumer dissatisfaction with an oligopolist's product quality.[17] There are two retaliatory weapons available to consumers. One is the transference of their custom to another supplier (exit), while the other is complaint about the good supplied (voice). These may be used separately, or, as Barry argued, in conjunction with each other. Hirschman contends that, in perfect competition, dissatisfaction with the goods supplied results in the exit of consumers from those who supply inferior goods to other producers. The incentive to the supplier to maintain quality is that if he lets it fall below that of his competitors he will cease to sell goods. In the long term, he will go out of business. On the other hand, with a monopoly, exit to another supplier is not possible, and consumers can only exercise voice. The extent to which this is effective in increasing general product quality will depend on two factors:

(i) the ability of the most effective exponents of voice amongst the consumers to maintain the supply of a higher quality good to themselves than is available to others;

(ii) the willingness of groups of consumers to incur costs, which may not be rational for the self-interested person, to promote group consumer action against the supplier.

The case of the oligopolist is different again, and the situation confronting consumers may be even worse than it is with a monopolist. Many consumers are likely to ignore voice in favour of exit when they become dissatisfied with product quality. When the most articulate consumers are amongst those who exit the potential lobby against the supplier is particularly weakened. Many of those who exit will be less willing to bear a cost in voicing a grievance against the supplier of a good they have already consumed, when they have hopes of getting a better product in the immediate future. The impact of voice is thus less than with a monopoly. Yet exit does not work in the way that it does in perfect competition, for the oligopolist is concerned with maintaining a particular share of the market. Unlike the perfect competitor who can sell all that he can produce, the oligopolist can sell in the short term no more than his approximate current share of the market. (In the long run, both his share and the total size of the market might be increased by advertising.) If he reduces the price of the good, he will provoke a price war with his competitors in which none of them substantially increase their share of the market and profits are small. Normally at some point they will collude to end it without any benefit from the war accruing to any of them. In a perfectly competitive market, when the quality of the goods of an individual supplier is lower than that of his competitors he must either improve it or quit the business; dissatisfied customers will buy elsewhere. However, in an oligopolistic market there are two reasons why the supplier of an inferior quality product is unlikely to be affected in this way. The first (and in this context less important) reason is that some consumers may be unable to exit: they cannot afford to buy the more highly priced goods of the competitors. The second reason is that, because the oligopolist differentiates his product from those of his competitors, many consumers may be unable to make a direct comparison between his product and that of his competitors. He may retain a fixed share of the market by virtue of consumers being imperfectly informed; this may be true of all the other members of the oligopoly. Consequently, the incentive for oligopolists to maintain quality in the long term is low. They gain as many customers exiting from other suppliers as they lose. Thus an oligopoly is likely to be a market in which many customers are not particularly satisfied with the quality of the product they are supplied with. It is also one in which voice is limited by exit, which, of itself, is not effective in maintaining control over the quality of the product.

Several arguments can be put forward which indicate that the major parties may be just as unconcerned about the interests and opinions of their voters as the oligopolistic firm is with customer satisfaction with their products. One consideration is the low level of political information possessed by voters; it is likely that this will be even less than their knowledge of the products of oligopolists. The man who is dissatisfied with his Ford car has some incentive to glean information about the comparable British Leyland model. He may lose considerably if there are quality differences and he chooses unwisely the next time. Furthermore there is at least some readily accessible information, of a formal and informal kind, about the comparability of current models of the companies. In the case of political parties, however, not only has the voter no incentive to acquire information, but also the available current information concerns the performance of the party in office only. All the information about opposition parties available is that of their policy proposals and their previous records in office, if any. Furthermore, most voters do not possess an ideology with which they can interpret political reality and differentiate between the parties. This is not to argue that electorates do not comprehend a difference between left and right, or liberal and conservative; rather it is to admit that these differences are not consistently understood.

Nevertheless, what is perhaps the most formal analysis of electoral competition between parties – that of Anthony Downs – in large part depends on the assumption that electorates have ideologies.[18] The most distinctive aspect of his analysis is the explanation of the behaviour of political parties faced by an electorate with sufficiently coherent ideologies that they can all be located on a left-right continuum. For different configurations of ideology within the electorate, Downs claims to show what will be the optimum number of parties in this polity and the optimum issue stances and ideologies for them to adopt. The 'standard' case is that of a 'normal' distribution of ideology for which the appropriate number of parties is two. Both parties will then try to provide an ideology which places them as close to the median voter as possible, whilst remaining on their 'own' side of the continuum (see Figure 3.1).[19] (Other configurations of voters on the continuum pose more complicated problems as they may entail multi-party systems. With the latter, the electoral ideology of the party will diverge from the policies it will support if it joins the coalition of governing parties.) The interesting point about this analysis is that it formalises one of the main conventional wisdoms of the free electoral system, namely that competition provides an incentive for the parties to align their policies closely to those of the interests and opinions of the electorate. For Downs this is achieved in a two party system, with normal voter distribution, by the attempt of the parties to adopt the ideology of the median voter.

This link between the electorate and parties becomes more complex if two assumptions crucial to the Downs analysis are rejected:

  (i) that new major parties can be formed if the existing ones move too far away from the electorate;

 (ii) that voters can be conceived as having a very weak ideology. Once again economists' studies of oligopoly, provide a useful heuristic device. This provides a framework for understanding the behaviour of parties.

It is appropriate to introduce this last point by outlining three of the main characteristics of oligopoly:

  (i) there is no incentive for firms to engage in price competition with one another and there is no incentive for them to improve the quality of existing product(s);

 (ii) firms are content with a fixed and stable share of the market;

(iii) firms attempt to differentiate their products from those of comparable brands of their rivals, and to this end they compete through advertising.

(i) *Absence of price competition*

In the 'standard' Downs' case of party competition an intense electoral struggle occurs for the central ideological position. As he assumes that one party cannot 'leap-frog' over another on the continuum, the ability of a party to get close to the centre in the two-party model will depend on the location of the other party. However, if the electorate is not consistently ideological, but rather has a complex set of weakly per-

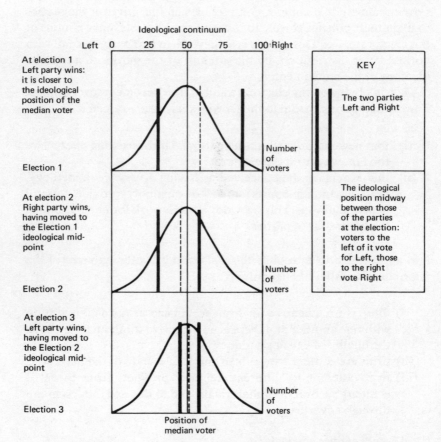

FIGURE 3.1   Party Strategies in a Two-Party System

ceived interests and a few incompatible policy preferences, it may be questioned whether there is a middle ground over which this competition occurs. As the parties will not be able to define the centre, they are unlikely to be immediately concerned either with shifts in it or in the position of the other party. Instead the parties will base their strategy on something that is more easily determined by them, and less likely to entail a risk of a complete debacle at an election. This is the definition of political reality – that is, of extremist positions and moderate ones and of the politically relevant socio-economic cleavages, that emerged from the last period of crisis in the party system. There is a customary definition of the areas of political conflict, one that developed when crisis forced the parties to 'reconceive' the nature of political divisions for the electorate. These crises are directly related to certain social and economic crises, the results of which threaten one or both parties with the loss of their position as either *a*, or *the*, major party in the system.

In Britain, political divisions are those that were established in the last period of party crisis – the 1920s. The decline of the Liberal party was not inevitable, as Downs suggests; it was not merely the effect of a franchise extension. Rather, there occurred in the period after the First World War a struggle between three parties to define for the public the nature of the relevant political divisions. Insufficient numbers in the electorate saw the specifically Liberal interpretation as appropriate as those of the other two parties, and the party drifted into being that of the 'protest' voter.[20] The causes of this crisis are directly attributable to the war. Both the socio-economic upheaval it produced and the split in the Liberal party, enabled the Labour party to escape from the ghetto of 'smallness' between 1918 and 1923. Immediately before the war the lines of political cleavage were not, as is argued in one well known book, being redrawn.[21] The Labour party did not make an electoral breakthrough after its initial success in 1906, which is best seen as the product of Liberal generosity in making electoral pacts with it. The last British party crisis, then, had exceptional causes and has set the pattern of electoral competition for over fifty years.

In the United States party crises have been somewhat more frequent, and have been explained by Walter Dean Burnham in terms of the inappropriateness of American political institutions in modifying the effects of rapid socio-economic change. The last redefinition of political reality was in the Great Depression. (This occurred not so much before the 1932 election, as in Roosevelt's programme afterwards, for his election campaign was not based on massive Federal government intervention in the economy.) Before that, the election of

1896 sealed the success of Republican politicians in defining politics in terms of the claims of industrialisation over those of primary production. A major theme in the analysis of these crises has been that they produce a system in which there is one major and one minor party, ı ather than two parties of similar size. Whether this is to be explained as somehow 'natural' to the U.S., or is the product of less deep-rooted institutional problems is an interesting question, but one that cannot be examined here.[22]

To return now to the idea of oligopoly. We noted earlier that parties dc not want to redefine the lines of division in the society, unless they believe that they have to. In doing so they may leave the way open either for their own demise (as with the British Liberal party) or for minority party status for a generation (as with the Democrats after 1896).[23] This behaviour is parallel to the pricing policy of the economic oligopolist, or to put it another way, the quality of goods he offers in a given price range. If he competes with the other suppliers in this way a price war will ensue. If not stopped by agreement, this would eventually force some of the suppliers out of business. Just as the party tries to stay in the middle of the lines of cleavage that it helped to draw, so the oligopolist prefers to maintain a stable price that renders above normal, if not exorbitant, profits.

Even when the oligopolist perceives that, by lowering the price, the demand for all goods in the industry will be increased to such a degree as to maintain or increase total profits, he may still be unwise to be the instigator of a price cut. To the new consumer, the products of his competitors may have more appeal (once they have followed his price leadership) than his own. Consequently both his profits and his share of the market may decline. There is no exact parallel to this in party competition, though there is a similar phenomenon. Parties that adopt a radical programme of reform, for which there is support and on which they are elected, may lose their majority at the next election even though their reforms are not rejected by their supporters or completely denounced by opposition parties. Because of the majority-minority party relationship, the U.S. offers no examples of this. However since the development of a two-party system in the 1860s in Britain, there have been three examples of 'radical' ministries. The governments of 1868–74, 1906–10 and 1945–50 all made significant changes in public policy as compared with the sequence of governments that preceded them. In all three cases the reforms seem to have been accepted by large sectors of the public; but the 1868–74 government was defeated, the government in 1910 lost its overall majority and became dependent on minor party support, and the Labour government in 1950 lost its effective majority and lost the subsequent election in 1951. These governments can be classified as liberal or progressive, but it could be argued that a similar experience would befall a 'radical conservative' government: indeed some might argue that the 1970–4 Conservative government was an example of this.[24] We may conclude from this that, even when they seek merely to change public policy fundamentally, let alone redefine divisions, parties run a great risk in doing so. Consequently, they tend to stay within a very narrow framework of policy reference.

(ii) *Stable market shares*

A second characteristic of oligopoly is the firms' concern to maintain a relatively stable market in which their share of the total market is constant. They do not collude in the sense that they conspire with each other to maintain similar prices, it is simply in their own interest to do so. Together with a competent advertising campaign, it usually assures them of maintaining their share of the market, without the risk involved in a price war.

Now, as far as the parties are concerned, we have already stated that there is no direct equivalent to the maintenance of a given market share, as it would seem that parties would want to win each election. (As has been suggested, the case of systems with no majority party is entirely different.) Yet it can be argued that there is a phenomenon that is not too dissimilar which may be considered in this context. This can be explained as follows. However attentive a government is to the interests and opinions of its electorate, the electorate's perception of its performance to a large extent can only be measured against the standard which the party's performance in government has established. For an ill-informed electorate, there is no more objective standard to which they have an incentive to turn. Clearly, a government perceived as competent, when its predecessor was regarded as the opposite, may generate support for several elections. This certainly happened during Roosevelt's first term of office, following public disenchantment with the hapless Hoover. But the apparently successful ministry will also raise public expectations of how a government should perform, and when the government falls below this standard it may lose office to a party of less talent. An example from recent British political history may make this point clear.

In 1959 the Conservative government based its election campaign on the success of its policies in providing economic growth that had made possible the boom in the consumption of consumer goods of the previous two years. By convincing many voters that the apparent affluence was partly its responsibility, the party helped to set a standard of what was expected of government control over economic prosperity. When government policy for controlling an imbalance in the balance of payments resulted in a mild recession and a slower growth rate the government lost much electoral support. For example, in by-elections in the later period the party did worse than it had done under similar conditions in 1957. Yet in the period 1960–4 the government's economic policies were arguably more imaginative in many ways than previously, and the government from 1962–4 certainly included more men of political talent than earlier. Yet although the policy differences between the two major parties were not great, the Conservatives lost the 1964 election when five years earlier they had had a landslide victory in terms of seats. This was an example of a party deliberately raising public expectations about what a government could achieve; but the same argument would apply to a government that had actually achieved policy success: it may be judged by the standards it sets. In the case of the Conservative party the following period (1964–75) was electorally their worst for 60 years.

The incentive for the parties to provide policy results which the public wants is tempered by the need not to raise public expectations of government to a degree that may be difficult to maintain in the future. It may rebound on the party at future elections. Like the oligopolist, the best strategy for the party will be to concern itself with gaining a certain minimum share of the market – in this case as measured by the proportion of elections that it wins in the medium term (for example, a 15 year period). The safe strategy is one which does not raise public expectations too much, since its failures may provide the basis for several electoral victories for the other party. When both parties informally adopt such a strategy the result is likely to be a regular turnover of governments at elections. The dissatisfied voter can only exit to the other party, which in turn will be keen not to 'over-achieve' or claim 'over-achievement'.

(iii) *Product differentiation*

So far the arguments have been directed towards explaining the limitations on party competition. Yet it is quite obvious that the parties in western democracies are not collusive; in some ways they compete very intensively with each other. The problem for political science is that of how to interpret this competition. The argument presented here is that it is best seen as a form of product differentiation that is stimulated by advertising. However it is necessary to be clear about the exact nature of this claim. We are not arguing that political parties do not put forward policy programmes, or that they do not maintain ideologies. 'Advertising' is not simply used to refer to appeals to sentiments and images that attach to party labels.[25] Rather we claim that ideology and specific policy programmes, of the kind put forward by British parties are most usefully conceived as a form of advertising: they are not a form of price competition. As this may seem paradoxical, we must commence with an account of the concept of product differentiation.

Comparable products of rival oligopolists do not resemble each other in every respect. As everyone knows there are differences between a British Leyland model and a similar one from Ford, just as there are between the competing products of washing powders from Proctor and Gamble and Unilever. The products of oligopolists, therefore, are unlike those traded in some commodity markets where there is no difference between the product of any suppliers. It is these differences themselves, and the differential performance that result from them, that form the basis of the claims that can be used to attract customers through advertising. Yet if this is so, it might be asked: on what criteria can we judge that one product is similar to that produced by another firm?

Sometimes the manufacturers themselves define the various categories of their product range; indeed much advertising is directed toward informing the customer that products from a rival firm that might be considered similar, are inferior. But in many cases the producers do not wish to tell their public which of their rivals' products are similar to theirs, because this may limit their market if the similar product is considered an inferior type of good by some sectors of that public.[26] Again, the customers' appreciation of their similarity is inadequate; the most successfully marketed goods are those for which a large number of consumers believe there is no direct competitor. Both of these methods of identifying equivalent products are often a useful 'shorthand' way of doing so. Yet if a government were considering control of some oligopolistic practices it would obviously need standards that were, on the one hand less biased, and on the other, more informed. Objective criteria related to the product's principal functions would obviously have to be used.

The characteristic form of competition for an oligopoly is product differentiation. Advertising is the means by which the public becomes aware of it. Advertising is designed to be 'disinformative' to the consumer; the term disinformation perhaps best describes the main purpose of advertising. (Its secondary purpose is that of stimulating the growth of the industry's market.) We do not imply in speaking of disinformation that the producer attempts to lie or even deliberately mislead the consumer, in the way that we speak of false or *mis*leading information, or of someone being misinformed. Nevertheless, the advertiser does provide a partial picture of the product's performance so that the consumer is imperfectly informed about the performance compared with that of the competing products. (The extent of this imperfection, in part, obviously varies with the length of the normal lifetime of the product.) Thus, if the consumer report informs, the advertising campaign disinforms. Consumers can normally only acquire information at a cost to themselves (subscriptions to consumer associations etc.), and many of them are not prepared to pay for this when disinformation is free. Advertising disinformation is partial in three different respects. First, it draws attention to only some aspects of the differences between the performance of a product's primary functions and those of other products. Second, it emphasises 'secondary function' competition that is, competition over criteria that are inessential for the sale of goods of that kind. (Cars would still be bought irrespective of their colour or finish. Yet since the days of Henry Ford's dictum, 'any colour supplied providing it's black', competition over such features has become prominent.) Third, it helps to stimulate total demand by drawing attention to secondary uses or features of the product. (The 'status' aspect of car ownership has been emphasised particularly in sports car advertisements.)

Competition by product differentiation does not perform the social function that price competition does. The latter is a mechanism for regulating both the quality and quantity of the good offered for sale at a particular price. By making consumers sovereign on the matter, the perfect economy will ensure that a 'socially optimum' set of goods is produced, exchanged and consumed (the social optimum is a direct reflection of the consumers' wants). Furthermore, it also enables the consumers to be in a position to define their wants unconstrained. With disinformation this process is distorted: the consumer cannot be said to have defined autonomously what he wants because information is much less readily available than disinformation. He has 'wants' but these largely reflect how he has been exposed to advertising.

The relevance of this to party competition can now be explained. For the society, party competition should perform two functions. First it should be the means by which the public is educated about the major alternative conceptions of the nature of political divisions within the society, and about the political principles in terms of which the parties claim these divisions should be evaluated. That is, party competition should provide the members of the public with information to help them define what they want. Second, it should provide an opportunity to select leaders who will implement policies that resolve the overt mass-level conflicts that emanate from these divisions. But as we have argued there is no incentive for the parties to do this: in seeking electoral victory they have an incentive to portray themselves as occupying the middle ground of a socio-economic division that was defined many years earlier. They do not try to redefine political reality for the electorate.[27] The cost to the electorate is that it is much less informed than it should be: there is no mechanism that provides them with 'quality' control. However in order to gain office the parties must compete with one another, but do so in ways that minimise the risk of long-term exile from public office. Thus they compete in three ways that closely correspond to those of the oligopolist firm:

(i) on specific policy proposals that have always been central to the long-standing definition of political division (for example, in Britain this would include the nationalisation/denationalisation stances);

(ii) allegedly different, if unspecified, approaches on agreed policy goals (for example, the need for more hospitals, better schools etc.);

(iii) appeals to the sentiments and traditions of the regular voters of the party and campaigns that draw attention to candidates' personality and style.

It is only with regard to (i) that parties come close to 'primary' competition, but even this falls far short of it. Not only are the issues so long established that any public debate is certainly not an educative process, but, by their very nature they hark back to a vision of political reality that is probably obsolete.[28] Of course, socio-economic changes can and do promote crises in party systems which result in the redefinition of political division, but this happens surprisingly infrequently. Outside these periods, the pressure to search for new conceptions of political reality is small, and is most easily rejected when the party organisation is least open to mass movements. It is noticeable, for example, that the relatively 'open' Liberal party in Britain has become the home of most of those who want to change the focus of political argument. Indeed, it might be argued that the Liberal party itself has been unsuccessful in this redefinition precisely because it has too divergent a set of 'radicals'. Within the two major parties attempts to do this have also failed, and the implication of the arguments presented in this book is that this is because the parties have not been open. The parties normally reject any redefinition of the political universe. This was true of both the ill-conceived Gaitskell challenge to the party's vision of its *raison d'être* in 1961 and the 'Selsdon experiment' in the Conservative party a decade later.[29]

We have argued that party competition in western democracies is not well conceived as a choice between ideologies, as it was by Downs. An ideology, at least as it is portrayed by Downs, is 'a verbal image of the good society and of the chief means of constructing such a society'.[30] It provides its adherents, with a set of ideal types of policy in terms of which all policy proposals can be evaluated. Neither the good society nor the chief means for attaining it change over time. We have suggested that it is exactly such rigidity in attitude toward public policy that is characteristic of one form of competition by product differentiation. Nevertheless, it is mainly used not with respect to the public, but to the party membership. It provides a theme around which to unite the organisations and membership, hence the intensity of opposition to Gaitskell's attempt to remove 'Clause 4'. This need for the party leadership to take account of party ideology greatly increases the pressures on it to accept the conventional perspective of relevant political cleavages. Again, those whose views do not conform to the party's mainstream ideology do not become members. Because of this there is no tendency for 'amateur' activist movements to develop from within, such that new definitions of the political universe can emanate from within the party.[31] In parties not 'locked in' by their own ideology such movements can more easily develop, and this appears to have happened within the Democratic party in America in the last decade. The variety of political leaders that has emerged in the party in this period refutes a popularly held view that the new activists are best regarded as liberals of a similar type. (As yet, though, it remains uncertain whether the Democratic party, by virtue of its role as the major party ('the sun' according to Lubell's analysis), is too large a forum within which a clear redefinition of political division can emerge.) We will return to this theme in Chapter 5 when we argue that mass movement of citizens into the parties is necessary for both the stimulation of genuine competition between parties and the political education of the citizenry.

4 Party Strategies in a Two-Party System

In the last chapter it was argued that, as oligopolists, teams of candidates organised into parties will limit their form of competition with each other. In this chapter we consider a further argument about the restriction of party competition. If this argument were to prove valid then the proposal presented here for removing the first restriction – internally democratic parties – would be undermined. This second problem has been raised by Joseph A. Schlesinger. He contends that when parties come to be concerned with the distribution of benefits they will tend to restrict the size of their electoral coalition to that of a minimum winning coalition.[1] That is, they will not seek to maximise their total vote. Only if parties consist of loosely united individual candidates, motivated by a desire to maximise their political careers, will each candidate running for office under a party label seek to maximise his own vote. Against Schlesinger we argue that the calculations candidates will make regarding optimal strategies are more complex than he suggests. *A priori* there is no reason for believing that non-cohesive , non-programmatic parties will provide for more extensive competition than programmatic ones. The starting point in this discussion is what Schlesinger saw as the main limitation in the application of Down's analysis to the United States: parties in America are not cohesive units.

For Downs, political parties are teams of individuals, the members of which compete for the citizen's votes so as to occupy the positions of leadership in the polity. They have no deeply-held positions of their own on issues. Both their ideology and their stance on particular issues are merely responses to electoral pressures in the political market. The occupation of a political candidate is similar to that of an entrepreneur: the men who enter either politics or business will have to understand the laws of the market if they are to be successful. The laws of electoral competition require that candidates act as brokers between the different interests and opinions in the society. On specific issues of public

53

policy elected officials act as brokers between competing pressure groups; their freedom to distribute benefits is circumscribed by the need to seek re-election at regular intervals from an electorate that is much larger than the pressure group leadership. Again, at elections the politician serves as a broker between extremes of opinion. In a two-party system a party will hold office only so long as its candidates' policies are closer to the centre of public opinion than those of its opponents. Electoral competition thus forces the politician to be a broker.

Downs, of course, conceives politicians as members of teams (parties) rather than as individuals who compete for the electorate's vote for particular offices. Moreover, he assumes that at any given election the party would aim to maximise its total vote. Yet this strategy is only a means to an end – the end being that of control of government. But in the Downsian analysis it is not plausible to assume that parties will simply want control of government now. As an approximation, we may assume that they will want to maximise the number of future years in which they control government. An electoral victory now might well be valued much more highly than one in 5 or 10 years time, but no party will invariably choose victory now if this entails a high probability of exile in opposition for a much longer period. In other words, within the Downsian framework the ultimate goal of a party is best conceived as: *the maximisation of its chances for having as much control as possible of government in the future*, when the value of each possible period of office can be compared with the immediate control of government.[2] However, although with a vote-maximising strategy, an immediate goal of victory can conceivably be the best means for achieving this, it might not be.

It might be thought that this discussion of the incentive for parties to win elections is related to a distinction drawn by William E. Wright between ('rational-efficient') theorists who believe parties 'define goals to win elections' and ('party-democracy') theorists for whom parties win 'elections in order to implement goals'.[3] However, his bifurcation conceals the fact that programmatic parties do (and should) define policies to win elections, just as non-programmatic ones do not (and should not if they are to maximise their long term prospects for office) concern themselves solely with creating images and policies with which to win the next election. If the former type of party is not concerned with its electoral competitiveness then the citizens are as badly served as they would be by volunteer-type candidates. If the latter type of party ignores longer-term strategies (by defining its policies so as to win the next election) it may be working against its own self-interest. As a party-democracy theory, the present analysis suggests that parties should define their policies so as to win elections (though, not necessarily every election). However, we do not accept that all electoral strategies are desirable for the society. If the parties do not try to win, the citizenry might conceivably be forced to choose between ideologies or proposals that bear little relation to the existing socio-economic divisions of the society. Yet whilst the view that parties should define goals to win elections is correct, its implication is not what many political scientists have assumed it is. If the electorate is ill-informed, unable to evaluate policies, and unclear as to the nature of existing socio-economic divisions, the parties should not compete by attempting to mirror the electorate's incompetence. Rather, the voters have truly autonomous choice only if the parties compete by providing voters with alternative conceptions of political reality and elementary conceptual tools with which these can be evaluated. Parties are 'educators'; if competition is to be worthwhile, the electorate must be in a position to choose, and a necessary condition of this is that party competition educates them so that they are placed in that position.

An alternative framework of analysis of electoral competition is provided by Joseph Schlesinger in *Ambition and Politics*, which in America has attracted almost as much attention from specialists in U.S. politics as has *An Economic Theory of Democracy*.[4] In his rational-choice analysis, Schlesinger sees parties as collections of individuals sharing the same electoral label. In opposition to the 'economic' competition of party teams, he postulates another form of competition, that between individual politicians in the furtherance of their own political careers. In the important extension of this argument, Schlesinger attempts to reconcile what he sees as being an inconsistency between the analysis of Downs and that of another rational-choice theorist, William H. Riker. Whereas Downs argues that parties will pursue a strategy of vote maximisation, Riker contends that they will seek to limit the size of their electoral coalition to the minimum necessary to win elections. This latter strategy seems plausible if it is assumed that the components of the party's coalition will not only wish to maximise their control over government in the future, but will also want to maximise their own share of the benefits derivable from government. Schlesinger's attempt to reconcile these seemingly incompatible strategies is founded on a distinction he makes between two kinds of participant in political parties: office-seekers (politicians as political brokers) and benefit seekers (politicians as pursuers of benefits). What Schlesinger has tried to show is that, from the viewpoint of the political broker, the optimal party strategy is the maximisation of his plurality over other parties combined with the maximisation of his total vote. On the other hand, those parties composed of candidates and supporters seeking benefits will, to the extent that they can affect the size of their electoral victories, seek to minimise both their plurality over other parties and the total vote. That is, benefit seekers will opt for the Riker minimum winning coalition strategy. Schlesinger's claim, then, is that Riker and Downs were concerned with two different kinds of party creature: Downs' parties were composed of office seekers whilst Riker's participants were benefit seekers.[5]

The relevance of Schlesinger's analysis to the arguments presented in this book may now be explained. It is that, if he is correct in suggesting that benefit seekers are vote minimisers and office seekers vote maximisers, our solution for overcoming the weakness of the electoral mechanism is inadequate. For we argue that parties are most likely to provide genuine competition when the leadership is constrained to a large extent by policy-seeking activists. However, if benefit seekers in a party normally try to limit the size of their coalition to that of a minimum winning one, the scope of the competition is restricted. The parties will not attempt to incorporate new electoral interests, and will not attempt to redefine political reality; rather they will concern themselves with the preservation of their traditional electoral alliances. This would reinforce the tendency of the parties to pursue the conservative electoral strategy that was explained in the last chapter. Party democracy would thus not overcome the limitations of oligopolistic competition. Conversely, on Schlesinger's argument, a party of office seekers would be more likely to take account of new interests in the electorate. Its candidates would compete more fiercely for the votes of those not currently within their electoral coalitions.

Although Schlesinger considers strategies from the viewpoint of office seekers and benefit seekers, it is more useful to analyse them from three points of view: the office seeking candidate, the supporters of an office-seeking candidate; and the benefit-seeking candidate and his supporters. The reason for this is that Schlesinger's bifurcation between the participants in a political party is not a symmetrical one. Candidates can be either office seeking or benefit seeking, but other participants can only be benefit seekers, irrespective of what kinds of reward they seek. Except for the limiting case in which the officeseeker's campaigns are entirely media-based and presumably directed by an advertising consultant without a 'victory bonus' in his contract, any party necessarily consists mostly of benefit seekers. The workers, activists and supporters of a party are benefit seekers whatever rewards they seek: material (patronage or the opportunity for a career as a political broker in the future), solidary (the love of the political game), or purposive (changes in public policy for others as well as themselves).[6]

A. THE OFFICE-SEEKING CANDIDATE

Schlesinger argues that the optimal strategy for this candidate is the maximisation of both his plurality and the size of the vote he receives. He further claims that the former is more important for him than the latter. He cites two arguments in support of this strategy. In the first place, the larger the plurality the more free the winner becomes from those who would make claims on him for benefits. Secondly, large victories (high pluralities with high turnout) make a candidate more likely to be considered as a contender for higher office in the future than do small victories.

The first problem with his account is that Schlesinger seems to assume that, at least for the 'big' election winner, there is little connection between the payments he makes after one election and the electoral support he will gain in the next one. That is, Schlesinger conceives the payment of benefits (from the viewpoint of the candidate) as payment for 'services' already rendered. They are better seen as advance payments for the support he requires at the next election. The candidate's large plurality in a high turnout election is only one factor which potential supporters will take into account when considering what resources to commit to him at the next election. Another factor is the 'pay off' they have received from the candidate during his period of office. If he has made no payments whatsoever, then there is no incentive for them to contribute anything at the next election. Even the most optimistic supporter would cease contributing at some point were the candidate to default continually on payment.

What the potential supporter will examine in deciding whether to contribute to a candidate's coalition is whether the opportunity cost of the contribution c exceeds the predicted level of payment y multiplied by both the probability that the candidate will be elected e and the probability that he will make the payment p. If $c \rangle yep$ then he will not make the contribution. Obviously, when a contribution to more than one candidate would be worthwhile he would further estimate the effects on y and p should he distribute his divisible resources between several candidates. He might either divide his contribution between opposing candidates or contribute to only one of them.[7] Schlesinger correctly observes that the larger the victory at the last election, the more likely it is that the supporter will accord a high value to e, but he ignores the effect of non-payment on the value of p. The supporter will estimate this partly from the candidate's promises for the future, but mainly from the responses to his contributions in the past, for it is these which are a guide to the credibility of the promises. When the value of p is low for many of his potential supporters, the candidate may not have a winning coalition, despite his large victory previously. In other words, whilst Schlesinger rightly suggests that a large plurality and turnout enables a candidate to reduce the level of payment to his supporters, there is a limit to this reduction beyond which he would risk subsequent electoral defeat.

One interesting aspect of Schlesinger's analysis is his assumption that the independence of office seekers derives from the irrationality of attempts by their erstwhile supporters to defeat them. This parallels an argument of Michels.[8] For the rational participant, the possibility of defeat is only one factor that forms part of the calculation he makes in deciding whether to discipline elected representatives.

A second problem is that the Schlesinger strategy forms only half the calculation a candidate will make in deciding electoral strategy. If we assume that he wishes to maintain a career at the same level of office, the office seeker will balance the winning of the immediate election against the need to win subsequent ones. For the former objective, the optimal strategy is that described by Schlesinger. However, the long term considerations require a minimum-winning coalition strategy which, if possible, he would combine with a vote-maximisation strategy. At future elections the office seeker wishes to prevent any free-riding by members of his coalition who, believing he will both continue payments to them and remain in office, will seek to reduce the cost of their own contributions. In order that the supporters continue to believe that it is rational for them to make the full contribution, he has to attempt to minimise his plurality. The lower the plurality the more likely will each member of his coalition see his own contribution as vital to the election effort, and the less likely he is to attempt to free-ride at the next election. This is the long-term optimal strategy for all but an avid risk bearer for it secures him future support. At the same time, the candidate who wishes to maintain his career will also want to win the next election, and the best means of ensuring that is a plurality-maximising strategy. Thus in choosing a strategy the candidate will weigh his immediate electoral uncertainties against his longer term interests. In a secondary respect, these two do not conflict, for with both it is preferable to maximise rather than minimise, the vote. In the longer term, this will decrease the risk that any of his supporters in the future will perceive a good chance of mobilising a coalition for a new candidate from both their own ranks and those of the non-voters. However, as the cost of free-riding is less for his supporters (it is a negative one) than is the cost of 'conspiracy', the office seeker will be more concerned in the long term with plurality minimisation than with vote maximisation.

Only the risk bearer will want to free himself from his benefit-seeking supporters. The truly conservative strategist would give considerable weight to the Rikcr Strategy. This is because the benefit seekers surrounding the winner of a close election will perceive the threat of his defeat, and will thus maintain their effort for him, even if his campaign should commence adversely. Some support for the argument that, because large pluralities may produce insufficient party effort on behalf of candidates in the next election, plurality maximisation is not the optimal strategy for those intent on preserving their careers, is provided by an examination of the recent experience of U.S. Senate incumbents.

The Senate is the best kind of office in which to test the Schlesinger hypothesis, because Senators are less tied to party effort on their behalf and are more reliant on their own electoral machinery than virtually any other office holders in the western world.[9] The Senators under consideration here are those who were elected for a full 6 year term of office which they served in either 1966, 1968, or 1970. To minimise the bias that would be introduced by including Senators from states where one of the two major parties has not been competitive in Senate races in recent years, all Senators from states that did not have at least one Republican and one Democrat Senator at some point during the years 1962–77 have been excluded. Consequently the re-election performances of 22 of the 100 Senators are not considered. Of the remainder, 24 either did not seek re-election, were excluded from the general election ballot, died in office, or retired from office in the middle of their term. This leaves 54 Senators, of whom 16 (29 per cent) were defeated in the general election, whilst 38 were re-elected in either 1972, 1974, or 1976. The names of these 54 Senators are contained in Table 4.1.

TABLE 4.1: Results of 1972, 1974 and 1976 General Elections Contested by Incumbent U.S. Senators

Percentage of total vote obtained in 1966, 1968 or 1970 election	Result of Election		
	Defeated for re-election in 1972, 1974 or 1976	Re-elected in 1972, 1974 or 1976	TOTAL
Less than 51%	Hartke (Ind.) Cook (Ky.) Beall (Md.) Buckley (N.Y.) Taft (Ohio) (5)	Gravel (Alaska) Weicker (Conn.) Mathias (Md.) Eagleton (Mo.) Javits (N.Y.) Packwood (Oreg.) (6)	11
51–55%	Brock (Tenn.) Montoya (N. Mex.) (2)	Cranston (Calif.) Ribicoff (Conn.) Chiles (Fla.) Bayh (Ind.) McIntyre (N.H.) Bellmon (Okla.) Hatfield (Oreg.) Schweiker (Penn.) Bentsen (Texas) Hansen (Wyo.) Byrd (Va.) (11)	13
More than 55%	Tunney (Calif.) Allott (Colo.) Dominick (Colo.) Boggs (Del.) Miller (Iowa) Smith (Me.) Moss (Utah) Spong (Va.) McGee (Wyo.) (9)	Goldwater (Ariz.) Roth (Del.) Inouye (Hawaii) Church (Idaho) Percy (Ill.) Muskie (Me.) Kennedy (Mass.) Brooke (Mass.) Griffin (Mich.) Curtis (Nebr.) Cannon (Nev.) Case (N.J.) Williams (N.J.) Young (N. Dak.) Burdick (N. Dak.) Pell (R.I.) Thurmond (S.C.) Hollings (S.C.) McGovern (S. Dak.) Baker (Tenn.) Tower (Texas) (21)	30
TOTAL	16	38	

What is immediately apparent from the table is that there is no direct relationship between the size of a candidate's earlier plurality and his likelihood of being re-elected at the next election. Certainly those with the smallest pluralities were the most vulnerable, although only 45 per cent of those with less than 51 per cent of the total vote in the previous election were actually defeated. However, the 'average' defeated Senator had only a fractionally smaller plurality in the earlier election than his counterpart among the successful incumbents: the median percentage of the vote obtained by defeated incumbents was 55.5 per cent, and the median for the successful ones was 56 per cent. More interesting than this point, though, is the fate of those with large pluralities. Those with more than 55 per cent of the vote in the earlier election were no more likely to win re-election than the whole group of 54 Senators. Of those who got more than 55 per cent of the vote in 1966, 1968, or 1970, 30 per cent (9 out of 30) lost their bid for re-election. This group can be contrasted with those who had had pluralities of between 51 per cent and 55 per cent: these were Senators whose seats did not look safe, but who could be accorded a reasonable chance of future success by their supporters. Of this group of 13 incumbents, only 2 (15 per cent of them) lost their seats in the following election. In effect, they were Senators who tended not to suffer from free-riding by their supporters, because the nearness of their defeat was only too obvious to the latter. On the other hand, theirs had not been so close a margin of victory that the seat would be discerned as an easily winnable one by the opposition. It is argued, therefore, that to the extent that a candidate could control his margin of victory, he would want a reasonably close electoral victory. He would want to avoid the dual dangers of a large plurality and an exceptionally narrow one. The former may result in decreased supporter effort on his behalf; attempting the latter may not only cost him victory now (he may miscalculate), but also result in exceptional efforts by his opponent in the next campaign.

There are two main types of candidate who will be more likely to adopt both a vote and plurality-maximising strategy. One of these is the person who does not want to seek further election after the next contest: he is free to concentrate on the maximisation of his chances of winning this particular election, and this entails a vote-maximisation strategy. The other type is the newcomer who, because he has not previously held office, has had none of the office-specific benefits to distribute to his would-be supporters. Consequently, in order to obtain this advantage, he will adopt the Downs strategy, realising that winning the first election is considerably more difficult than re-election will be. Having gained office in this way, the risk-averting newcomer will not wish, and indeed may not be able, to maintain his career with a continuation of this strategy (for the reasons outlined above). He must establish a body of support that is sufficient to provide him with victory in the future, but not so large as to encourage his supporters to free-ride. Thus, if his plurality-maximising strategy was successful, he must decrease the size of his initial coalition and some of his supporters will consequently receive no benefits from him. Furthermore, the candidate might choose to pay some groups who did not support him in his first election, and in doing so he may fail to pay off many of those who were part of his coalition. This can occur when, for reasons beyond his control, his opponent had been able to gain the support of a group whose members were amongst the least likely section of the electorate to attempt free-riding. By paying off this group he will bid for their support in future elections, a policy which may make more secure his continuance in office should he at sometime miscalculate the size of his coalition.

Another limitation of Schlesinger's analysis follows directly from this last point. A candidate who has progressive career ambitions (that is, he aspires to higher office than he presently holds) may be faced by an electoral constituency other than his present one. He also may decide to 'pay' those who have not previously supported him, or distribute a large share of the benefits to those who form only a small part of his present coalition. Contrary to Schlesinger's assumption that when a candidate does distribute benefits they go to his previous supporters, this candidate will take account of three factors in deciding to whom to distribute benefits. These are: (i) his optimal coalition for winning the next election; (ii) his longer term optimal coalition for securing continued re-election to this office; and (iii) his optimal coalition for securing election to a higher office with a different electoral constituency. An example of a future career oriented strategy is that of Jimmy Carter. On becoming Governor of Georgia in 1970, he was seen by some observers as 'paying off' black voters by his immediate commitment to racial integration, although this had certainly not been a major part of his electoral promises in the campaign. This commitment did not harm his bid for the Presidency in 1976, when crucial support was won by several black politicians in other states who worked as party activists on his behalf. Obviously the particular weight an office seeker will give to his career progress in determining his overall best strategy will depend on four variables: (i) the value he places on the higher office(s) as compared with his present one; (ii) his perception of the probability of attaining it; (iii) his attitude to risk taking and risk aversion; (iv) the difference between the constituency he requires to maintain a minimum winning coalition in his present office and that necessary to maximise the likelihood of victory in the office to which he aspires.

In this section it has been suggested that there are three major difficulties with Schlesinger's account of the optimal strategies for office seekers. (A fourth one is considered in the next section.) In the first place, Schlesinger does not recognise that the minimum level of payment an office seeker can make to his supporters is determined by several factors other than the size of his electoral victory. Indeed, in many circumstances a large victory may not increase his independence of action in benefit distribution. Secondly, whilst a minimum winning coalition is not optimal in the short term for an office seeker, it is the best long-term strategy, and as such will be taken into account by him in devising a strategy for a particular campaign. Thirdly, the distribution of benefits is future-oriented: they are payments for coalition support at elections in the future, particularly the next one. To this end he may not pay off those who have supported him in the past because with his projected career a change of coalition might be optimal. This can occur when his current electoral support is 'thin' (prone to free-ride), or when he has plans to seek election to an office with a different constituency.

B. THE SUPPORTERS OF AN OFFICE-SEEKING CANDIDATE

All supporters of political candidates are necessarily benefit seekers. According to Schlesinger the optimal strategy for benefit seekers is the minimisation of both the candidate's plurality and the total vote. He argues that this will entail that benefits are then distributed amongst the smallest number of people, thereby maximising each share of the total. We may examine the validity of this argument by first considering the conditions in which supporters will make a contribution. As was shown in section A, the benefit seeker will decide to make a contribution only if the expected returns from it produce greater benefits, or smaller losses, than any other available alternative. The payments the office seeker makes now directly affect one element in this calculation (the value of p), in that they are an indication of how he might distribute them in the future. Nevertheless, they are not the sole determinant of p. The supporter's perceptions that the office seeker may seek to change his coalition (either as an anti-free-rider or a 'career progression' strategy) will lead the supporter to reduce the value of p if he believes he may be excluded later. Thus, in these circumstances, the supporters may still reduce or cease their contributions even if the office seeker has paid them off. In a rational choice model the benefits are future-oriented for the supporters, as they are for the office seeker; they affect their behaviour at the next election and they are not perceived as payment at the end of a contract (for the services provided at the last election).

A further problem with Schlesinger's analysis is that he is concerned only with the distribution of benefits, and not with the question of what will result when the total amount of benefits is inadequate. For if the maximum amount of benefit the office seeker can pay his supporters is too small then supporters will cease to contribute, irrespective of whether they obtained the *share* of the benefit they wanted. That is, if y is anticipated to be sufficiently small by all potential contributors, even very high values of e and p may not produce any contributors. If elected officials cannot provide the radical changes in policies which are required to produce the benefits the potential contributors seek, it will not be worth their while contributing to any campaign. Alternatively, if non-elected officials can affect the distribution of benefits, then benefit seekers may redirect their resources towards, for example, contacts with the administrative sector of government.

Assuming that some contribution by the potential benefit seekers is rational, the important question is whether Schlesinger's argument – that their optimal strategy is plurality minimisation – is valid. He is correct to suggest that, with a fixed total amount of benefits transferable one between another, it is the optimal *short term* strategy. However in the long term, as we have already suggested, a small plurality over his opponents will be of advantage to the office seeker. This enables him to claim support from the benefit seekers on the ground that, if it is not forthcoming, the party will be defeated. This strategic position allows the candidate the opportunity not to pay out the maximum benefit, which he would otherwise have to do. Indeed, the longer he remains in office, the more likely it is that an office seeker with continually small pluralities will be able to regulate his payment of benefits and distribute the minimum necessary to retain the support of his coalition. In other words, vote minimisation allows him to squeeze the level of payment he has to make to his supporters, because he does not have to guard against free-riding, and supporters cannot make comparable returns on their 'investment' elsewhere. By maximising his plurality, the supporters minimise their initial commitment to the candidate, thereby forcing him to pay larger-than-minimum benefits. This then becomes the only way in which he can obtain an insurance policy against possible loss of support in future elections. Whether the gain they make in this respect, in preventing benefit squeeze, offsets the loss they incur from the decline in their share of total benefits, will depend on the amount by which the total benefits that could be paid out exceeds the minimum payment that must be made. Furthermore, as we suggested earlier, vote maximisation favours the office seeker; its minimisation favours benefit seekers who are faced by office-seeking candidates. This is because vote minimisation reduces the cost to the benefit seekers of forming a new coalition should the office seeker default on payment. (This argument rests on the assumption that in opposing an incumbent it will cost benefit seekers less to mobilise non-voters than it will to join the coalition of his earlier opponents.)

At this stage a major assumption made by Schlesinger needs to be scrutinised. For the argument that supporters will prefer plurality minimisation rests on the claim that there is a limited amount of benefit to be distributed, such that every group added to a coalition necessitates smaller shares for everybody. Now there are two related objections to this assumption. The first is that each group may seek different kinds of benefits; there is no fixed supply which is either distributed or retained by the office seeker. This objection is exactly the same as the claim made by American pluralist theorists, such as Dahl, that qualified-majority decision making procedures enable more benefits to be distributed than simple-majority rules. The claim is that societies are composed of minorities, each of which is seeking benefits which are different in kind from those of the others. Although even America is not as pluralistic (in this sense) as Dahl maintained, it is clear that not all the demands made on governments in western societies can be reduced to any one unit, such as money. Nevertheless, it could still be argued that some goods such as time are required by all those who make demands on office seekers, and that there is a fixed supply of these goods.[10]

A second, and more important, objection is that the perfectly-informed electorate, which is assumed in Schlesinger's model, does not correspond to political reality. Once this assumption is weakened very different conclusions can be drawn about optimal strategies. This exposes a major difficulty in the direct transference of economic theories of perfect competition to political analysis. With respect to the level of voter information, Downs, at least, recognised the importance of weakening this 'economic' assumption. However, in Downs's model the electorate adopted an ideology as a means by which they could evaluate the performance of governments, and this too can be criticised for its lack of correspondence to the real world. Indeed the acquisition of an ideology by a voter would normally seem to entail him bearing a fairly high cost, rather than it being a cost-free means by which he can evaluate political information. This is because he has to develop a framework for understanding political reality which is in partial competition with alternative frameworks that are acquired elsewhere in his social interactions. Only when these provide the same ideology will the cost be low: it is exactly for this reason that the Italian Communist Party, for example, has attempted to monopolise the arenas of social interaction of its members.[11] It is more plausible to assume that the larger part of the electorate is often unable to evaluate the effects of most policies in comparison with the alternatives an opposition party might have initiated. The types of benefit upon which electors can judge are not substantive ones, but are either solidaristic or related to the style, rhetoric or personality of the candidates. Only the smaller part of the electorate is able to determine whether or not it has been supplied with material or purposive rewards by the office seeker.

We suggest, then, that there are two markets for political goods, one of the kind recognised by Schlesinger and another, for very different kinds of goods, which exists because the customers (voters) lack the skills necessary to participate in the first market. This dual market enables the supporters in the substantive market to pursue a plurality-maximising strategy amongst voters in the other market, without affecting their own share of the substantive benefits. In conjunction with this, they may still employ a minimum-winning coalition strategy in the substantive market should they wish to. However, they can only do this if the narrow span of this coalition is either of no concern to the members of the other market or those members are unaware of it. One main way in which both the latter can identify a narrow political base in a party and also, more importantly, how its opponents can successfully expose the base to this electorate, is for the party to have a readily identifiable ideology. For substantive benefit seekers, an ideology that unites the activists in the party is of considerable disadvantage. It will impede their attempts to pursue a plurality-maximising strategy.[12] Conversely the office seeker, by emphasising party ideology or allowing his supporters to do so, can limit the size of his coalition. He can thus bind his supporters more closely to him and thereby reduce to the minimum the payments he has to make to them to induce their continued contributions to his electoral coalition. In other words, we suggest that an ideology is not a device by which benefit seekers can retain control over the policies pursued by office seekers, but instead it is one by which the latter can restrict the former's control over them. In chapter 5 we further contend that the form of party organisation usually associated with the most ideological parties – the membership type – does not in all respects, as is traditionally believed, further the interests of the benefit seekers. Rather, its style of nomination is appropriate for the office seeker.

C. THE BENEFIT-SEEKING CANDIDATE AND HIS SUPPORTERS

In the absence of office seekers, benefit seekers still face a choice with regard to optimal party strategy – that between a long- and a short-term strategy. In this case there may be two aspects to such a choice. In the first place, the nature of the benefit may be such that there is a choice between: (i) a radical policy change now, with high benefits in the short term but accompanied by a decreased probability of future electoral success (which would increase the probability that an opposition party would modify the policy in the long term), and (ii) a moderate policy change now, with lower short term benefits in the inter-election period but with greater prospects of subsequent electoral victory. Secondly, when a candidate and his supporters are seeking different benefits, or differ over the priority to be accorded to benefits maturing at different times, there may be a conflict of interest over strategy. Those wanting immediately maturing benefits will opt for a plurality-maximisation strategy, because this will maximise the probability of victory, following which they can default on payment to the additional supporters whom they have induced to contribute. Those seeking benefits which mature over a longer period of time will pursue that strategy which maximises the likelihood of continued electoral success. When it is important for the members of a coalition that their *share* of the benefits remain as high as possible, a tendency toward a minimum-winning coalition strategy would result, as Schlesinger suggests. The need to prevent free-riding would also encourage the use of this strategy.

When there is a conflict of interest over the type of benefit to be distributed between the benefit-seeking candidate and his supporters, both will attempt to maximise their own contribution to the coalition vote. However, to the extent that there is no such conflict of interests, the optimal strategy will resemble the plurality minimisation one outlined by Schlesinger only in a superficial way. For, in the substantive benefit market, both candidate and supporters will try to maximise the number of interests embraced within the coalition. They will do so until the point is reached at which the amount of the benefit distributed to any coalition member declines. This will only be a plurality minimisation strategy when the diversity of the benefits being sought by the different interests in the electorate is already fully embraced by the minimum-winning coalition. Furthermore, the coalition will also seek to maximise its plurality in the non-substantive benefit market, something which normally entails vote maximisation.

What conclusions may we draw from this analysis of the optimal electoral strategies about the possible kinds of participant that a party might have? In the first place, Schlesinger is incorrect in his argument that office seekers will seek to create as large a coalition for the party as possible. When they take account of long-term considerations of future electoral success, they will tend to pursue a minimum-winning coalition strategy. It is only the short-term consideration, of winning the next election, that will tend to direct them towards a maximisation of their plurality. In other words, if the parties were composed entirely of office-seeking candidates, it would be very unlikely that they would seek to establish for themselves as broad a coalition as possible. On the contrary, in order to bind their supporters to them as closely as they can, they will want a coalition that is large enough to win, but not so large that their activists or voters will attempt to free ride at future elections. If they can choose between several minimum-winning coalition strategies, they will opt for that which maximises their total vote. But this is a secondary factor, and one that does not seriously alter the conclusion that teams of 'electoral brokers' are unlikely to be fierce competitors for the vote of the whole electorate; they will concentrate on preserving, or creating, a winning coalition. Normally this will entail retaining the support of their previous coalition, and seeking to supplement it with some marginal or independent votes. However, in some circumstances, an office seeker might be advised to bring about a major shift of the core groups in his coalition, although this is a tactic he cannot use frequently.

A second conclusion we may draw in relation to optimal party strategies is that it is normally in the interest of the supporters of an office seeker to extend his electoral coalition so as to prevent themselves from being tied too closely to him. Schlesinger's conclusion that benefit seekers will seek the smallest plurality possible for the party's candidate rests on the assumption that they are concerned entirely with maximising their share of a benefit in a world in which there is only one type of benefit. However, there are serious disadvantages for the supporters in obtaining a small plurality. They are likely to be concerned more with the absolute amount of the benefit they receive, than with maintaining a fixed share of it irrespective of the total amount available. Furthermore, there may be more than one kind of benefit, so that the supporters may, without any cost, be able to take into a minimum-winning coalition extra supporters who seek a different benefit from the kind they themselves seek.

Finally, when both candidates and supporters are benefit seekers, the polity does not degenerate, as Schlesinger implies, into rival coalitions seeking to minimise both their own support, to the size of a minimum winning coalition, and the total electoral vote. They would only do this if there were a fixed amount of a single benefit, and in the real world this is obviously not so, particularly given that mass electorates are characterised by an absence of coherent policy demands. The mobilisation of these voters can be attempted by the parties precisely because no reduction in benefit for those seeking substantive benefits is necessary. The problem for the society in the mobilising of this electorate, however, is that the parties may compete for the vote through advertising, and thus fail to create a more informed electorate. It is for this reason that we need to examine whether democratic procedures within the parties are likely to lead them to provide a more genuine form of competition.

5 The Theory of (Intra-) Party Democracy

In Chapters 3 and 4 objections were raised to theories of popular control over government which rely on competitive elections to achieve accountability of elected representatives. In this chapter a theory, the origins of which predate Schumpeter's theory, is introduced to explain how the balance between governmental responsiveness and responsibility can be attained. This is the theory of party democracy. It explains why there is a need for political parties to be both internally democratic and centralised, and why their policy goals should be determined as far as possible by their activists, or members. The origins of it are twofold. In the first place, it derives from the arguments of 19th-century socialists that political parties needed to be internally democratic if democracy at the level of the state was to be attained. (It was this assumption that Michels also accepted, and which allowed him to conclude that democracy was impossible.) Secondly, it is embodied in some party government theories.[1] It is a theory that has remained largely dormant in political science literature since the 1950s, although some of its arguments and assumptions have been rehashed in the party reform debate in America in the early 1970s.[2] The most important statement of it is found in a well-known report of a committee of the American Political Science Association which, at the time and subsequently, was derided by its critics.[3] Nevertheless, a more recent commentator has noted the far-sightedness of many of the points the report made about the future of the American political system.[4] This chapter is devoted to an account of this theory, together with a consideration of some possible criticisms of it.

A. PARTY DEMOCRACY AND CONFLICT DISPLACEMENT

In the late 1940s E. E. Schattschneider acted as chairman of the committee of the American Political Science Association that was set up to examine the working of the American party system. His was, and was seen to be, the guiding hand behind the report. Many of the proposals submitted in the report reflected his own ideas, and it has become the most important, and also the most notorious, blueprint for party democracy. It proposed a series of reforms of party structure which many critics were quick to point out were both unlikely to gain much public support and ran contrary to the American political tradition and the constitutional framework of its institutions. The object of the reforms was to make the parties more responsible, in the sense that they would perform what Schattschneider had seen as their main function – that of implementing, in government, policies that took account of a wide range of interests, and not just those that were organised. They were to be responsible *to the electorate* in that the citizens would know (by inspecting the parties' clearly defined policy programmes) which interests each party was promoting. They would be able to vote out of office any party that did not embrace the more general interests in the society. In distinguishing between party competition over policies and programmes and that over 'wild fictions . . . used to excite the imagination of the public' the APSA committee recognised that not all forms of competition between parties are qualitatively the same for the public.[5] Consequently, it came close to identifying what is claimed here to be a major function of parties: the education of the public in relation to the socio-economic and political divisions of the society. The committee believed that the main problem of electoral politics was that the citizens would not be able to check the parties effectively if there were no clear policy alternatives presented by both parties. However, we argue in this book that this criticism of disinformative electoral competition needs to be taken further. The problem is not simply that ambiguous or inconsistent policy 'packages' make the choice of party a meaningless one; it is also that the citizen cannot develop adequate skills for evaluating the performance of governments if the parties do not enlighten him about what government can be expected to achieve.

A second aspect of the committee's report was its proposal to initiate widespread participation in the parties by their activists, and it devised institutional structures to give the latter control over the policies promoted by the party leadership. The justification for this was that responsibility *to party members* was a means by which the party's responsibility to the electorate could be enforced.[6] It was assumed that, unless the party leaders were accountable to their membership, there was no guarantee that the clarity of electoral choice needed to make the electoral mechanism effective would be forthcoming from the leadership. Responsibility to the membership was thus an aspect of the party's responsibility to the electorate, and the former was not seen as an alternative source of authority to that of the latter.[7] The conventional interpretation of this aspect of the Report, including Austin Ranney's, is that membership was interpreted to mean all party voters. This is misleading. It is quite clear from the discussion in Section 9 of the Report that two kinds of membership were envisaged for the reformed parties. On the one level there were party voters to whom electoral appeals would be made in primary elections. On another level there were the regular activists who, through such devices as pre-primary conventions, would determine the nature of these appeals to the primary electorate. Given the virtual absence of issue-activist control in the late 1940s, the Committee's main concern was to improve their position (APSA Report, pp. 69–70); this is far removed from the ticket-voter notion of membership attributed to the Committee by Ranney.

Party activists were seen by the committee as being voters whose perceptions of the nature of the political universe are derived less directly from the party leadership's current concept-disputes and image projections than are those of the majority of electors. They constitute a group of citizens that could provide a check on the leaderships' inclinations to engage in the kind of competition that in Chapter 3 was identified as disinformative advertising. They engage in politics in order to realise in public-policy output their own view of political reality. They would not be satisfied with a style of leadership that merely accommodated organised interests and competed with opponents in presenting the public with 'wild fictions'. Hence the participation by party activists advocated by the committee was of an 'instrumental' kind, in that it assumed that they would participate only because they wanted to obtain policies from the leadership that accorded with their own view of political reality.[8] Yet at the same time this participation would also serve developmental ends. For, because there are only two parties, the activists would learn to modify their own demands and would take account of the wider interests of the society.[9]

This developmental effect of party democracy described by the committee is of obvious relevance to what would seem to be an important function of political parties in a liberal society. Members of the public need to be enlightened about the value of their shared interests and, if the argument outlined above is correct, widespread participation in internally democratic parties would be a means of achieving this. Clearly, the committee accepted an argument that is a commonplace amongst participatory theorists of democracy: by participating with others, citizens come readily to accept the legitimacy of the claims that others might make, and this will tend to direct their attention to interests common to all.

Now two points need to be noted about the logic of the APSA Report's argument about participation within internally democratic parties. The first is that it was likely that wide-ranging interests would be taken into account only if there were two parties; this form of political education was incompatible with multi-partyism. Yet at least one commentator on the party democracy conception of political parties assumes that multi-partyism is normally desired by its proponents.[10]

The second is that the committee believed that the party leadership had to be responsible to the party's active workers. Nevertheless, it recognised that a fully participatory party, with a large number of activists, would not follow immediately from institutional reform. Like most developmental theorists, the committee did not make the simple-minded assumption that a large number of voters would instantaneously involve themselves in the work of the party. Therefore, in maximising participation in the short term, it sought to provide a means by which the party voter as well as the activist could affect the nomination process, whilst policy formulation was placed in the hands of the activists. Thus the nomination process was to be reformed by the abolition of the open and cross-filing primaries, and by making national conventions reflect state party voter strength rather than electoral college strength. The party was to be responsible to its members, but the Committee's notion of membership was a deliberately broad one so that it would include both activists (who would take part in policy discussions) and party voters (who could vote in primaries). The activist influence was obviously to be greater even in the nomination process, and the committee supported pre-primary assembly procedures to restrict the number of candidates on a party ballot.[11] This point has been missed by one of the Report's most prominent critics – Austin Ranney.

Ranney assumes that a party must either be responsible to its 'party-workers' or to its 'ticket-voters', but apparently not both.[12] He argues that the logic of the APSA report commits it to the latter kind of responsibility. Clearly this analysis over-simplifies the pattern of responsibility outlined by the committee, for there is no reason why party leaders should not be constrained by the policy demands of activists (through a complex committee structure), and have their nominations controlled at one stage by the activists and at another by the party voters. Indeed, as we argue later, a looser, non-membership element in the nomination procedure (a primary following a party convention) helps to prevent the atrophy of party democracy.

A decade after the APSA Report was published Schattschneider addressed himself to a new theme of direct relevance to party democracy. He had come to see that, of itself, party competition is not a process by which the parties mirror pre-existing conflicts in the society. For:

> There are billions of potential conflicts in any modern society, but *only a few become significant.* The reduction of the number of conflicts is an essential part of politics. Politics deals with the domination and subordination of conflicts. A democratic society is able to survive because it manages conflict by establishing priorities among a multitude of potential conflicts.[13]

And this establishment of priorities determines who will get elected to public office and who will not:

> Political conflict is not like an intercollegiate debate in which the opponents agree in advance on a definition of the issues. As a matter of fact, *the definition of the alternatives is the supreme instrument of power*; the antagonists can rarely agree on what the issues are because power is involved in the definition. He who determines what politics is about runs the country, because the definition of the alternatives is the choice of conflicts, and the choice of conflicts allocates power.[14]

Schattschneider had come to recognise that what is of central importance in politics is how an issue is defined, for it is possible to define a conflict, or socio-economic division, in any number of ways, all of which will result in very different levels of benefit accruing to those affected:

> The substitution of conflicts is the most devastating kind of political *strategy.* Alliances are formed and re-formed; fortresses, positions, alignments and combinations are destroyed or abandoned in a tremendous shuffle of forces redeployed to defend new positions or

to take new strong points. In politics the most catastrophic force in the world is *the power of irrelevance which transmutes one conflict into another and turns all existing alignments inside out.*[15]

The mainspring of politics, then, is conflict between those who seek to define the dominant cleavages in the society. The ability to make a division a dominant one provides an advantage, and not just a short-term one, to the party that does so. Now the 'theory' of electoral competition indicates that when this occurs the losing party will recognise it, accommodate itself to the dominant groups, yet seek itself to gain an electoral advantage, by emphasising other, newer, lines of division. But Schattschneider himself came to see that the electoral mechanism may be defective in this respect:

The danger is that diehard minorities which want to continue old fights *may simply freeze obsolete alignments* and become permanently isolated minorities.[16]

He then proceeds to expand on a theme he had developed earlier: how the lines of division laid down in America in 1896 had permitted sectional politics and the consequent rise of decentralised parties. These were parties that could not serve as a mechanism through which a serious challenge could be mounted to those who had newly redefined the lines of division. The Southern wing of the Democratic party, being unchallenged in its own area, was content for the party to remain a minority party nationally if the price of not doing so was a threat to its own interests and hegemony. It was not until the 1932 election that this atrophy of the party system was reversed.

Schattschneider's claim that in some circumstances there are defects in the mechanics of two-party competition, that lead not to the frequent supplanting of existing lines of division but to the entrenchment of these divisions, has been taken further in the analysis of Walter Dean Burnham.[17] For Burnham also, the election of 1896 represents the triumph of a business ruling class which defined the political universe for the next generation. However, he sees the creation of this particular party system as part of a more general pattern in U.S. politics. He argues that lines of division are established every 30–40 years, and are then replaced in the period surrounding a critical election.[18] In effect, he is maintaining that party competition as a mechanism only provides for the periodic redefinition of political reality, and that these redefinitions take place at a time of social and/or economic crisis. The crux of Burnham's theory is that there is an incompatibility between an American economy that has been developing continually and a political system that has not developed at all.[19] The two main features of this underdevelopment have been a decentralised party system and the dominance of the laissez-faire ethic in the electorate, both of which have made radical changes in public policy difficult. But economic development is not a smooth process, and when social dislocations result from it the groups that are adversely affected will normally seek governmental assistance. As this is rarely forthcoming in America, at least to the extent required by these groups, the social conflicts are played out in the only available arena – that of the mobilisation of electoral coalitions. The result is periodic electoral crises normally characterised by the temporary rise of third parties.

Like Schattschneider, Burnham sees the consequences of the 1896 election as an example of how political advantage gained in an election may be used to entrench the position of those who have benefited. Thus he examines how the dominant party within most of the states restricted the size of the electorate after 1896, by a variety of devices, so as to prevent effective party competition. Again, as in Schattschneider's account, one particular social group is seen as the main beneficiary of this political upheaval – the business community. Yet for both writers, the subsequent insulation of these interests from political control in the period 1896–1932 was not the product of a conspiracy, nor was it preordained by their control over economic resources. Both, though in somewhat different ways, argue that in 1896 one definition of what was politically relevant won, and this made possible the dismantling of effective party competition. In turn, this enabled one part of the winning coalition (business) to retain its autonomy for nearly 40 years. Particularly in his most recent account, Burnham is emphatic that he is presenting what may be called an 'institutional bias' explanation rather than a 'power' explanation of this phenomenon:

> ... the process was largely unconscious and sociologically determined at all levels. It was certainly not a matter of conspiracy but of circumstances that things turned out as they did during and after the realignment of the 1890s, ... much of the demobilisation and anti-partisanship of the post-1900 era was achieved by a common mass consensus – at least among those who were still left in the shrinking electoral universe. As for the dissidents and dropouts, what viable

alternative did they have? Granted the manifest absence of conditions favouring class-solidaristic substitutes for the political confessionalism of the vanishing nineteenth century religious cosmos, what other vision of the commonwealth and human liberty than one or other variant of liberal capitalism could survive the transition.[20]

At this point, what needs to be borne in mind is that both Schattschneider and Burnham are concerned to explain how flaws in political structures or processes can prevent new conflicts from displacing old ones. For Schattschneider, the 1896 election was an aberration because the sectionalising (or 'de-nationalising') of politics made possible non-competitive party systems. For Burnham, it was the underdevelopment of American political institutions that made for an electoral cycle of hegemony and periodic revolution. In contrast with this, we argued in chapter 3 that it is not merely flaws in particular polities that prevent party competition over the redefinition of political divisions, but also the logic of the electoral mechanism itself. The reason for this is that parties are competing oligopolists and not perfect competitors. The logic of oligopolistic competition is that competitors, for their own survival, will seek to compete in ways that do not threaten their position as oligopolists. One result is that the parties are prepared to accept, as long as they possibly can, the given, conventional definition of political reality, and compete with one another in the manner described in chapter 3. Because the parties are not prepared to risk minority status, they permit the electorate to misunderstand, and sometimes conflate, new lines of social and economic division. This is not a conspiracy, for it comes about because there is no incentive for the electorate to understand new conflicts except within the older framework.

What happens when this framework is under threat from autonomous social movements, as it was in America in the early 1890s? The political party leadership can still shape and redefine these emerging divisions; in the South 'economic' populism was tamed, and by the later 1890s had become a force for the maintenance of racial segration. The Jim Crow laws followed directly from this. However, at times of party realignment during crisis, there are few constraints on how the leadership redefines the patterns of public division, for these periods of crisis are of short duration. This is the central weakness of a cycle of politics in which political reality is redefined only occasionally: what emerge as the major lines of division in the society are more likely to reflect the strategic position of *certain* organised minorities, than the overall pattern of those who are mobilised. In other words, there is no accountability by the party leadership for the way they have shaped politics. The result may be an increase in political inequality, some advantaged groups benefiting disproportionately in comparison with the rest. Schattschneider and Burnham believe that this was what happened in the realignment of the 1890s. When there is no accountability, and can be none, the political universe will be identified, for the public, to the maximum advantage of the party leaders; indirectly this may greatly benefit others. Taken to an extreme, one partyism and greater economic inequalities may be the outcome and this is why the realignment of 1896 is of such fascination to the political scientist: it is an extreme example. The problem for the democrat, then, is how to make the parties more aware of new social divisions, so that the redefinition of political divisions becomes part of normal, and not crisis, politics. Once again this leads to the idea of intra-party democracy.

B. THREE PARADOXES OF PARTY DEMOCRACY

The argument that is being presented here is that parties that provided for real control over policy goals by their activists would come to have a leadership that took account of new conflicts. To respond to these conflicts, the leadership would attempt to identify anew the political universe for the electorate, and in doing so parties would be performing a major function that they have in a liberal society. In terms of Hirschman's analysis, party democracy would provide a 'voice' mechanism, to complement the 'exit' alternative already available to voters, an alternative that by itself does not function effectively under oligopoly. In some ways, therefore, activist participation in a party is akin to the operation of an association of consumers concerned to maintain the quality of goods. However, there are two important differences. First, the party activists are only concerned with the single product of one oligopolist and not with a range of products. Second, unless the party activists can, and do, remove party leaders from public office when they deviate from the goals of the party there is no other means by which they can get a product of satisfactory quality. A consumer association, on the other hand, although it faces similar problems in making the 'exit' mechanism effective, has other alternatives open to it. In particular, it can lobby government to impose standards on the producers with regard to certain kinds of quality control. There is no such higher level of appeal for the party activist.

Now if effective party democracy means that party leaders follow the policy goals of the activists becaue they fear dismissal by them, it might seem that this produces a paradox. Why should we assume that party activists will concern themselves with broad-ranging issues (how the political universe is to be defined, how policies are to resolve the conflicts within it, etc.) rather than with the promotion of sectional, or special, interests? That is, it might be argued that mass control over the parties could make for a populist, and not a liberal, polity. In support of this view, it might be argued that one special interest – labour unions – in both Britain and in some states in America (such as Michigan) have used their control over party organisation to further their own interests.[21] How much greater might their involvement be if policy making was a function of party organisation?

Three arguments can be brought against this line of criticism and they suggest that the paradox is more apparent than real. In the first place there is Schattschneider's claim that no party can afford to be identified with only a few interests.[22] If all interest groups are fairly small minorities, then no party with a narrow appeal that would result from promoting only a few special interests could win an election. And, if it attempts to promote more than a few interests, the compromises involved would hardly make for special interest politics. Again, it is possible to agree with Schattschneider that groups rarely mobilise 100 per cent behind one party, so that the potential for a small minority having undue influence over the goals of a party are small, however responsible leaders are to their activists. Nevertheless, it might be argued that there is a flaw in this argument – namely that some groups are, at the very least, large minorities with a high potential for introducing a bias into party policy. Yet even the trade unions in Britain, of whom this claim is most usually made, have not had enough active members to take over most local Labour party organisations. Rather, trade union influence over Labour party policy has been made possible by two factors: their institutionalisation in the party (and particularly its annual conference) since the 1918 reorganisation; and the large share of election financing borne by them. Indeed it is the latter which constitutes the greatest problem in the maintenance of parties that are largely free from the influence of special interests. For the organisation of a special interest cannot as easily mobilise its members to participate in the party organisation as it can allocate funds to that party. It is not surprising, then, that the public financing of elections should have become a central issue in the debate about the autonomy of parties in Britain and America during the 1970s.[23]

Secondly, it can be argued that the real problem in attempts at party democratisation has not been the complete responsiveness of leadership to activists, but the ease with which the former can become autonomous within a seemingly democratic structure. Just as party platforms in America do not bind party candidates for public office, so in Britain party conferences rarely prevent a government from implementing the policy the leadership has chosen.[24] Various accounts have been given to explain this failure of popular control in parties. For Michels, it was a combination of unavoidable organisational constraints and certain psychological dispositions of the masses which led to the creation of an oligarchy.[25] Yet as Gordon Hands has argued, the evidence for this claim can be rejected partly on the ground that many supposedly 'democratic' parties were set up by small cadres of professional organisers who believed the membership party best served their own interests.[26] Again, the superiority of information available to those in government has been held to be the decisive advantage enjoyed by the leadership over activists. Furthermore, there is the problem, which is mentioned later, of the development of team loyalty that transcends differences over policy goals between leaders and activists. What is not in doubt is that it is the unresponsiveness to new demands by party leaders that is the more likely danger facing a party than total responsiveness to such demands.

Thirdly, there are the well known arguments from the developmental effects of participation. The authors of the APSA report correctly believed that participation would direct activists toward the promotion of common, rather than sectional or special, interests. In this respect they made assumptions about the developmental effects of participation similar to those made by most participatory theorists from Rousseau onwards.

So far it has been argued that mass participation in parties, with a membership style of organisation embracing committees at all levels involved in the setting of policy goals, is conducive to the political education of the citizenry. But it might be argued that there is a second paradox to be discovered here. It might be asked: is it not the case that some of the membership parties of Western Europe have been remarkably unable to discipline their leaders for deviating from the stated goals of the party?[27] If membership parties are appropriate to the internally democratic party but enable the party leaders to become independent of the membership, it would seem that party democracy is impossible. However, this difficulty disappears if a distinction is introduced between the membership style of organisation (control over public-policy goals by the activists) and the membership style of nomination for public office. For it is the latter, a nomination process in which only the membership is involved, which is one of the causes of the phenomenon that Michels and others have sought to explain – the seemingly democratic organisation that is controlled by its leadership. There is no logical connection between a membership style of organisation, with regular meetings to examine the attainment of, and barriers to, the party's public-policy goals, and the exclusive control over nominations by the same caucuses. The danger of this latter procedure is that, when the party becomes identified with a particular ideology or viewpoint, no recruit will join the party unless he shares that ideology. If he does not share it, he cannot, by appealing to those outside the party, break this hegemony unless he can persuade others to bear the unreasonable costs (in terms of time and other resources) of membership. Since there arise no battles to be fought inside the party between those who have rather different views of the political universe, the party can only become a service organisation for its office seekers. There are no other tasks for its members. And in a service organisation (raising funds, getting out the vote etc.), its members tend naturally to develop a sense of loyalty to those for whom they are providing the service. When loyalty is established it has to be relatively easy for new or dissident activists to mobilise to challenge those whom they believe are deviating from the stated party goals, if party democracy is not to be a fiction. But this is the vicious circle, for it is not easy to mobilise: the costs are high for those who wish to do anything at all to redirect the party to its original stated goals.

The remedy for this malaise of parties was outlined, perhaps unwittingly, by the authors of the APSA report in their support for pre-primary assemblies. For, on the one hand dissident groups must not have to bear overwhelming costs in challenging loyalists. On the other hand, there is equally a danger if the nomination process enables either a small minority, or those who merely have campaign funds or a 'name' with which the public identifies, to secure the nomination of a party.[28] There are three characteristics that need to be built into the nomination process for public offices to prevent either this Scyla or Charybdis from taking its toll. However, since all three are related to a style of nomination that involves the use of a particular kind of party primary, it is first necessary to state briefly some of the main characteristics of the primary system in America.

America is the home of the primary, a device introduced in many of the states at the turn of this century to counteract apparent 'boss' control in local parties. Although the primary is rightly associated with the Progressive era, it had both older origins than this and also failed to become universally used in the American states until 1970. The first recorded primary was held in Pennsylvania in 1844, but it was employed comparatively rarely elsewhere until the beginning of this century. The first law to require the statewide use of the primary was passed in Wisconsin in 1902. Thereafter most states rapidly followed suit. Connecticut was the last to do so; it did not pass a law providing for a primary until 1955 and there was no statewide primary contest until 1970. Moreover, it could be argued that Indiana has yet to capitulate, for whilst it has primaries for nominations to the U.S. House and the state legislature, nominations for statewide offices are made in party conventions.

Yet talk about *the* primary conceals the most obvious fact about primaries in the various states: their great diversity.[29] The two most important ways in which they differ are related to the questions of who can vote and who can stand as a candidate in them. At one extreme some states require that a would-be voter must be a voter for the party in whose primary he wants to vote; he may have to register to vote in the primary a considerable time before the election, or, rather less restricting, he is required in some states to state on oath that he will vote for that party at the general election. Toward the opposite extreme from the closed primary is the open one in which a voter merely asks at the polling booth for the ballot of the party in whose primary he wants to vote at that particular election. Providing for even less party control than the open primary is the blanket primary, in which the voter can choose to vote in one party's primary for one office and in another party's primary for other offices. In determining who can run, the law in some states merely requires that a prospective candidate obtains the signatures of a specified number of voters in support of his candidacy. In others he has only to pay a small filing fee to get on the ballot. In contrast to this, a few states have the requirement that only those candidates who have obtained a certain percentage of the votes at the party's convention or assembly are allowed to be placed on the primary ballot. In Colorado they must have got 20 per cent of these votes, and state law also provides for open and fair procedures in the selection of delegates to these assemblies. A contention of this book is that it is this last kind of nomination procedure that permits both party government and internally democratic parties, that is cohesive parties that are not merely instruments of the party leadership. However, in making this claim an argument is being presented against a long-standing assumption in politicial science.

This assumption is that all types of primary weaken the political party: if party organisations cannot determine who is to run for office, then two consequences ensue. First, the party in the legislature is less able to enforce discip''ne there. Second, a candidate who has a viewpoint that has little in common with those of the regular party activists may gain the nomination despite their opposition. Obviously, with open direct primaries, and when any citizen who wants to can run under a party label, V. O. Key's conclusions about the effect of primaries on the demise of party may be justified.[30] But with the pre-primary assembly system need the results be similar to this? One study conducted in Colorado suggested that although this system ameliorated the defects of the primary it did not remove them.[31] And if these arguments were valid, they would counteract the benefits of the open, non-membership nomination style outlined in this book. Yet, against their arguments, weight may be given to two factors which suggest that there is no such inherent defect in the pre-primary assembly nominating process.

In the first place, the key to party cohesion in a legislature is control over patronage. In Britain the ability to effectively deny an M.P. renomination merely reinforces the power of the executive over his career. (Of course, it is the local constituency party that renominates the M.P., though its freedom to do so is restricted if the M.P. has had the whip withdrawn or has been expelled from the party.) Party discipline in Parliament was slack before the rise of constituency party organisation in the years after the 1867 Representation of the People Act, but equally there was less centralised patronage. Not only were there fewer executive positions at a Prime Minister's disposal, there were also many uncontested seats and few career (as opposed to 'volunteer') M.P.s. Patronage was also crucial in making for a high degree of party cohesion in the U.S. House of Representatives in the fifteen years before the revolt against Speaker Cannon in 1910. After this date the power of the Speaker was dissipated for he could no longer appoint Congressmen to committees and he had no seat on the Committee on Rules. His loss of patronage led to the rise of 'baronies' – rule by the Committee Chairmen of the House; since their appointment depended largely on seniority, the House became a gerontocracy.[32] However, even within this framework, Congressmen have been unwilling to enforce party cohesion except in the business of organising the House. In short, when party has control over officeholders' renomination, party cohesion is nearly absolute; but a high degree of cohesion could be established in its absence provided that the party's legislative leadership has a monopoly of house patronage and that the majority of legislators are prepared to let their respective leaders use it as an instrument of power. Naturally, this raises the question of *when* legislators will submit themselves to party rule through patronage, and we contend that the existence of a party policy programme is of central importance in this respect. This point will be examined further in chapter 6.

Secondly, with an assembly rule similar to the 20 per cent rule employed in Colorado, it is difficult for an outside candidate to mobilise support at an assembly unless he has won over some party 'regulars'. As a first approximation, we may say that, in the absence of widespread support amongst the 'regulars', he will find it difficult to wage a successful primary campaign except under two conditions: (i) the office for which he is running is so much more important than any other in his region (or state) that not only is it profitable for him to buy a considerable amount of television time but individually he also receives a disproportionate amount of television news coverage; and (ii) the parties are not the sole distributors of campaign resources, particularly finance, and there are no limits on the amount that a candidate can spend in the campaign. When both these conditions are met a candidate with a different viewpoint from the party's activists might be able to gain the nomination. However, it will be seen that, in their absence, a pre-primary assembly would permit intra-party competition without the danger of party becoming merely a label for which those of a variety of political views compete in their search for public office. (We shall see in chapters 6, 7 and 8 that there are other factors that in fact weaken party and prevent full intra-party democracy based on pre-primary nomination procedures.)

Clearly, the argument outlined here seems to be contrary to one presented by Leon D. Epstein.[33] Epstein argues that it is the parliamentary system, rather than the type of external party organisation, that makes for cohesive legislative parties. We do not deny that, as in Canada, legislative-executive links are a sufficient condition to provide this cohesion. Nevertheless, we contend that it is not a necessary condition. None of the systems Epstein compared – Britain, Canada and the United States – have had internally democratic parties. What may be called the 'we-are-all-in-one-boat syndrome' of parliamentary parties can be developed elsewhere if legislators are actually accountable to party activists through their acceptance of a party programme. In the case of parliamentary parties, the objective of organising the executive provides an incentive for legislators to 'hang together' and use the distribution of patronage to achieve this end.

The three characteristics which we maintain are necessary to provide for effective control through the nomination process of elected representatives by a large number of party activists can now be identified.

The first is that the nomination process must be completed within a fixed and short period of time, so that dissidents can plan their mobilisation and are not faced with having to 'make news', or bear monetary or other costs (for example, attendance at numerous meetings) over a long period of time. If an activist does not know *when* he may successfully remove an incumbent he is unlikely to concentrate his mind, or his resources, in an effort to do so. The second is that the party activists must have complete control over which candidates will be presented for selection by a primary electorate. To make it impossible for 'name' candidates to disrupt the selection process, the party rules must be such that no more than 2 or 3 candidates can get on to the ballot and anyone doing so must have demonstrated at least substantial minority support within the party. (This point was recognised by the APSA Committee in their support for pre-primary meetings of the parties.) Third, it should be possible that at the primary election both defeated dissidents and loyalists (if they are more than a small minority of the activists) have the opportunity to demonstrate that it is their opponents who are isolated from the mainstream of the party. The primary can thus serve as a means by which the vicious tie of loyalty to incumbents in a party can be broken: the costs of voting for the supporters of a dissident movement are much less than those involved in active membership of a party. Dissident movements are not then doomed to failure.

This argument can be illuminated by considering a claim put forward by Joseph Schlesinger: a claim which seems to be a false one. Schlesinger did not recognise the distinction between the membership style of organisation and the membership style of nomination process: he assimilated the two. His argument is that membership parties (of the Western European kind) are appropriate to benefit seekers rather than to office seekers.[34]

He argues that the rationale for the membership party is that it is one which is concerned with the distribution of benefits, for it is most noticeably through membership that the contribution of a supporter will be apparent to an office seeker.[35] Thus membership is a device by which the former control the distribution of benefits from the latter. ('Without a membership to make claims and a clearly identified structure to enforce them, what can keep the officeholder in line?'[36]) The office seeker, on the other hand, wants a looser organisational structure so that he can 'achieve the manoeuvrability which is one of his most valuable assets'.[37] In fact, the question Schlesinger poses about the constraints on the office holder who is not dependent on a party membership is not an empty or rhetorical one. It is plausible to assume that an office holder will normally be most aware of the nature of his coalition if he regularly has to compete openly against others for the nomination of his party in an electoral contest. Such open competition will be most effective as a means for identifying the bases of party support if it includes provisions for both the designation of candidates at a party assembly and their nomination in a subsequent primary election. At the latter, the office holder may observe centres of opposition of which he was not aware at the former. Furthermore, party activists can more easily enforce their claims the fewer constraints there are on their considering potential alternative candidates to the incumbent. And it is argued here that the membership style of nomination does indeed provide such constraints by inducing loyalty to office seekers on the part of the party members.

Now Schlesinger's account of the rationale for the membership party is supportive of one of the longest standing pieces of conventional wisdom in political science -- namely that the European socialist parties adopted the most appropriate form of organisation for their activists when they made them members. For the period of growth of a party to major party status in a polity it is probably true that this was the most effective form of organisation. By being able to confer selective benefits on members, the party would be able to overcome the disadvantage that all associations have in providing a collective benefit when a large number of contributors is required. However, in their maturity political parties do not need members, save for the few required to perform the essential administrative functions, including fund raising.[38] It is not surprising, therefore, that in nearly all western countries there has been a decline in the membership of political parties. And somewhere along the way the members lost what control they had over the policies pursued by office holders. Even though Michels accounted for this in terms of the growth of oligarchy, it can be argued that in the case of Britain, at least, a cursory examination reveals a rather different explanation of the failure of party democracy.

There would seem to be three factors which have prevented local party officials, or dissident members of the party, from directly having any great control over the policies pursued by the parliamentary leadership. First, particularly in the case of the more obviously membership-type party (Labour), the rules governing the refusal by a local party to readopt an M.P. give the party's central organisation opportunities to intervene. This extends indefinitely the period over which an anti-incumbent campaign has to be sustained. 'Incumbent-dumpers' have no specific meetings, after which the issue of the party's nomination is finally settled, to direct their campaign towards. As with Mr. Reginald Prentice's dispute with the Newham North East Labour party (which began in 1974 and only ended with his defection to the Conservative party), the issue may recommence each year with the annual election of the local party's officials. Enquiries into procedures and threats to disaffiliate a local party further increase the cost to those planning to challenge a candidate.[39] Even when it is not designed to assist an office holder, intervention by the central party has the effect of doing so because it extends the nomination process. Second, local parties have become the service organisations of the national parties; the tasks they have to perform (particularly fund raising) leave no time for overtly political activities, including the setting of policy priorities and the enforcement of these priorities in the nomination process. The result is that, although party members are ideological, they join the party to perform functions which provide only solidaristic rewards. Jim Bulpitt has described the apolitical character of British local party organisations in the following way:

In many ways the 'performance' at elections became more important than the actual result: *organising* for elections was the *raison d'être* of the local party. . . . The important point is that the central parties benefitted in two ways from all this. On the one hand they received a certain amount of money and ensured that the local organisation operated throughout the year, on the other hand they kept the local parties so busy (or thinking about being busy) that there was precious little time, let alone energy, to engage seriously in other matters, such as policy discussion. . . . But undoubtedly the principal reason why administrative and social activity dominated party work was that this was what most members wanted. It is a mistake to think that party activists were interested in politics. Many were not, and many recognised that policy discussions caused divisions, and many were prepared to leave politics to the national party.

What all activists were interested in was not politics but organisation. Those peculiar people who joined the party to discuss politics could be shunted off to party auxiliary organisations or socialised into accepting the prevailing culture of *apolitisme*.[40]

Third, as a consequence of the priority accorded the activities that are supportive of the national parties, local party officials develop a sense of loyalty to an incumbent. This means that discontent with the latter must probably be made overt by those who are least able to generate a successful campaign against him. There is thus little incentive for the discontented party members to coalesce to plan a campaign; some support for this claim, about the inefficacy of local parties in disciplining office holders, can be found in Jackson's study of the constituency constraints on British M.P.s who defied the parliamentary whip.[41]

In contrast to the inefficacy in controlling their office holders of the party members in Britain, it is interesting to note the relative ease with which issue-oriented activists in the First Congressional District in Colorado (Denver City and County) were able to secure the removal of their Congressman, Byron Rogers, in 1970. Many of the supporters of Rogers' opponent, Craig Barnes, were purposive reward-seeking Democrats, whose prime concern was with Vietnam war policy and other national political issues. They were exactly the sort of party contributors whom Schlesinger believes would be better off in a membership party. Yet despite the fact that Barnes only became a candidate shortly before the precinct caucuses, and that Rogers was a 20-year incumbent who had not been challenged within the party since his first election, at the county assembly Barnes won first line designation for the primary by 967 votes to 871, and then won the primary.[42] Three aspects of this exercise of activist control are relevant here. First, those who wished to present a challenge to Barnes knew the exact period over which they would have to concentrate their resources: precinct caucuses and a county assembly were held in May 1970 with the primary in early September. This made it easier for them to mobilise support at all three stages of nomination. Second, although some party officials might have been as concerned with solidaristic rewards as their British counterparts, there were many other activists in the party who were in just as good a position to lead a challenge to Rogers on the question of the purposive rewards he distributed. Because the party was composed of more than those mainly concerned with supportive, administrative functions (the equivalent of the British party members) challenges to an incumbent within the party were possible. Third, the assembly-primary system was a mechanism for overcoming loyalty within the party. Because their efforts at persuading 'fringe' Democrats to attend the caucuses were successful, the insurgent benefit seekers could show strength amongst party activists; the primary campaign gave them an opportunity to take their claims to a wider group in the party from the vantage point of their candidate having the top-line designation. Even had they lost, they would have been more able to demonstrate their contribution to the Democratic coalition in Denver, than any issue-oriented activists in a membership party in Britain could have done. Not only are the claims of activists in a non-membership nomination system visible, but these activists work through a process in which direct control of office holders is possible.

Against Schlesinger it can be argued that, in conjunction with a membership style of nomination, a membership style of organisation *can* be appropriate for the office-seeking candidate. It will provide him with a loyal organisation which is less likely than a looser structure to attempt to free-ride after he has obtained a particularly large plurality. Again, the formal rules of membership, and the type of activist whom the party attracts, make his removal more difficult. He will have to pay out only the minimum benefits to the membership, and thus maintain the manoeuvrability which Schlesinger justifiably assumes the office seeker will value. It is perhaps no coincidence that the British Labour party, with its formally democratic organisation and its much publicised internal disputes on public policy, has had only four leaders in the last forty years. Of their former leaders, two retired from office after a long period of leadership (Attlee and Wilson) and the other (Gaitskell) died in office. In this period, the less formally democratic Conservative party had eight leaders, of whom only two (Baldwin and Churchill) were clear cases of entirely voluntary retirement. One (Chamberlain) resigned in wartime after the defection of 113 Conservative Members (including abstainers) in a parliamentary vote in the House of Commons, and two were forced by party pressure to resign or seek relection, which was lost (Douglas-Home and Heath, respectively). In the case of the remaining two (Eden and Macmillan) party pressure, apart from their ill-health, has been thought by some to have hastened their decisions to retire.

To conclude: against the claim that an internally-democratic, membership-style organisation is the same as a membership style of nomination a separation of the two aspects of membership has been suggested. Moreover, it has been argued that a more open style of nomination (involving a particular type of party primary) is more likely to make intra-party democracy possible than is the kind of nomination process associated with the European type of membership party. Having said this, what might be alleged to be another paradox of party democracy may be disposed of more quickly.

The argument that a more open, non-membership style of nomination process prevents the atrophy of internally democratic parties, might be held to be the source of a third paradox of party democracy. For if the party is open to new elements, and if nominations are in the hands of local parties, why should not diversity between the regions of a country give rise to Tweedledum and Tweedledee parties? That is, it might seem that if control over the nomination process is not centralised, there is nothing to prevent both parties from embracing the same interests at the national level, thus being indistinguishable from each other. Indeed this argument has been propounded as an explanation of why there is a lack of coherence of viewpoint in the American parties at the federal level of politics. ('Because the natives of Massachusetts and Arkansas have exclusive control over nominations in their own state, it is only natural that the Republican party in the former will be more "liberal" than the Democratic party in the latter.')

However, there are three arguments that can be brought against the claim that there is a genuine paradox here. First, there is the general point made in the APSA report that even when a party does not have stated objectives:

> ... it is the hope of accomplishing common aims that leads people to act together. The very idea of party implies an association of broadly like-minded voters seeking to carry out common objectives through their elected representatives.[43]

In other words, those who seek purposive benefits will want to act on a national basis in concert with those who have similar views, rather than in a team embracing the whole range of current political views. Indeed it can be argued that the similarity of the Congressional parties in America until the 1950s was made possible by the fact that the majority of activists in many states were not concerned with purposive benefits but with solidaristic ones. With the influx of issue-oriented activists in the Republican party after 1960 and in the Democratic party a few years later, the Congressional parties have become more distinct.

A second argument is derived from 'ambition theory'. Where there is a minority wing of a party that is more akin in views to the opposition party than to its own (for example, the liberal Republicans of the North East), office seekers from this wing will find their route to the highest offices blocked. Even if office holders do not leave the party (as did, for example, New York mayor John Lindsay) their experience of being blocked will encourage those of similar views, about to embark on a political career, to join the opposition party. Since 1960, the last year when it seemed possible that a moderate or liberal Republican might gain the presidential nomination of his party, the numbers and influence of this type of politician has declined.[44]

Finally, the most important reason for the existence of look-alike parties is the willingness of legislators to tolerate voting defection by their fellow representatives. This willingness is fostered by the absence of a standard by which the party activists can evaluate performance in office, the most important standard being a party policy programme. Even though they cannot control the nomination of those with radically different views, the majority of a party in a legislature has a variety of devices to force dissidents to choose between a change in what policies they will support or a change in party. These range from withdrawal of support for the dissident's pet projects to refusing to provide him with any benefits given to other members (for example, centralised campaign funds) to the non-recognition of him as a party member in organising the legislature. In fact, being largely free of activist control and anxious to maximise the benefits they can supply to their constituents through being in a majority party, most American legislators tolerate any deviation in views by a fellow party legislator. The most extreme case of this failure to discipline a dissident was perhaps that of U.S. Senator Harry Byrd Jr. of Virginia. There is considerable evidence that when a party in America does attempt to impose discipline, it has the weapons necessary to do so. For example, the dumping of three committee chairmen in the U.S. House in 1974–5 led one senior Democrat (Jarman of Oklahoma) to switch parties and other senior Democrats to consider retirement more seriously.[45] But, of course, in a parliamentary system there is the important additional weapon available to the majority in a governing party: executive patronage. Whilst its absence in a system of separated powers makes it more difficult for the parties to cohere, and hence to provide for political education by outlining different definitions of the political universe, it does not make it impossible. As is seen in the next three chapters, the main problem in the U.S. is that legislators are often unwilling to impose discipline within their party. And this unwillingness is shared by both those who see themselves as independent of their party activists and those who believe they should partly reflect the views of their activists on public issues.

6 Party Democracy and the Denver Democrats

This chapter is concerned with the question of whether the pre-primary assembly system has enabled a high degree of internal democracy to emerge within the Colorado Democratic party or whether the results have been less than might be expected.[1] The chapter divides into three unequal sections, the first being devoted to the effects of the pre-primary system on Congressional nominations in Denver. The second section is devoted to the Senate contests, and not 'major statewide contests' because in the period covered by this study there has only been one contested nomination for the Governorship: 1974. In 1970 there was no challenge to the party's then most senior office holder, Lieutenant Governor Mark Hogan, in his bid for the Governorship. In the third, and much the longest, section the discussion is focused on nominations in Denver for the state General Assembly, but there more general problems about the factors limiting the extent of party democracy in the American system of government are raised.

By way of introduction, however, it is necessary to explain why this particular party was chosen for the case study. In the first place, as we have seen, it appears to have the kind of nominating process that is most appropriate for maximising party democracy. Secondly, at least until the early 1960s, these nominating procedures prevented the kind of atrophy of parties that had occurred in many other states where the progressive reformers had introduced primary elections. Thirdly, its political culture, what Elazar calls a 'moralistic one', is most supportive of 'issue competition' between the parties.[2] Fourthly, in recent years it has experienced an influx of the kind of political activists who are most likely to use these procedures of internal democracy. In the 1950s the issue-oriented, liberal wing of the party organisation gained supremacy over the older elements in it, both in Denver and statewide. Beginning in 1968, these activists were joined by an increasingly large number of new 'amateur' participants, many mobilised by the issue of the Vietnam war. This participation had many manifestations, not the least being in attendance at party caucus meetings.[3] This very high level of participation, in comparison with most other parties in America and elsewhere, has continued in the 1970s. This study focuses primarily on the party organisation in Denver, although this is certainly not the only centre of increased activism. The main reason for this focus is that Denver is the most important constituent of the state party, and although an urban area, it is largely suburban in character and hence is not unlike most of the other populated counties in Colorado.

A. THE U.S. HOUSE OF REPRESENTATIVES

From 1950 until 1970 Denver was represented in Congress by a Democrat, Byron Rogers, who faced no primary opposition after his first election until his defeat by Craig Barnes in the 1970 primary. Although one prominent state legislator had been approached by a group of Democrats in 1968 with a view to him challenging Rogers, he ruled this out as inappropriate. He may have been correct – much of the effort of his potential supporters was then being directed towards either the Presidential election or the contest for the U.S. Senate nomination. However, by the end of the 1960s Rogers had become vulnerable for two reasons. In the first place, whilst he was not a vigorous supporter of the Vietnam war, he was not an opponent of it. He thus became an obvious target for the anti-war organisers of the 1968 Kennedy-McCarthy coalition in Colorado. (This, one of the few successful coalitions that year, endured until after the National Convention.) Secondly, he came from an older political tradition – one that was only a minority element in the party organisation even in the early 1960s.

At the beginning of 1970 a group of former McCarthy supporters began a series of informal discussions and interviews with a view to finding a candidate to challenge Rogers. Nevertheless, even just before the party caucuses there was no agreed candidate. At a meeting of this group in April, Barnes was asked to speak alongside some possible candidates of the group. Barnes had already been approached earlier in the year and asked to run against Rogers, but he had declined. At that meeting, with no desire to emerge as a candidate, he felt free to demand 'that the Democratic party change the world', and his inspiring performance there led many to insist that he challenge Rogers.[4] The style of his approach at this meeting was to set the tone of his campaign: it was a crusade for the intrusion of morality into politics, and the placing of clear alternative policies before the electorate. Although he announced his candidacy only a few days before the caucuses, his approach had an enormous impact on many activists, and he was able to win first-line designation on the primary ballot against the incumbent at the district assembly three weeks later. That the sort of views he was stridently putting forward were listened to sympathetically amongst a wide range of Democrats was reflected also in his subsequent victory in the September primary. Yet the narrowness of his victory was indirectly responsible for his loss to the Republican in the general election. For Rogers invoked a law suit, claiming that Barnes's 27-vote margin of victory should be overturned because some of the votes were invalid. The current party chairman, Monte Pascoe, has argued:

> Had the dispute with Byron Rogers been resolved the day after the primary, in short had it been clear that Craig Barnes had won the primary, we could have spent 3 or 4 weeks trying to mend our fences with Byron Rogers. Instead it wasn't concluded until some time in October and up to about the time it was concluded we were still talking about having another election with Byron Rogers [as the candidate]. And that was very divisive.[5]

Obviously, the disunity in the party that followed from Rogers's refusal to accept the result of the election did affect the campaign effort. However, some party activists have maintained that the real cause of his defeat was his close association with 'busing' litigants in the city, an issue that was raised by his opponent during the last week of the campaign. Whether either of these factors was in itself sufficient to produce the Republican candidate's 7 per cent margin of victory is now merely a matter for speculation. What is less doubtful, though, is that the campaign period itself was decisive in the loss of the election: a poll taken in late September showed that Barnes had a 55 per cent - 30 per cent lead in the sample surveyed.[6] On the surface, then, there is no evidence that the challenge of an incumbent by a dissident group was responsible for the Democrats losing the district.

The Barnes candidacy has undoubtedly been of enormous importance in shaping attitudes in the party towards elections. For one thing, as is shown in the next chapter, it was a turning point in the way in which the party presented the busing issue to the electorate. However, it also helped to mould opinions about the desirability of opposing incumbents or clearly front-running candidates for the nomination of the party. Although on the one hand the Barnes case demonstrated the potential of the pre-primary system for removing unpopular incumbents, on the other hand it reinforced beliefs in the costs of such opposition. In short, it was seen as sustaining the argument that internal opposition damaged the party's chances of winning the general election. Certainly, in 1972 the Chairman of the Denver party was acting on this supposition when he attempted to dissuade Patricia Schroeder from running against the man he believed would be the eventual nominee for the Congressional seat – Arch Decker. However, this fear of the primary when the incumbent is a Republican is not a typical view: amongst Executive Committee members there were more believers than disbelievers that a strongly contested primary helps the Democrats (Table 6.1). But with a Democratic incumbent, 71 per cent of the Committee members believed that the Democratic party is not helped by a strongly contested primary (Table 6.2). It is this perception of a supposed cost to the party in challenging incumbents that places a limit on the willingness to employ the weapon of denying renomination to an incumbent.

Of course the divisive primary can promote disaffection amongst party activists.[7] Nevertheless, even in the most bitter and ill-tempered recent Democratic primary in Colorado (the Haskell-Vollack 1972 Senate contest) the winner did not suffer from lack of party effort because of it, and unexpectedly went on to defeat the Republican incumbent. Indeed there is some evidence from elsewhere that a divisive primary does not harm a candidate's election prospects.[8] Moreover, of the 'peace' candidates who defeated incumbents for the party nomination to the Congress of the United States in 1970, Barnes was the only one to lose at the subsequent general election. And this seems mainly to have been the product of either the challenge in court to the primary result or Barnes's role in the Denver busing controversy. The main point at issue here, however, is not whether the party's leading activists were justified in their belief that strongly-contested primaries involving incumbents hurt the party, but that they in fact took this view of the primary. One lesson they learnt from both the 1968 coalition effort and the Barnes candidacy was that the nomination mechanism in Colorado did make it possible to influence public affairs directly. But the other lesson they took from 1970 was that challenging an incumbent hurt the party. Even though the Executive Committee is now dominated by former Barnes supporters, there is a common assumption that the primary imposes a cost on the party –

TABLE 6.1: *DDPECM: View of the Effect of a Strongly Contested Primary with a Republican Incumbent*

Will you say whether you strongly agree, mildly agree, are undecided, mildly disagree, or strongly disagree with this statement:

'When the incumbent is a Republican, a strongly contested Democratic primary helps the Democratic party.' (N=67)

	Percentage of respondents in each category
Strongly agree	22
Mildly agree	30
Undecided	8
Mildly disagree	24
Strongly disagree	16
TOTAL	100

TABLE 6.2: *DDPECM: View of the Effect of a Strongly Contested Primary with a Democratic Incumbent*

Will you say whether you strongly agree, mildly agree, are undecided, mildly disagree, or strongly disagree with this statement:

'When the incumbent is a Democrat, a strongly contested Democrat primary helps the Democratic party.'

(a) All respondents (N=66)

	Percentage of respondents in each category
Strongly agree	8
Mildly agree	12
Undecided	9
Mildly disagree	30
Strongly disagree	41
TOTAL	100

(b) Those who reported support for Craig Barnes in 1970 (N=40)

	Percentage of respondents in each category
Strongly agree	8
Mildly agree	2
Undecided	7
Mildly disagree	38
Strongly disagree	45
TOTAL	100

indeed recognition of this apparent cost is more extensive amongst Barnes's erstwhile supporters than in the Committee as a whole (Tables 6.2 and 6.3).

TABLE 6.3: *DDPECM: Support for Craig Barnes in 1970*

At the time, did you support, oppose, or remain neutral in the campaign of Craig Barnes in the 1970 Congressional primary against Byron Rogers? (N=58)

	Percentage of respondents in each category
Supported Barnes	71
Opposed Barnes	14
Neutral	8
Not active then	7
TOTAL	100

The absence of overwhelming support for the view that a Democratic primary helps the party against a Republican incumbent (Table 6.1) is perhaps as surprising as the activists' views about primaries involving a Democratic incumbent. A study of the Colorado nominating system in the 1960s had revealed support for the primary among party leaders in the state, as a way of stimulating voter interest, providing that the primaries were unlikely to involve bitter personal exchanges.[9] In addition, in 1976 the party activists generally, and the members cf Executive Committee in particular, were dominated by those who had supported Patricia Schroeder in the 1972 primary. At the time Schroeder was seen by some as the 'outside' candidate who was forcing the contest. There is no evidence that the primary campaign hurt her general election contest: rather it enabled her to become well known to both potential activists and the general electorate.[10]

Like Barnes in 1970, Schroeder was first approached by an informal group of activists shortly before the party caucuses, and was persuaded to seek the Congressional nomination. She was then unknown to the vast majority of Democratic voters, having never previously run for any public office. (Her husband had unsuccessfully run for the state General Assembly in 1970.) Her opponent for the Democratic nomination, Arch Decker, was a moderately conservative, long-serving member of the State Senate, of which he was then minority leader. His main claim for the nomination thus lay in his seniority and the fact that his name was known by the voters. Some effort was made by the county chairman to dissuade Schroeder from running; what seemed to lie behind this was the belief that the identification of the party with 'liberal' politics during the primary would harm the party's general election prospects. There were two grounds for supposing that a candidate identified with liberal views could no longer win in Denver. In the first place, after the 1970 Census a Republican Governor and General Assembly had redistricted Colorado in such a way as to make it easier for the incumbent Republican, Mike McKevitt, to win. They removed from his district part of the heavily Chicano – and thus Democratic – western portion of the city and placed it in a predominantly suburban (and Republican) adjacent district.[11] Secondly, the controversy over busing was thought by many to work against any candidate who was not identified with a strong anti-busing stance. Yet if Schroeder was an outside candidate in one sense, she was not from outside the party. She had worked for the party for several years, had been a prominent young Democrat, and, unlike Decker, represented the sort of views that had become dominant in the party. At the district assembly she accordingly won by a margin of $919\frac{1}{2}$–445. (A system of proportional representation in the selection of delegates to assemblies and conventions makes possible the phenomenon of the casting of a half-vote at an assembly.) But without the subsequent primary she would have been less able to present herself as a serious candidate for the general election. Her 4 per cent margin over McKevitt at the latter election owed much to the free publicity that she obtained during the primary, particularly in a year with both a Presidential and a Senate election; with several controversial referenda on the ballot this publicity was invaluable.

In recent years then, there have been two major contests for the Congressional nomination in Denver. The willingness to employ the primary mechanism as a last resort against incumbents was also apparent at the same time in other parts of the state. Yet, as we have argued elsewhere, these other two cases are not examples of the kind of intra-party accountability with which we are concerned here.[12] That intra-party accountability has been limited in Colorado is also revealed when an examination is made of the incidence of primaries for nominations to the state General Assembly from Denver: it is seen that there have been very few primaries involving the defeat of incumbents, far fewer than might be expected of a party with an activist base that has recently changed in character (Section C).

B. THE U.S. SENATE

The main feature of nomination for the Senate in recent years has been the decreasing importance of first-line designations in the primary. That is, the candidate who wins the most votes at the state party assembly and consequently has his name placed first on the primary-election ballot, is now less likely to win that election than were first-line candidates in earlier years. Under Colorado's nomination procedures (as also in five other states) the majority of party activists should have a substantial, but not overwhelming, advantage *vis-à-vis* Democratic voters in the selection of candidates.[13] It is this advantage which makes for party accountability though it is, of course, the availability of an appeal to the party's electorate that prevents the party from being 'captured' by either office holders or a small minority within the electorate. Two benefits then accrue to the activists. Firstly, only those would-be candidates who obtain more than 20 per cent of the vote at the appropriate assembly can get on to the primary ballot. Secondly, the most preferred candidate has the advantage of being first-lined. This advantage results from the propensity of two kinds of voter to vote for the first-line candidate. The first, and smaller group, consists of those who, knowing little about the candidates, vote for the candidate whom they know to be the choice of the majority of activists. In other words, they respect the party's ability to choose a suitable candidate, and are supportive of the party. The other group is composed of those who also know nothing of the candidates, but whose inertia leads them to vote for the first name on the ballot. Obviously, if this mechanism is to work effectively there has to be a fine balance struck between excessive and insufficient party control. On the one hand, it must not be too difficult for candidates to get on to the ballot, and to present their case to the electorate. On the other hand, if the advantages of first-lining are too easily overcome, then the party has too little control over candidates to provide it with an effective mechanism for making office holders accountable. The achievement of this balance necessitates that the candidate who is responding to interests that are underrepresented by the party's activists, has a genuine opportunity to mobilise an electoral majority in the party against them. Thus the resources (particularly financial ones) available to candidates for the campaign must not be too unevenly distributed in favour of the party's choice. But the balance can only be attained if the voters' recognition of a lower-line candidate's name or political style is, by itself, insufficient to overcome the advantages of the first-line candidate. In particular, in the era of television campaigning there would have to be a limit to the amount of publicity of which a candidate can avail himself if the election is not to be determined by factors other than the mobilisation of unrepresented interests.

In the period between 1928 and 1962, success in the primary seems to have been closely associated with ballot position in Congressional and Gubernatorial nominations. Counting Democratic and Republican primaries together, over 90 per cent of first-line candidates were successful in these elections.[14] In Senate elections the first-line candidates had a slightly lower success rate, but still managed to win 70 per cent of the contests. However, recent Democratic Senate primaries suggest an important change in this pattern of nomination. In the last three elections (1968, 1972 and 1974) a second-line candidate has won. In 1968 and 1972 fairly close assembly wins by the first-line candidate were followed by substantial defeats in the primary; in 1974 the reverse was true: a large margin of victory at the assembly preceded a narrow (6 per cent) defeat in the primary.

The 1968 election between former Governor, Steve McNichols, and an out-state legislator, Ken Monfort, was perhaps the last successful Senate primary campaign of an older style of politics. Monfort had obtained the first-line designation at the assembly as an anti-war candidate. It was largely a by-product of the Kennedy-McCarthy coalition success of that year that he had even become a serious challenger for the nomination.[15] In part Montfort's primary loss can be attributed to the decline in enthusiasm of the anti-war activists after the Chicago National Convention. In part it was due also to the fact that McNichols himself was not a Vietnam 'hawk', and many party voters at that time were not fervently against the war. But to a large extent also McNichols was the *party* candidate – he was able to organise the vote in Denver, thanks to his long-standing connections with the party. Because the activists were less organised, and because the war was still not of such prime concern for many Democrats, the traditional methods of getting out the vote could not be overcome. It was perhaps the last success in a partisan election for the remnants of the Denver political machine that had been prominent in city politics in the 1930s and 1940s. More importantly, it seems to have been the last Democratic Senatorial nomination for which mobilisation through the party was decisive.

As in many other states in America, Senatorial campaigns have decreasingly been dependent on *party* effort on behalf of candidates.

Indeed, Colorado provides a good example of how parties have been disintegrating in the United States in the 1970s. The rate of disintegration of the parties in respect of Senate elections is perhaps more advanced in this state than in some others but it is not a unique phenomenon. In 1972, and more especially in 1974, a new style of campaigning emerges in which there are three crucial elements. The first is the availability of 'free time' before the election year for a candidate to build up a body of personal support partially inside, but mainly outside, the regular party organisation. Obviously some 'party' support is necessary to ensure that the candidate does obtain 20 per cent of the votes at the assembly, which as an 'outside' candidate he may be uncertain of getting.[16] Secondly, he needs to have access to adequate campaign funds. Since the office of Senator is such a valuable one, it is worthwhile both to hire polling firms and purchase advertising time from local television stations: the latter enables the candidate to get Democratic voters to recognise his name and style of politics. Thirdly, he can gain a considerable amount of free television time by developing a 'media strategy' – making news with well-timed statements and meetings. Because of the uniqueness in an election year of a Senate contest in the state, the primary contests for it will receive more attention than all other elections, save those for the Presidency and perhaps the Governorship. Certainly, the television stations will give more time to this contest than to Congressional or other races.

The 1972 nomination contest is best seen as an intermediary case between the older style of party politics and the new, extra-party campaign with which Gary Hart succeeded in 1974.[17] Neither Gary Hart nor the 1972 nominee, Floyd Haskell, was a candidate of the party activists. Haskell did not become a Democrat until 1970, following a period he had served in the state senate as a Republican. His nomination as a U.S. Senate candidate in 1972 followed a primary campaign against Anthony Vollack. For liberal activists both Haskell and Vollack were somewhat unattractive candidates in the year of the McGovern campaign, the Schroeder campaign, and several radical initiative referenda. They suffered from a double liability: they were too 'moderate' to attract active support from many party regulars and, until just before the general election, it was not widely recognised that incumbent Gordon Allott was vulnerable. Thus, after the state assembly at which liberal activist support was divided between the two candidates, Haskell's campaign organisation remained one that owed little, except tacit support, to those who had taken over the party organisation after 1968. In effect, Haskell demonstrated that an office seeker could set himself up in the party and, providing his views were not too far removed from those of most activists, organise his own nomination and election.

Two years later, Gary Hart demonstrated that, in regard to Senate nominations, the activists in the party organisation were not king-makers; he defeated a candidate who was the popular choice of most of the liberal activists. Hart's campaign strategy is of particular interest because it was founded on the assumption that not only could the candidate of the organisation activists be defeated, but that any candidate whose support was mainly party support was at a disadvantage. Haskell had merely shown that in a party of issue-oriented amateurs an 'outsider' could be successful; Hart was to show the limits of party control over nominations, even in a state with a pre-primary assembly system. To understand how he achieved this it is necessary to return to the three characteristics of the new campaign style identified above.

It is a disadvantage for a prospective Senate candidate to have a full-time job, or even to be the occupant of another public office, in the period leading up to the election year. As elsewhere in America, lawyers and similar professionals are advantaged in this respect – both the 1972 and 1974 Democratic nominees were lawyers who held no political offices in the two years preceding their election. With his free time the candidate can establish a personal following that he will need both to get on the ballot, and during the primary campaign itself. Of Hart's preparation for the 1974 campaign, his campaign manager Harold Haddon said:

> He spent a lot of time talking to people at a time when he had the luxury of not having to be everywhere at once – which is what happens when the campaign really starts to roll. He started so early and he met so many people on a one-to-one basis that he attracted a personal following – people who really believe in him personally.[18]

But during this period the candidate can also work out his standard kind of response to policy issues that are likely to arise in the campaign. He certainly does not want to develop specific proposals, but he does have an incentive to guard against two problems that may emerge in the campaign. He may be accused by opponents of being ambiguous on issues, or if he has a specific proposal it may be shown to be defective. He has to do what Benjamin I. Page describes as 'putting a limit on his ambiguity.'[19] That is, he establishes 'positions' that cannot be readily described as ambiguous, but which avoid a high degree of specificity. Moreover, he needs to familiarise himself with the subtleties of his particular stances. It is in the pre-campaign period that he can do this. This is the background work to his media strategy; he can make statements and respond to events in the campaign by relating them to the stances that have been worked out, and learnt, much earlier.

Perhaps the greatest lesson that Gary Hart took from being George McGovern's campaign manager was the value of the pre-campaign period to the candidate in allowing him to familiarise himself with his unspecific issue stances. In comparison with the ideal strategy, McGovern had been both unduly specific and had had the stances worked out for him only just before the campaign. The result was that he was too easily criticised for propounding unworkable and inconsistent policies during the campaign, and this hampered him severely. In contrast, Hart had his own positions drawn up months before the party caucuses.

The preparation for a campaign also requires a certain amount of finance. As well as having a job that would support him and also provide him with free time, Hart had to pay for a private opinion poll. The first poll was commissioned in early 1973 to test his prospects in a race against incumbent Republican Peter Dominick 18 months later. The poll revealed both a surprising lack of support for Dominick, and also that Hart was not suffering from a handicap through his association with McGovern. However, it is during the campaign itself that an adequate supply of finance is crucial. In a public reaction to Watergate, Hart's main opponent, Herrick Roth, refused to accept contributions of more than $19.74. Eventually he was to spend approximately one half the amount that Hart and the other Democratic candidate, Marty Miller, each spent in the primary campaign. Finance permits the candidate to buy two commodities that an army of activists cannot provide: detailed opinion poll information and 'name recognition' through television advertising. Roth, the first-line candidate, did not commission any polls during the entire campaign, and could afford very little prime-time advertising. However, Harold Haddon was certain that 'bought' name recognition was not the main difference between the Roth and Hart campaigns. Rather, he saw it as Hart's ability to create 'free' news that would be covered by the television news programmes, something at which the Hart campaign team was adept whilst Roth's was not.

Aside from developing his 'position' statements, Hart had earlier launched a study which was to reveal an association between Dominick and the 'laundering' of milk fund money in the 1972 Nixon campaign. ('Laundering' is the term given to the process of disguising some sources of campaign funds when candidates are required by law to report the donors of their funds.) This gave Hart considerable free publicity at the start of the primary campaign, but publicity which was gained without alienating the regular activists. This was essential because Roth was the preferred candidate of many of the new activists, although he was not one of them. He was nearly 60 years of age and had been the long-serving head of the state AFL-CIO (the American equivalent of the TUC). Yet his credentials were sound ones for his party activist 'constituency' – he had been sacked by George Meany for attempting to give official AFL-CIO endorsement to the McGovern campaign in Colorado and, as a former teacher, he was an 'intellectual' who had always been on the radical wing of the party.[20] In early 1974, from a field of six, Roth emerged as the candidate with the strongest party support. In Hart's perception, his own task was to outmanoeuvre Roth in the primary campaign rather than attempt to outorganise him at the precinct level beforehand.

Now this method of campaigning in the primary was possible with a set of activists many of whom were not regular Democratic workers. Apart from some support inside the 'regular' party to legitimise his candidacy, and to assist in obtaining 20 per cent of the assembly vote, Hart did not want a party-centred campaign:

> We prefaced our entire organisation from the outset on the theory that we were going to have our own people and we weren't going to rely on county and state party organisations in any way. The problem of relying on those kind of functionaries is that they have a lot of loyalties, conflicting loyalties .. and they've got five or six different races to concern themselves with. And our focus was just to get people in the precincts and districts who were working for Hart and weren't concerned with any other race. I think a lot of our best workers were people who had never been involved in politics before.[21]

This type of candidate strategy raises a major threat to parties as the main determinant of nominations. For it is clear that in Senate contests the Colorado party activists cannot only be bypassed, but deliberately bypassed by the candidate. In this case, the candidate, Hart, was not attempting to mobilise underrepresented interests in the party electorate, but to create an efficient campaign organisation. What encourages this decline in party is the potential for a direct appeal to an electorate by a candidate on the basis of his name, style, and personality. This potential exists mainly for two reasons. The first is the uniqueness of the office, which places it above nearly all others in terms of the attention it receives. The second is the absence of a *party* monopoly over campaign resources and, in particular, the absence of rigid restrictions on campaign expenditure. The result is that the balance required of a nominating system, to which attention was drawn earlier in this section, has been disturbed. In Senate elections therefore, the party's ability to determine who will be their candidate has been seriously undermined.

This last point can be illustrated by comparing recruitment in the cases of Patricia Schroeder in 1972 and Gary Hart in 1974. Hart was self-recruited – he decided to run for the Senate, and built up his staff, personal following and 'positions' well before the county and state assemblies. He deliberately set out to involve 'non-regular' activists. Schroeder was recruited by a group of party regulars together with some irregulars. Although her first campaign was partly characterised by the bringing in of outsiders in the primary to those precincts which supported her opponent, many of the precincts were organised by regular activists, precinct committee members, and captains. First-line designation in the primary enabled her to rally support as the *party* candidate, whilst Hart had been unconcerned about his position on the ballot (he merely wanted to make sure he was on the ballot).

C. THE COLORADO GENERAL ASSEMBLY

In the five elections between 1968 and 1976 a combined total of 102 seats in the Colorado House and Senate was at stake in Denver. Of these seats, 57 involved Democratic incumbents seeking re-election after the county assembly. Yet only about 5 per cent of the incumbents were defeated in a primary, with two out of the three instances occurring in the party's cataclysmic year, 1970 (Table 6.4). Because intra-party conflict that year was more intense than in any other year in the immediate past, it is necessary to digress at this point to outline the arenas of controversy then.

There were three main arenas, the first being over nominations for office. In Denver, whilst Barnes was obtaining the first-line designation for the primary election against Rogers, there were 13 primaries with 7 incumbents seeking re-election being challenged. Elsewhere in the state, Congressman Wayne Aspinall had his first primary challenge for 22 years. A second area of dispute was the party organisation. The controversy centred on the non-residence of several 'old-style' captains in the districts they represented. A compromise was eventually reached, but the county party chairman resigned soon afterwards. Thirdly, the gubernatorial nominee and many organisation Democrats were involved in a dispute about the former's right to 'recommend' to the state assembly a nominee for Lieutenant Governor. Clearly the disputes within the party in 1970 were not simply a repeat of the 'Anti-war Coalition'–Humphrey division of two years earlier. Nor were they merely a 'new participant–old guard' battle. Even less were the splits purely between 'liberals' and 'conservatives'. There was no clear-cut battle between two well defined sides, but rather a whole series of small disputes, which reflected a period of change in the composition of the party. By 1972 it was a very differently balanced party that was to meet at the county and state conventions.

TABLE 6.4: *Competition for the Democratic Nomination in Denver for Seats in the Colorado General Assembly (House and Senate): 1968–1976*

	1968	1970	1972	1974	1976	TOTAL
Total number of seats at stake	22	22	19	20	19	102
Total number won by Democrats	15	15	13	15	12	70
Total number of incumbents nominated at assembly	10	5	8	8	11	42
Total number of incumbents facing primary opposition	2	7	2	4	0	15
Total number of incumbents not 'top-lined' at primary	0	5	1	1	0	7
Total number of incumbents defeated in a primary	0	2	1	0	0	3
Total number of non 'top-line' candidates winning	3	2	0	1	2	8
Total number of primaries	5	13	5	10	3	37

1970, then, was the only election year of the last five in which even a majority of the incumbents seeking re-election faced primary opponents. The minor sanction against an incumbent, that of being 'second-lined' in the primary, was meted out to only 12 per cent of those seeking renomination, and 5 out of these 7 instances occurred in 1970 (Table 6.4). Thus the denial of renomination to a legislator has not been extensively used as a means of disciplining Democrats in the General Assembly. Of course, the evidence on which this conclusion is based does not take account of those legislators who abandoned their plans for renomination either before or after the caucuses and assemblies, through fear of defeat. There were certainly a few such cases, although not apparently very many. But how is this unwillingness to challenge incumbents to be explained for a period when the composition of the party's activists changed, and the party organisation fell into the hands of issue-oriented amateurs?

One explanation of it might be that the natural turnover of legislators in the last eight years produced a new generation with whom the activists shared a similar political outlook. However, superficially this seems implausible, for whilst the sorts of issues with which the activists have been concerned have changed in the last decade, there has not been a corresponding change in the agenda of the General Assembly, even when the Democrats regained control of the lower house in 1974. There were different emphases (though not radically different) in much of the legislation from those of the preceding years. Again, the activists on the Executive Committee see their own political outlook as being dissimilar to that of the majority of legislators from Denver. Whereas 69 per cent of the Committee people describe their own viewpoint as either liberal or left wing, and 92 per cent of them describe their fellow activists in this way, only 38 per cent of them see this as the philosophy of the majority of Denver Democrats in the General Assembly (Tables 6.5, 6.6, and 6.7). Indeed 45 per cent of the committee members perceive a substantial difference between their own philosophy and that of the majority of legislators, the most common response being that of the self-defined liberal who believes the legislators to be moderates.[22] A further 15 per cent of the committee see a partial difference between their philosophy and that of the legislators.

Obviously what lies behind these perceived differences in political philosophy are disagreements over specific policy areas. Differences of priority and emphasis have arisen in several issue areas in recent years, and two of these are worth mentioning. The first is the development of opposition in 1971/2 to the public financing of the proposed 1976 Winter Olympic Games to be held near Denver. Opposition amongst Democratic activists was substantial. A private survey conducted at the 1972 Democratic state convention showed that nearly three-quarters of the Denver delegation (and over two-thirds of the whole convention) were opposed to the Denver Olympics because of their

TABLE 6.5: *DDPECM: Own Political Philosophy*

It is sometimes said that a person's political viewpoint or philosophy can be described as either right wing, conservative, moderate, liberal, or left wing. In terms of these descriptions, how would you describe your own viewpoint? (N=67)

	Percentage of respondents within each category
Left wing or Liberal-to-Left wing	3
Liberal	66
Moderate-to-Liberal	6
Moderate	24
Conservative	1
Right wing	0
TOTAL	100

TABLE 6.6: *DDPECM: Perceived Political Philosophy of Other Democratic Activists*

It is sometimes said that a person's political viewpoint or philosophy can be described as either right wing, conservative, moderate, liberal, or left wing. In terms of these descriptions, how would you describe the viewpoint of the majority of Democratic activists in Denver? (N=66)

	Percentage of respondents within each category
Left wing or Liberal-to-Left wing	4
Liberal	88
Moderate-to-Liberal	4
Moderate	4
Conservative	0
Right wing	0
TOTAL	100

alleged environmental effects.[23] The present Executive Committee of the Denver party was even more opposed to the Olympics at that time (Table 6.8). But with the exception of a tiny minority, the Democratic legislators were much less opposed to the Games. Certainly the roll-call votes on state financing of the Games in 1972 does show the Democrats voting as a group against financial support. But amongst legislators opposition to, and also support for, the Olympics was muted. Laura Katz Olson has argued that:

TABLE 6.7: *DDPECM: Perceived Political Philosophy of Denver Democrats in the General Assembly*

It is sometimes said that a person's political viewpoint or philosophy can be described as either right wing, conservative, moderate, liberal, or left wing. In terms of these descriptions, how would you describe the viewpoint of the majority of the Denver Democratic members of the State General Assembly? (N=67)

	Percentage of respondents within each category
Left wing or Liberal-to-Left wing	0
Liberal	38
Moderate-to-Liberal	18
Moderate	40
Conservative	4
Right wing	0
TOTAL	100

TABLE 6.8: *DDPECM: Attitude towards the 1976 Denver Olympics*

Will you say whether you strongly agree, mildly agree, are undecided, mildly disagree, or strongly disagree with this statement:

'At the time in 1972, I was opposed to the proposals to hold the 1976 Winter Olympics in Colorado.' (N=66)

	Percentage of respondents in each category
Strongly agree	73
Mildly agree	17
Undecided	0
Mildly disagree	4
Strongly disagree	6
TOTAL	100

... the low visibility of legislative combat was perpetuated by the parties and legislators themselves. Although House Republicans voted strongly in favor of the Games, and Democrats voted in opposition to them, most legislators were unwilling to take a position publicly. Even when CCF attempted to poll representatives in 1972 so as to provide the electorate with the information, most of the Representatives refused to be interviewed. In addition this researcher discovered substantial differences between public statements and actual voting behavior.[24]

Moreover, 55 per cent of the present Executive Committee believed that the Democrats in the General Assembly should have taken a more definite stand on the issue (Table 6.9). There is thus considerable evidence of disagreement between activists and legislators over one of the most controversial single issues in recent Colorado politics.

A second issue on which there has been a disparity between the priorities of the legislators and those of the activists is tax reform. This has been an item on every set of resolutions of the Democratic assemblies since 1968, and in response to assembly resolutions even the 1974 state platform called for a more equitable distribution of personal and corporate income taxes. However, in 1972 the legislators reacted very differently from the activists to a tax reform which Common Cause had campaigned to place on the ballot as an initiated referendum. Between its formation in 1971 and about 1973, the

TABLE 6.9: *DDPECM: Attitude towards Democratic Party Opposition in the General Assembly to the Denver Olympics*

Will you say whether you strongly agree, mildly agree, are undecided, mildly disagree, or strongly disagree with this statement:

'In 1971–2 the Democratic members of the General Assembly should have taken a more definite stand than they did on the issue of the 1976 Olympics'. (N=66)

	Percentage of respondents in each category
Strongly agree	32
Mildly agree	23
Undecided	24
Mildly disagree	15
Strongly disagree	6
TOTAL	100

Common Cause Colorado Project was in effect the forum through which the new activists in the Democratic party attempted to directly influence Colorado government and administration. It was a public interest group, its idea of the public interest being that of the liberal wing of the Democratic party. Hence it became concerned with issues such as tax reform, and not merely with more non-partisan machinery of government problems. Its proposal was to replace the regressive local property tax as a means of funding education in the state with increased corporate income tax rates and the introduction of a severance tax on mineral extraction. (The severance tax would have taxed companies that extracted minerals in the state directly in relation to the quantity of minerals removed.) Not surprisingly, given the source of this initiative, only 10 per cent of the present Executive Committee in Denver denied having supported it (Table 6.10). A majority of them also saw this as being a partisan issue for the Democrats rather than a non-partisan one (Table 6.11). On the other hand, amongst the

TABLE 6.10: *DDPECM: Attitude towards 1972 Common Cause Property Tax Initiative*

Will you say whether you strongly agree, mildly agree, are undecided, mildly disagree, or strongly disagree with this statement:

'At the time in 1972, I supported the Common Cause referendum to replace local property taxes with a tax on mineral extraction as the means of financing education in Colorado.' (N=65)

	Percentage of respondents in each category
Strongly agree	35
Mildly agree	40
Undecided	15
Mildly disagree	8
Strongly disagree	2
TOTAL	100

TABLE 6.11: *DDPECM: Attitude towards Partisan Involvement in the Mineral Tax Issue*

Will you say whether you strongly agree, mildly agree, are undecided, mildly disagree, or strongly disagree with this statement:

'The issue of the mineral tax is the sort of issue which should be mainly promoted by the Democratic Party, rather than a nonpartisan organisation like Common Cause.' (N=66)

	Percentage of respondents in each category
Strongly agree	24
Mildly agree	28
Undecided	15
Mildly disagree	24
Strongly disagree	9
TOTAL	100

Democrats from Denver in the General Assembly between 1973 and 1976, few claimed to have supported this proposal and even fewer did so actively. That their opposition was not merely to the principle of the electorate being allowed to decide on tax measures was demonstrated by the exclusion of the abolition of the property tax from their legislative proposals after they won control of the Governorship and the lower house in 1974.

In the two years after this, the General Assembly did not pass any major reform of either the property or the income tax laws. This failure was not primarily due either to the Republicans' control of the Senate or the presence of rural Democrats in the Democratic party coalition, although both were contributory factors. For many of the Democrats from Denver and other urban areas were simply uncommitted to the sort of tax reform favoured by the activists. In 1975, not unexpectedly, the Republicans in the Senate defeated a Democratic tax package. In itself the package was not a radical one, certainly not an obvious response to resolution 42 of the 1974 Denver assembly which demanded that 'the tax system should undergo substantial revision toward more progressive forms of taxation'. In 1976 two of the 1975 bills' components were reintroduced – an increase in corporate income tax (from 5 to 6 per cent), amounting to 0.3 per cent of Colorado's total taxes, and a mineral severance tax designed to raise $15 million, or about 0.6 per cent of total taxes paid in Colorado in 1971. The efforts of the legislators were concentrated on the latter.

The origins of the demand for a severance tax lie in the increased value of minerals extracted in Colorado in the early 1970s. A severance tax was popular with both environmentalists and liberal Democrats, and the issue first came up for public discussion in the 1972 initiated referendum. As a combination of both environmentalist and liberal, the Democratic Gubernatorial candidate in 1974, Richard Lamm, gave prominence to his support for a mineral severance tax in his successful election campaign. After the failure of the tax proposal to get through the Senate in 1975, the measure was reintroduced in the 1976 session. With the possibility of legislative failure again, and with no tax reform to show to the party activists for his two years in office, Lamm announced in the middle of March the possibility of starting a party-led 'initiative' (i.e. a referendum brought about by the circulation of petitions in the state) effort to legislate a severance tax at the November election.[25] Only the State Treasurer, a former 'new-wave' activist, and the state party chairman were extensively consulted before the announcement. It was apparent that they were worried about the activist backlash to the party's record on tax reform in the previous 18 months.

Like the 1972 Initiative, the proposal was a complex one, involving the substitution of a mineral tax and higher corporate taxes for the tax on food sales. The threat of an Initiative had one desired effect – it increased the willingness of the Senate Republicans to accept a mineral severance tax.[26] But it also exposed the fact that the Democrats in the General Assembly were uncommitted to 'substantial revision' of the tax system and to anything other than the establishment of a severance tax at a very low rate. Indeed, by the end of April a compromise between the parties in the legislature was approaching. With this kind of tax 'reform' in prospect Lamm faced a dilemma. He wanted the tax legislated but knew it was insufficient for the activists and thus, claiming Republican obstinance in compromising with the Democrats, Lamm commenced the initiative campaign.[27] It was a move to rally the Democratic troops against the opposition and avoid their probable revolt later against their own office holders. In part it succeeded – many activists did circulate petitions, and it probably did attract attention away from the party's failures in the legislature on tax reform. But in several respects the tactic failed. Many Denver legislators had no great love for the particular initiative proposal and resented Lamm's lack of consultation with them.[28] Nor were all the activists particularly enthusiastic about the proposal: Craig Barnes, for example, explained his refusal to get involved in the initiative campaign in the following way:

> I would get involved in a major income tax reform effort, to make it more progressive, or another shot at the property tax, but food tax just doesn't cut deep enough.[29]

To some degree the initiative campaign did help to disguise differences in priority between the legislators and the activists, even though many like Barnes did not become involved in it. But party unity in the future was not helped by the loss of the Initiative at the election by a margin of more than 2:1.

Having established that there has been conflict over policy priorities between activists and legislators, it is necessary to explain why this has not manifested itself in conflict over the renomination of legislators in recent years, with the notable exception of 1970. Five main factors seem to have been responsible for this, and we examine them in turn.

(i) *Single-member districts*

Between 1966 and 1968 Denver changed from having one multi-member district for the lower house to having single-member districts. With a multi-member district all party activists could be involved in attempting to remove an unpopular incumbent. For example, in 1962, a 'maverick' legislator was opposed by a majority of district captains, and she received a bottom-line designation at the assembly. Although she was well-known in the city, she was defeated in the subsequent primary.[30] However, with single-member districts some incumbents have few regular, issue-oriented activists in the districts with whom to contend. Certainly two of the present legislators who seem to have least in common with the majority of Denver activists come from districts with the lowest levels of activist participation. Single member districts have the additional effect of dissipating activist effort between a large number of campaigns. Combined with the effects of federalism and the separation of powers, this reduces the value of the activists' most important resource – manpower; with many offices to be competed for activist cohesion is reduced.

(ii) *Officer loyalty to incumbents*

A second factor in limiting the utilisation of the primary has been that the party officers themselves have tried to prevent challenges to incumbents. They have also, as in the Schroeder Congressional race, attempted to stop challenges to 'senior' public office-holders seeking election to another office. The problem of officer loyalty to incumbents is perhaps less than, for example, in a British Parliamentary constituency for two main reasons. First, because challenges do occur from time to time, the party Chairman cannot afford to be as completely protective of the incumbents as his British counterpart tends to be. Second, both the county and state chairmen have several different levels of public office-holder with whom they have to maintain a working relationship, and this precludes a high degree of loyalty to any one of them. But there will be occasions on which the office holders will want to 'cash in their credit' with the chairman and seek his intervention against the dissidents. One of the more extreme examples of this occurred in 1970:

> In 1969 [Waldo Benavidez] had been hired by the Democratic State Central Committee to boost Chicano participation in the party statewide. By May 1970 he had been fired by then state chairman Dan Lynch. Officially the story was that Lynch had an agreement with Waldo when he was hired that neither Benavidez would run for

office while Waldo was on the state party payroll. When Betty entered [a] legislative race, Lynch says, he sacked Waldo. Unofficially the reason seemed to be that Waldo was promoting Chicano candidates to run in primaries that year against Democratic incumbents in several districts. The incumbents complained behind the scenes that their own party should not be footing the bill to have them knocked off.[31]

(iii)　*The absence of party control over campaign finance*

Today the party organisation *per se* does not have a monopoly control over the supply of campaign finance either for the primary or the general election. However, in the 1960s Rudolph Gomez reported that there was a relatively high degree of such control in Denver for General Assembly contests.[32] This was possible because it was not worthwhile for candidates to raise much money themselves when running on a long ticket in a multi-member district. The primary would be won largely on the strength of ballot position, and the general election won on the party ticket and not by individual effort.[33] With single-member districts all candidates found it advantageous to raise funds for their own campaigns, and with no restrictions on private fund-raising, the candidates could become semi-autonomous from the party. Primary campaigns certainly have to be financed independently of the party organisation, and in some districts the Democratic candidate has been able to finance the general election campaign almost entirely through personal contacts.[34] But even when the candidate is not able to do this, fund-raising for General Assembly elections becomes fund-raising for a particular candidate rather than for the party, which then spends it on behalf of the candidate. And as was noted in chapter 5, the more that a party's activities are centred on fund-raising, the less able its activists are to engage in 'politics'.[35]

Undoubtedly if the party monopolised the supply of campaign funds, the legislators would be much more closely bound to the party and hence to the party activists. When legislators raise their own funds they are able to run for election with a coterie of personal support rather than as the party's candidates to whom they owe 'benefits'. But the problem of the party's resources in raising funds is not the only factor affecting this link between candidate and party. For the major offices in the state, a new form of fund raising has been utilised recently that with little effort can raise as much as exhaustive projects by the party. Colorado has been one of the first states in America in which rock singers and film stars have performed for the benefit of particular candidates. When candidates have access to such outside funds it is not surprising that their ties to the party decrease, however intensive the party effort is.

(iv) *The availability of the 'exit' option – the Initiative process*

Colorado has had a provision for initiated legislation since 1910 when the state adopted direct democracy as advocated by Progressive Republicanism. In 1942 the state law was changed so as to require would-be initiators to advertise their proposals in every county in the state. The resulting expense entailed for would-be initiators meant that the number of such issues on the ballot declined. Given the uncertainty of getting the signatures of 8 per cent of the electorate and of the legislation being passed, many attempts were discouraged. In late 1971, however, Common Cause, which had spent its first year gaining publicity from its defence of consumer interests against the utility companies, was looking for an outlet for its resources. Craig Barnes and other dissident liberal Democrats were drawn to the idea of taking some issues directly to the electorate rather than working through the Democratic party. By early 1972 there were plans to start four initiative campaigns, but the cost of advertising was thought to be prohibitive. In consequence, Common Cause challenged the constitutionality of the advertising requirement in the state courts, and in winning its case, cleared the way for a whole series of initiatives in the following three elections. In 1972 alone Common Cause had four initiatives covering very different policy areas – tax reform; the 'sunshine' (open-government) law; a consumer advocate; and a reform of car insurance ('no fault') – while the anti-Olympic initiative was arguably the most contentious aspect of the elections in Colorado that year.

The effect of the Initiative on party can be quite easily stated: it dissipates the strength of the activists. They tend to 'exit' to direct appeals to the electorate rather than stay to voice opposition within the party. Even when the Initiative is a party inspired measure, as was the food tax-mineral tax proposal in 1976, the effect is to divert the efforts of activists away from the control of office holders. Along with multi-member districts, federalism and the separation of powers, it reduces the potential for activist influence in the party. There is a further cost to party democracy entailed by the availability of the Initiative: initiative campaigns, unlike party ones, are unlikely to transform the activism of the single-issue participant into more general party activity. When citizens feel strongly enough about any one issue to contribute to a party effort in support of a candidate, their political involvement is more likely to be made permanent than it is by a specially created campaign group.

The irony of the Initiative phenomenon of the 1970s is that, with few exceptions, the dissident Democrats have been unable to effect important policy changes. In 1976 all the statewide Initiatives failed, as the people (to use John Mackintosh's dictum) 'did as they were told' – in these cases as they were told by the most highly financed campaigns. But this was to be expected on issues that did not embrace basic problems or emotions of the electors as, for example, busing did.[36] In Colorado many of the issues have been too complex to be understood immediately by the electors who were thus receptive to campaigns that brought information (or more accurately what was earlier termed disinformation) to their attention. The special interest groups quite naturally were prepared to expend funds when they saw their own interests threatened. As special interests they had greater access to funds than those trying to promote their own conceptions of the general interests of the society. Their ability to turn round support in a campaign, when the initiative proposers had a low-financed campaign, was sometimes spectacular. A private poll taken in March 1976 revealed that as many as 80 per cent of the electorate might vote for the repeal of the food tax and its substitution in part by a mineral severance tax. In the November election less than 39 per cent of the electorate voted for this initiative. To a large extent, what had given the liberal Democrats faith in the initiative process, a process which is known to favour special interests and tax-cutting efforts, was the success of the 1972 Olympics Initiative. Yet, as is shown in chapter 8, the success of this particular underfinanced activist campaign was due to circumstances that were unusual and highly favourable to the initiators.

(v) *The lack of criteria for evaluating legislators' performance in office*

In Colorado, as throughout the U.S., it is difficult for party activists to assess whether individual legislators have effectively pursued policies of which they approve. Superficially there seem to be two reasons for this, although it will be seen that they are related to one another.

On the one hand, in the House the Democrats only have party caucus meeting on budgetary matters and similar essential business. Indeed, all the Democratic legislators interviewed were opposed to the system used by the Republicans (particularly in the Senate a decade ago) whereby all members of the party were bound to vote for the caucus position in the legislature. In the Senate, as the minority party for the last ten years, the Democrats have scarcely caucused at all. Because on many issues that divide the parties there is no formal party line, the overseeing job of the activists becomes difficult in two respects. They cannot readily determine what sorts of policies Democrats in the legislature are in fact supporting; again, except in the most extreme cases, they cannot tell whether an individual legislator is supporting the majority of his colleagues or not.

On the other hand, a legislator's support of the party platform is not an adequate measure of his commitment to the sorts of views on public policies that most activists have. The state party platform is not even written by the activists, but by the candidates for public office after the primaries have been held. All that the activists can do is to adopt a set of resolutions at the state assembly which party rules dictate 'shall be submitted to the State Platform Committee by the State Chairman as the recommendations of the State Assembly for incorporation into the platform'.[37] And after it is written (a requirement under state law), the platform is usually not heard of again. It is rarely mentioned by candidates in the general election campaign, who state their own priorities in their campaign literature, and it is never referred to as the basis for establishing legislative priorities.

Before turning to examine the problem of legislative caucuses and party platforms in more detail, it is worth mentioning that the party activists do see opposition by a legislator to the caucus or the platform as a justification for opposing his renomination. 90 per cent of the Executive Committee members believed that a legislator who consistently opposed the majority view in a legislative caucus should be opposed in a bid for renomination (Table 6.12). Since there are so few caucus positions, 'maverick' behaviour in the state legislature has to be quite extraordinary before it becomes 'consistent opposition'. Yet most of the Committee members do not seem to want such a high degree of maverick conduct by Democrat legislators. For nearly two-thirds of the Committee believed that all candidates should be under an obligation to support the party platform, whilst only one-third would permit an incumbent who had failed to support the party platform an unopposed renomination (Tables 6.13 and 6.14). In other words, the activists seem to want to impose some discipline on public office holders, but one of the problems for them is the lack of clarity as to what a breach of discipline is.

Party caucuses in the legislature have traditionally never been strong in the western states of America. Colorado has been, and still is, no

TABLE 6.12: *DDPECM: Attitude towards Maverick Behaviour in the Legislature*

Will you say whether you strongly agree, mildly agree, are undecided, mildly disagree, or strongly disagree with this statement:

'If a Democratic legislator consistently opposes the majority view of the Democratic party caucus in Congress or the General Assembly, he should be opposed if he seeks the renomination of the Democratic party'. (N=67)

	Percentage of respondents in each category
Strongly agree	60
Mildly agree	30
Undecided	4
Mildly disagree	4
Strongly disagree	2
TOTAL	100

TABLE 6.13: *DDPECM: Attitude towards Democratic Candidates' Obligations to Support State Party Platform*

Will you say whether you strongly agree, mildly agree, are undecided, mildly disagree, or strongly disagree with this statement:

'All Democratic candidates should be under an obligation to support the main provisions of the state party's platform'. (N=67)

	Percentage of respondents in each category
Strongly agree	33
Mildly agree	31
Undecided	5
Mildly disagree	24
Strongly disagree	7
TOTAL	100

exception, although arguably both houses are organised on more partisan lines than in many of these states. Particularly in the Senate, the Republicans have been able to act cohesively through the taking of caucus positions. They have achieved this without being able to control their members' renomination. What they did have was a belief in party as policy maker. Undoubtedly many House Democrats, and some Senators, also had such a view of party, but they would not consent to

TABLE 6.14: *DDPECM: Attitude towards Office Holders' Failure to Support Party Platform*

Will you say whether you strongly agree, mildly agree, are undecided, mildly disagree, or strongly disagree with this statement:

> 'If a Democrat holding public office does not subsequently support the main provisions of the state party's election platform, he should be opposed if he seeks the renomination of the Democratic party.' (N=67)

	Percentage of respondents in each category
Strongly agree	22
Mildly agree	30
Undecided	15
Mildly disagree	19
Strongly disagree	14
TOTAL	100

the use of sanctions against mavericks in order to achieve this. For them, procedural democracy meant government by consent, even within the party. In consequence, the party leaders did not use the sorts of sanctions they can employ – poor committee assignments, loss of priority for the maverick's own bills and many others. Of course the Colorado Speaker has nowhere near the extensive patronage available to a party leader in a parliamentary system, but he has sufficient to discourage dissidents. To do so he needs the support of a majority of the legislative party.[38] Yet the spirit of 'openness' that had made for an internally democratic party organisation, when applied to the legislature, made impossible a cohesive party efficiently pursuing a complex of policy objectives. The result was that, despite the fact that the parties in Colorado have become more ideologically distinct in the last decade, there is no coherent party programme in the legislature on the Democratic side. And without such a programme, evaluation of the legislators' performance becomes difficult for the activists. This point clearly bears on the question posed by Schlesinger discussed in the last chapter: 'Without a membership to make claims and a clearly identified structure to enforce them, what can keep the office holder in line?'[39]

What keeps a legislator in line is party discipline in the legislature. And what makes for the acceptance of discipline is not merely a shared political outlook, but the acceptance by the legislators at their election of an agreed policy programme. For legislators may only be expected to bind themselves to one another, if they face rejection by the party for not carrying out the programme when they have a majority in the legislature. And it is this absence of a party programme, and not a party membership with a fixed ideology, that is crucial in explaining why legislative discipline is low in Colorado, and in America generally. Without a commonly agreed programme there is no need for legislators to submit themselves to party discipline. It is now necessary to return to the distinction, introduced in chapter 5, between a membership style of nomination process and a membership style of party organisation, and to consider the status of party platforms in Colorado.

The enforcement of a policy programme by the majority party in a legislature can only be expected when the legislators have an incentive to accept such enforcement. They will not subject themselves to party discipline unless they have to. To some extent the need simply to organise the chamber will generate such an incentive, and provide a system of leadership in which those who do not obey will have sanctions imposed on them such that they will be less able to satisfy the demands from within their electorates. But party activists have no guarantee that a sufficient number of their legislators will be prepared to submit to discipline to effect this. The Colorado Democrats have not done so. Neither can the activists be sure that the leaders will use sanctions to pursue policies of which the activists approve. It is through the adoption of a party policy programme that the latter can ensure the creation of a disciplined party in the legislature, and a party that is pursuing the policy objectives of which they approve. For if the legislative party deviates from the previously stated objectives, they can in turn invoke sanctions against the legislators, including the denial of renomination. A party programme provides a standard against which the performance of office holders can be evaluated. But a specific programme will not be voluntarily constructed by legislators, even if they are benefit seekers and not office seekers. For divergence of opinion is common (perhaps especially common) amongst those with a similar political outlook. This tends to make for an unwillingness to be formally committed to support the majority party line in the legislature. (Of course, office seekers will want to be free of such restrictions.) A party programme then has to be forced on to the legislators by the activists – it is they who must insist on a programme.

Now the ability of the activists to force a programme on the public office holders requires a 'membership' style of party, but not of the kind Schlesinger envisages. With the membership style of nomination, at meetings of those who have paid to join the party, the activists can supposedly control the benefits they receive from the office holders. Yet the ideological nature of the party first shrinks the number of potential participants, then makes the party organisation merely a provider of electoral services, and finally frees the office holder from the constraints of the activists' attitudes to policy. Equally a completely open nomination process, in destroying party as an intermediary, frees the office holder from the need to support a party programme. On the other hand, when the party can continue to determine nominations, but is not subject to the withering away experienced by parties of the voluntary association type, the activists are in a position to make demands for benefits from the office holders. For it is the availability of the primary mechanism, and hence open competition in the party for nominations, that prevents the atrophy characteristic of the membership party, and makes it possible for activists to obtain benefits from office holders. But if the membership style of nomination is not appropriate to the establishment of a party programme by the activists, a membership style of organisation is necessary. That is, for all levels of office, the party must have a formal structure of committees of activists to discuss, evaluate and set policy priorities. It must be formal in the sense that it has pre-arranged deadlines for the setting of agendas, the holding of investigations and debates and for the compilation of a programme. It must be a structure in that there is coordination between the different levels of party organisation in the setting of local and national programmes. In other words, a party programme cannot be compiled by *ad hoc* meetings of activists who discuss issues. Priorities acceptable to most activists, and clearly defined so as to be used as the basis for judging office holders' performance, do not come out of informal discussions.

Now the establishment of such a policy-forming structure within a party requires two conditions to be met as far as the activists' participation in the party is concerned. The one is that the activists must be issue-oriented (seeking purposive benefits), and this has been the case with the Denver activists. The other is that, in seeking to influence public policy, the activists must have an incentive to direct their efforts almost entirely through the party organisation. To the extent that there are other forums available, they will 'exit' rather than employ 'voice' within the party, thus diminishing their chances of forcing a programme on the party. In fact, in Denver there have been three main ways in which this monopolisation of political activity by the party has been broken, thus inhibiting the development of a party programme. In the first place, the parties do not extend down to a level of government at which policy-making activists could be seen to have some direct effect. There is no form of neighbourhood government in the city, and at the city level the offices are supposedly non-partisan. In fact, the parties are extensively involved in the nomination of candidates for mayoralty and city council, and in assistance to the campaigns of endorsed partisans, but their function does not extend beyond that of providing electoral services. Secondly, the increased independence of candidates, particularly with regard to the financing of their campaigns, at all levels of office has resulted in candidate-centred participation in the party, rather than party-centred activity. This trend towards candidate autonomy has been greatest in U.S. Senate contests. It results in the discontinuity of political activism, and decreases the potential for making candidates obliged to support a party programme. Finally, the availability of the initiative process for placing specific issues directly before the electorate has led to the focusing of public attention on some of these issues, but also to a diminution of effort within the party. Indeed, it was through the Initiative that much of the effort of Democrat activists was directed, especially in 1972.

It is not surprising, then, to discover that the upsurge of activist politics in Colorado has not resulted in a programmatic party. And without a programme the party activists have not had the means with which to evaluate the performance of legislators and, if necessary, challenge their renomination. However, there is quite clearly a gap between the kind of party the activist Democrats would like, and the actual relationship between public office holders and activists. The party platform provides a good illustration of this point. It has already been seen that in Denver a majority of the Executive Committee see the platform as something which office holders have an obligation to support, and support for which the activists have a right to enforce (Tables 6.13 and 6.14). And the Democratic platform in Colorado is not the short, platitudinous document that its instantaneous confinement to oblivion might suggest. Both the Denver County and Colorado State platforms are long documents containing specific proposals – in 1974 there were 74 specific proposals in the state party platform. Furthermore, the resolutions at the state assembly that formed one of the bases of the platform were the subject of extensive debate at that assembly.[40] As well as being discussed by the resolutions committee of the assembly, most of the subjects were previously debated at the county assemblies. It might be expected, therefore, that only one in six of the Executive Committee would claim that he was unfamiliar with the state platform (Table 6.15). Nevertheless, the attention it attracts in its compilation is not matched by the attention it receives after its publication, or rather its duplication on a machine in state party headquarters. That the platform is rarely mentioned in the general election campaign, or afterwards is witnessed by the fact that even the Executive Committee members could remember very few of the 74 specific proposals on the 1974 platform. Over one half of the Committee could recall none of the proposals and less than one third could remember more than three of them (Table 6.16).

Given that the party platform is clearly not a party policy pro-gramme, there has been some concern amongst the leaders of the party organisation to provide some channel of 'input' from activists to Democratic public officials. The result has been the 'issues confer-ence', the idea of which was that precinct workers and public officials would sit down together to establish policy priorities. The state party

TABLE 6.15: *DDPECM: Familiarity with the 1974 Democratic State Platform*

How familiar were you with the platform of the state Democratic party in 1974? (N=67)

	Percentage of respondents in each category
Very familiar	15
Partly familiar	48
Not sure	21
Unfamiliar	16
TOTAL	100

TABLE 6.16: *DDPECM: Recollection of Specific Proposals of the 1974 Democratic State Platform*

Without consulting anyone else, or any documents, can you remember any of the specific proposals of the state Democratic party in 1974? (N=67)

	Percentage of respondents in each category
None	52
One or two	17
Three	18
Four or more	13
TOTAL	100

'Recollections' of items not on the 1974 State platform were excluded in the compilation of this table.

held one in the spring of 1974 and another one two years later, while the Denver party held its own conference at the end of 1975. At the time of the Denver conference coordinator, Jim Raughton, said that its purpose was 'to have elected officials at the national, state and local levels listen to the ideas and suggested priorities of Denver Democratic precinct committee persons and block workers'.[41] This ideal, of activists and public officials just sitting down and working out priorities, was also reflected in the state party Chairman's assertion, when announcing the first conference, that 'the formulation of policy is too big a 'burden' to be borne alone by elected officials'.[42] Many activists themselves believe that the issue conferences do help the party to set clear priorities for the state, and fewer than one third of the Executive Committee members believe they do not do so (Table 6.17). Moreover, as many activists see the conferences as having some effect on the issue positions of public officials as those who think they do not (Table 6.18).

TABLE 6.17: *DDPECM: Attitude towards the Role of Issue Conferences in Setting Priorities for Colorado*

Will you say whether you strongly agree, mildly agree, are undecided, mildly disagree, or strongly disagree with this statement:

'The issue conferences held by the state Democratic party in the last few years have helped the party to establish a clear set of priorities for Colorado.' (N=65)

	Percentage of respondents in each category
Strongly agree	17
Mildly agree	35
Undecided	17
Mildly disagree	19
Strongly disagree	12
TOTAL	100

In practice the conferences have been far from serious arenas for formulating policy priorities. As an article in the *Colorado Democrat* stated after the 1976 conference, 'For many delegates, the issues developed at the conference were less important than the opportunity to hear speeches by the party's leading lights.'[43] The conferences have seldom come up with any new ideas, and the absence of formal resolutions means there is very little upon which the participants can be seen as having agreed. But then, as one participant observed, their purpose was issue *discussion* and it was 'only the beginning of a long process by which we would synthesise many ideas and eventually form the basis for party policy.'[44] The real weakness of the conferences is that the office holders, whose policies the conferences are supposed to help to form, are generally much less enthusiastic about them than the activists. The most sympathetic, and usually younger, Denver legislators believed that they became aware of some problems at them – particularly those of the rural areas. But many legislators felt that the conferences were a waste of time, allowing those who had no worthwhile opinions to air their views. Some did not bother to attend them, and one legislator believed that their main purpose was to enable public office holders to inform the activists of what the issues were. The majority of legislators believed that they were merely listening to the same sorts of views that they heard at every party occasion.

TABLE 6.18: *DDPECM: Perception of the Effect of Issue Conferences on Democratic Public Office Holders*

Will you say whether you strongly agree, mildly agree, are undecided, mildly disagree, or strongly disagree with this statement:

'The Democratic party's issue conferences are unlikely to have any effect on the positions on issues taken by Democrats who hold public office.' (N=65)

	Percentage of respondents in each category
Strongly agree	11
Mildly agree	31
Undecided	15
Mildly disagree	34
Strongly disagree	9
TOTAL	100

Because they bind office holders in no ways whatsoever, issue conferences in their present form are not even the antecedent of an internally democratic party in which the activists set the policy objectives for a programme. At some point their novelty will probably wear off, and they will fall into either disuse or disrepute. Sam Brown, formerly one of the leading 'new wave' activists and in 1976 the State Treasurer, was under no illusions that issue conferences were not a substitute for a system of accountability of office holders to activists:

It may be inherent [that legislators do not take issue conferences very seriously] unless you do what we've talked about on the national level with the Presidency. That is, have an interregnum accountability conference, where you bring people back and say 'This is what you said you'd do when you ran for office, and this is what you've done, and in these following seven places it doesn't match.' But I don't see any concentrated effort to do it, but in order to get it done somebody's got to believe in it enough to go out and proselytise for it . . . and I don't see anybody who feels that strongly about it. God knows, I'm not going to go out and organise people to whom I have to go back and say, 'Look I screwed up – I told you the first time that I would do that, and it turns out I couldn't do it.'[45]

Supporters of the principle of party accountability, such as Brown, have not in recent years attempted to change this basic aspect of the relationship between office holders and activists. Without accountability and in particular through a party programme, it becomes virtually impossible for activists to have criteria with which to evaluate the performance of office holders, and if necessary oppose their renomination. In Brown's own case, becoming an office holder meant that he no longer advanced the cause of accountability. Obviously not all the regular activists who came into the party after 1968 became public officials, and Brown's own career provides an indication of the main reason for this halting of party democratisation short of party accountability. For Brown made his name as one of the three organisers of the referendum to stop the Denver Olympics in 1972. For those concerned with changing public policy, the Initiative has often seemed an attractive direct route for doing so, that takes comparatively little time to produce results. In contrast with this, the continued reform of the Democratic party seems a slow and difficult route. As mentioned earlier the intensity of party conflict in 1970 was unusual for the Democrats – it was not typical of the level of intra-party conflict, especially over nominations, of the following three election years. It was not typical because after it much of the effort of the dissident Democrats was either channelled towards mobilising the electorate directly or was dispersed among a large number of campaigns. Thus whilst the formal procedures of the party after 1970 were made even more open than previously and the party continued to attract a large number of activists, it did not develop a membership style of organisation through which activists could directly affect public policies. Some pressures for such arrangements were present, and the result was an embryonic 'membership' device, the issues conference.

To conclude: whilst the Colorado pre-primary system of nomination is appropriate for the development of an internally democratic party, the Colorado Democrats have succeeded in only partially democratising their party. What they did not achieve was a mechanism by which they could more easily control their public office holders; their failure to develop a party programme meant that a disciplined party promoting shared goals became unattainable. One product of this, as is seen in the next two chapters, is that candidates for public office have tended to obscure their stance on issues and, in particular, an emerging social cleavage in the state has not been made comprehensible by the party to the electorate. The limitations of the electoral mechanism have thus not been overcome by the party's partial democratisation; perhaps more important, this democratisation has occurred when office seekers have been able to become more independent of party activists. Partial democratisation would appear to have been accompanied by party decomposition.

7 Party: Issue Clarity and Ambiguity

The point has now been reached at which it is necessary to link together some of the main themes of the last four chapters. In Chapter 3 it was argued that, of itself, the electoral mechanism is unlikely to provide for the political education of the electorate. It was contended that it is only through the interpretations of political leaders that the majority of citizens can develop a coherent understanding of the economic and social divisions in the society. But the electoral mechanism does not furnish an incentive for the parties either to identify new lines of cleavage or to present to the electorate comprehensive and comprehensible alternative policies for resolving these divisions. It was suggested that with internally democratic parties an incentive for party leaders to compete with the other party 'team' in primary, rather than secondary, ways would be introduced.

In Chapter 5 the possible structure of an internally democratic party was examined. It was argued there that a long-standing assumption in political science – that membership parties of the European type were the most appropriate form of organisation for maximising the control of party activists over leaders should be rejected. A distinction was drawn between the membership style of organisation and the membership style of nomination. Whilst the former is necessary for party democracy, the latter (as in Britain) can lead to the atrophy of party at levels below that of the national legislative party. What is appropriate for the maximisation of activist control is a style of nomination which provides for party dissidents to take their case against established leaders to the party's electorate in a primary election. But it was further argued that only when there were restrictions on the number of candidates who could get on to the party's primary ballot was there a means of preventing another kind of party atrophy.

In Chapter 6 the experience of a party that had become highly participatory in recent years was analysed, one which has a style of nomination process – a pre-primary assembly system – which matches the criteria for maximising party democracy. However, it was seen that the Denver Democratic party was not fully democratised. The dissidents who came to take over the party did remove some public office holders in the early 1970s, but in their place they did not put leaders who reflected their own views and concerns. They lacked the ability to do anything other than remove those with very different views from their own, partly because their efforts became dispersed and partly because there was no standard by which they could evaluate the performance of office holders. In particular, they had not evolved a party programme which would serve to tie legislators to one another in the state's General Assembly, and the enactment of which would provide the clearest indication of leadership responsiveness to the viewpoint of the activists. We further contended that the failure of the Denver activists to transform platforms and issue conferences into programmes is connected with the availability of the initiative process.

It can now be seen why the conduct of democratic politics requires that the parties, as teams, place before the voters in an election packages of policies in which the priorities are clearly stated. From the standpoint of the citizen, the two parties are the major sources from which he can acquire a coherent view of the political universe. In part this entails the creation of images of the polity – images, that is, as opposed to rational arguments and coherent policy proposals. But the politics of electoral competition in which specific types of policies, and sets of policy alternatives, are not presented to the voters in an unambiguous and comprehensible way does not serve to educate the electorate. That is, 'dreams' of the good society that do not lay down the exact priorities that have to be followed in realising such dreams tell the voters very little about how a candidate sees the political universe. The problem is not that the voter does not know what 'goods' he is buying when he votes, but rather that he is not being provided with the intellectual equipment to decide later whether he prefers the new political world or not. The candidate has then not made the voters more autonomous in their electoral choices at future elections. A 'dream' of 'A New Frontier' or 'A Great Society' in which the priorities and costs are not clearly explained is likely to result in the political alienation of those who come to see others benefitting from policies whose goals the former were unaware of.

For the voters, then, electoral competition involving policies is a necessary part of the process by which political reality is defined for the electorate by political leaders. The purpose of it is not to provide a 'shopping list' for the voter who at the next election can then check a candidate's (or government's) performance against its promises. But for the activists, this *is* precisely the purpose of party competition. It is the activists who force the public office holders to be genuinely competitive in the electoral game. It is they who ensure, through their control of nominations, that new interests are taken account of, and old social cleavages clearly identified. But they can only make effective use of the nomination process when they insist that candidates commit themselves to a party programme. In doing so, they in turn provide the candidates with policy priorities with which to construct their picture of political reality for the electorate. In the absence of a programme of policies, clear policy alternatives and the identification of new lines of division in the society are less likely to be presented to the electorate by candidates. Thus when an examination is made of whether either *party* positions on issues, or an emerging new social division, has been clearly identified by the Democrats in Colorado, we see that the partial democratisation of the party has not resulted in the presentation of coherent alternatives to the electorate. We show that on the Vietnam war issue a discernible Democratic position did develop, but with regard to busing the policies of the Democratic candidates increasingly became unintelligible to the electorate. Again, in chapter 8, we show that in respect of the expansion of Colorado's population and economy, about which mass concern became increasingly evident in the 1970s, a distinctive Democratic approach to the alternatives available to the state government failed to emerge. It is argued that the partial democratisation achieved by the Colorado Democrats has been insufficient to promote the sort of competition between the two parties' candidates that provides for the political education of the citizenry.

The starting point of this discussion is the difference in attitude between professional and amateur activists towards the role of policy issues in campaigns. For the former, the activist who is seeking either material or solidary benefits, the discussion of issues by the candidate is at best a necessary cost that has to be borne in winning a particular election. At worst, it is seen as counterproductive to the main object of the campaign – ensuring that the candidate is elected. But for the amateur, the discussion of issues is an essential part of the campaign – whether he sees the taking of issue positions as the essential ingredient of a contractual relationship between voter and candidate or sees it as a means by which the candidates educate the voter. This difference between professionals and amateurs is best illustrated by comparing the attitudes towards issues Snowiss found in his study of inner-city Chicago with those of the Democratic Executive

Committee members in Denver. Of the Chicago activists Snowiss has written:

> The predominance of material incentives and the need to maintain the unity of a rather complex organisation have contributed to an ethos which tends to inhibit the use of issues for obtaining either personnel or public support. The organisation is able to maintain unity through intricate bargaining over the allocation of patronage. Issues, on the other hand, are deemed irrelevant at best, and dangerously divisive at worst. Under such conditions, skills at bargaining, negotiation, and compromise are fostered and rewarded.[1]

In contrast to this, the majority of Denver activists did not believe that the discussion of specific issues hurt the party in the winning of votes: about one quarter of them thought issues adversely affected a candidate's poll whilst over 60 per cent thought it did not (Table 7.1). Nor did these activists take the cynical, self-interested view that policies should only be discussed if that would win votes for the candidate – only one quarter of the respondents saw this as appropriate behaviour in the electoral market (Table 7.2). Virtually all of them saw the discussion of issues in contractual terms – the voters being entitled to know what policies the candidates would support if they were elected to office (Table 7.3). Furthermore the majority of the respondents believed that it was the duty of the party's candidates to educate the electorate even if their discussion of issues entailed a risk of losing the election – less than one quarter of the Committtee disagreed with this objective (Table 7.4). There is, then, considerable support amongst these amateur activists for the discussion of issues and policies in election campaigns, and it is now necessary to examine an example of an issue area in which the Democratic party came to clarify the alternatives for the electorate – the Vietnam war.

A. THE VIETNAM WAR 1966–1972

Perhaps more so than in any other state, the Democratic party in Colorado did serve as a channel through which alternative views about the war were discussed, and a clear understanding of what sorts of policies the party stood for was conveyed to the electorate. By 1970 a distinctly Democratic position on the war had developed such that office holders who did not support it were likely to be challenged, and activists who did not found themselves isolated from the party's mainstream. By the time of the primaries in September of that year even 20 year Congressional incumbent, Byron Rogers, who was not known as an opponent of the war, felt it necessary to explain that he would have voted for the Hatfield–McGovern amendment had he had an opportunity to do so.[2] At the state convention in June 1972 the widespread support for this common line was demonstrated in the responses to a survey conducted by the Vietnam Veterans Against the

TABLE 7.1: *DDPECM: Beliefs about the Electoral Effects of the Discussion of Specific Issues*

Will you say whether you strongly agree, mildly agree, are undecided, mildly disagree, or strongly disagree with this statement:

'Normally if a candidate discusses specific policies he will lose more votes than he wins.' (N=66)

	Percentage of respondents in each category
Strongly agree	5
Mildly agree	21
Undecided	12
Mildly disagree	38
Strongly disagree	24
TOTAL	100

TABLE 7.2: *DDPECM: Beliefs about the Circumstances in which Candidates should Discuss Issues*

Will you say whether you strongly agree, mildly agree, are undecided, mildly disagree, or strongly disagree with this statement:

'The candidates of the Democratic party should only discuss specific policies in the general election campaign if this will win them votes.' (N=65)

	Percentage of respondents in each category
Strongly agree	9
Mildly agree	16
Undecided	9
Mildly disagree	35
Strongly disagree	31
TOTAL	100

War – four-fifths of the respondents favoured an immediate cessation of American bombing and a withdrawal of America's land forces by no later than April 1973.[3]

The emergence of a consensus on this issue within the party (and hence a *party* position that was visible to the electorate) was largely made possible by the openness of the party with respect to nomination procedures. Again the assembly/convention system enabled op-

TABLE 7.3: *DDPECM: Attitude towards the Voters' Right to know what Policies a Candidate will support if he is Elected*

Will you say whether you strongly agree, mildly agree, are undecided, mildly disagree , or strongly disagree with this statement:

'The candidates of the Democratic party should discuss the relevant issues so that the voters will know what kind of policies they will support if they are elected.' (N=65)

	Percentage of respondents in each category
Strongly agree	74
Mildly agree	25
Undecided	0
Mildly disagree	1
Strongly disagree	0
TOTAL	100

TABLE 7.4: *DDPECM: Attitude towards Political Education through the Discussion of Issues by Candidates*

Will you say whether you strongly agree, mildly agree, are undecided, mildly disagree, or strongly disagree with this statement:

'The Democratic party's candidates should discuss political issues and state their policies clearly so as to educate the electorate in the long term, even if this involves a risk of losing the next election.' (N=66)

	Percentage of respondents in each category
Strongly agree	29
Mildly agree	39
Undecided	8
Mildly disagree	21
Strongly disagree	3
TOTAL	100

position to the war to be mobilised much earlier than it was in states where there was no public forum in which the nomination process could be linked directly to public-issue debates. It is not unfair to say that, at each stage of its development, opposition amongst Colorado Democrats was two years in advance of that elsewhere. Conflict engendered by a minority, feeling itself to be excluded from power, characterised the 1968 National Convention. Yet this had been experienced in Colorado in 1966.[4] Fifteen months after Johnson's commitment of ground troops to Vietnam, concerted efforts were made in Denver, and more especially in Boulder, to send anti-war delegates to the assemblies.[5] These delegates succeeded, as did the Kennedy–McCarthy forces nationally two years later, in sending a large minority of sympathisers to the state assembly. A further similarity between the state party in 1966 and the national party in 1968 was an acrimonious dispute between the dissidents and Johnson supporters over procedures at the State Assembly and National Convention. In the 1966 Colorado state assembly this took the form of a walk-out by some of the dissidents after being refused recognition to speak on a resolution that in effect censured the Johnson administration on the war issue. Nevertheless, a vote was taken on this resolution which lost by a margin of only 2:1, and many of the dissidents at least seemed satisfied with the extent of support within the party for their viewpoint.

The assembly system had provided the opportunity for new attitudes to the war to be heard, but the fact that party served merely as an electoral services organisation meant that, until the conventions of 1968, the party could not be the main centre of public debate about the war. In other words, the party could not be a forum through which public opinion about the war could be educated over the next two years. It was not until the end of 1967, with Eugene McCarthy's announcement that he would be a Presidential candidate, that an attempt could be made to develop a clearly visible anti-war stance by the party. In Colorado the dominance of this position within the party was established in 1968, a stage not reached in most other states until 1970.

Between 1966 and 1968 the political parties as such did not define alternative positions on the Vietnam question. Opposition to the war was bipartisan, and in the case of many Republicans was a strategic device to employ against the Democrats. Among legislators in the General Assembly in Colorado, opposition was not only bipartisan but also very low key. In January 1967, ten Republicans and five Democratic assemblymen memorialised the U.S. Congress requesting that it initiate hearings to determine whether the war was in the national interest. Many of these Republicans merely wished to embarrass the Johnson administration. Moreover, Colorado, unlike California and Massachusetts in 1969–70, did not experience attempts to legislate 'against the war' at the state level. There were two main reasons for this. In the first place, the Republicans controlled both state chambers and the Governorship in the period when the 'Johnson war' had become the responsibility of Richard Nixon. There was little hope that extensive hearings on the war would be initiated by a Republican Assembly when these could only embarrass a Republican national administration. Secondly, the anti-war Democrats in the legislature were a minority even of their own party, and they quite naturally believed that there were more important priorities. Leadership opposition to the war could only be brought about by changing the party's public office holders, and this change was only occurring in the period 1970–72, when the war effort was already being run down.

The visibility of a party stand on the war to the electorate was apparent in the party's nominees for the U.S. House and Senate. Between 1968 and 1972 the Democrats increasingly came to select candidates who identified themselves with a policy of immediate cessation of overt American involvement. In 1968 only one such candidate, Ken Monfort, put himself forward. In the wake of the Kennedy-McCarthy coalition success, Monfort received top-line designation, but he failed to win the primary against former Governor McNichols. With the main effort that year being directed towards the Presidential nomination, neither of the state's conservative Democratic Congressmen was challenged for renomination and the single Republican incumbent's opponent was not notably a 'peace' candidate. As mentioned earlier, one prominent state legislator was approached in 1968 and asked to run against Byron Rogers, but this Democrat declined, arguing that it was not an appropriate time to do so. But by 1970 an unmistakable Democratic stance on the war was emerging. Craig Barnes's successful challenge to Byron Rogers, and his subsequent general election campaign, was centred on the issue of American withdrawal from Vietnam. Incumbent Wayne Aspinall also faced an unsuccessful attempt by a peace candidate, to deny him renomination. In the remaining two districts in Colorado, the Democrats nominated an anti-war candidate to run against the Republican incumbent, Donald Brotzman, whilst in the Third District a Democrat, now sympathetic to the policy of withdrawal from Vietnam, was renominated. In 1972 a united Democratic position on the war was achieved. Alongside McGovern as the Presidential nominee (McGovern having been the overwhelming choice of the Colorado Democrats) all five Congressional candidates and both Democrats who sought the Senate nomination favoured withdrawal. The Democrats did not attempt to conceal from the electorate the fact that they advocated the recognition of Vietnam as a 'lost' war. That this was an attempt to educate the electorate about the best alternative available, rather than to follow popular sentiment, can be shown by the lack of support amongst American voters for declaring the war to be lost. A survey published in May 1972 revealed that only 19.6 per cent of those surveyed favoured 'admitting defeat and giving the North Vietnamese whatever they wanted to get back our prisoners of war.' In contrast to this 38.9 per cent 'advocated stepping up the war for total victory' whilst 25.3 per cent favoured continued negotiations with the North Vietnamese.[6] Of course, this stance by the Democrats played little part in enabling the voters to decide what sort of policy priorities they wanted on the war issue. They were pre-empted by the Nixon administration which concluded an agreement with the North Vietnamese in early 1973 that was to lead to a communist military victory two years later.

The resolution of the Vietnam war issue by President Nixon may indeed be seen as an example of the antithesis of the process of political education that has been described here. The electorate was not informed of the available alternatives, nor was it provided with clear statements on why one alternative should be preferred to others. Instead, after his election, Richard Nixon set out to remove the two features of the war around which the greatest controversy had centred – the large number of casualties and conscription. The war strategy on the American side increasingly became one of aerial bombing. But this policy was incompatible with any hope of removing communist forces from South Vietnam. By 1972 the war could only be lost, in the sense that communist influence over much of the country was inevitable in the medium term, for President Thieu's forces were by themselves incapable of imposing a military solution. The only problem for the Nixon administration was to reach an accommodation with the North Vietnamese that would not make the withdrawal appear a defeat for America. With this in sight, the administration was able to portray itself as pursuing a policy of peace while only a few years earlier, and particularly in the 1970 mid-term elections, its rhetoric had been that of hostility to opponents of the war. Nixon's method of resolving the issue through the development of confusion rather than clarity amongst the electorate has been described in the following terms:

By ... two acts, reducing American casualties and reducing the threat of conscription, he succeeded in diverting a good deal of public attention from the war and in cutting most of the ground from under the critics of his war policies. As Secretary of Defense Melvin Laird commented, 'The American public understands the difference between addition and subtraction'. These steps seemed to blur even his critics' memory of the president as the man who watched a football game while youthful protesters staged a demonstration against the war in the nation's capital and who referred to the protesters at Kent State University as 'bums'.[7]

The cost of such an approach is political alienation amongst the citizens when they come to realise the results of policies are very different from the priorities they thought they had opted for in choosing their leaders. To prevent this alienation, the political leader who believes that the interests of the electors are different from some of their wants for policies, has to explain to the citizen why the promotion of their interests requires that these wants are not satisfied. But those who did not want to 'lose' the war in Indochina were never told of the abandonment of this goal. In the spring of 1975 they simply had to watch the consequence of the Nixon policy as the communist forces won their military victory.

Like the Great Society programme before it, the policies of the Vietnam war were largely carried out in the belief that the reaction of large segments of the population were irrelevant. The citizens would accept any results, providing some of the obvious consequences of the policies were initially shielded from them. But the politics of ambiguity over priorities in Vietnam and other national policy areas gave rise to the politics of disenchantment with politics itself. This growth in public disenchantment in America was observed in a variety of ways. Voter turnout in elections declined continuously between 1960 and 1976, making for an increasing gap between the United States and western European democracies in respect of mass participation at elections. Confidence in the activity of government declined, as response patterns to a variety of questions in political surveys changed between 1966 and 1973. The point has been well summarised by John F. Manley:

Alienation takes many forms. 'People running the country do not really care what happens to you', rose from 26 to 55 per cent. 'The rich get richer and the poor get poorer' went from 45 to 76 per cent. Seventy-four per cent believed that 'special interests get more from Government than the people do.' Sixty per cent agree that 'most elective officials are in politics for all they personally can get out of it.[8]

In clarifying their view of the priorities with regard to Vietnam, the Colorado Democrats had little effect in educating the public and reducing alienation. By the time a clearly Democratic position had been evolved, the war was already being wound down by the Nixon administration in a way that would leave many citizens confused about what the priorities had been. But at least the Colorado Democratic party was attempting to make the alternatives obvious to the electorate by 1972. In turning to examine a second major controversy that has concerned Colorado it appears that the Democratic party position went from clarity to obscurity. For on the busing issue it became increasingly unclear what policies the Democratic party stood for.

B. RACIAL INTEGRATION IN DENVER SCHOOLS 1968–74

The controversy over the busing of children to achieve racial integration in the pupil composition of Denver schools became one of the most contentious political issues at the mass level of politics at the end of the 1960s. It played a direct part in several types of election within the city and also affected elections for statewide offices. Two features of this need to be emphasised. First, the Democratic party in the city began by appearing to have a united attitude towards the problem which later dissolved into an apparent plethora of positions. To some extent this movement away from a clearly identifiable party position can be explained by the fact that the original position was largely created by the party organisation, not Democratic public officials. When Democratic public office seekers were drawn directly into the debate, they came to espouse rather different views, and there then ceased to be a coherent and comprehensible *Democratic* point of view or policy. Second, as the debate proceeded, Democratic candidates increasingly tended to obscure from the electorate the real alternatives and the real costs. This made for a sound electoral strategy but it did little to increase the understanding of a citizenry that saw itself as having busing imposed upon it. Indeed, it provides a good example of how the logic of party competition led candidates to compete with their opponents in ways that did little to educate the public about the nature of the choices facing the community.

Like the early consolidation of opposition to the Vietnam war in Colorado, busing in Denver has a small niche in American national history. Denver was the first major non-southern city in the country to have a programme of court ordered busing reviewed by the U.S. Supreme Court.[9] The impetus for racial integration in the Denver school district came from largely middle-class elements in the black community – a community which comprises about 9 per cent of the population, and the children of which form 19 per cent of the school population. Opposition to the reorganisation of the schools to make them racially mixed came from sectors of the Chicano and Anglo (white) populations. The origin of this conflict was the same as in other non-southern cities – the vast increase in the black residents during the last 40 years. In 1940, Blacks had formed only 2.4 per cent of Denver's population. But in Denver, unlike most other cities, a large proportion of blacks are middle class, most of them living in a particular area of the city – Park Hill. However, this is not an all-black area, and the immigration of blacks into it has not led to 'white flight' from what is, in effect, an inner-city suburb. It was in this neighbourhood that the demand for racially-integrated schools developed; it was a demand from white-collar workers that their children be educated in schools other than all-black ones. For, over a period of years, the Denver School Board had employed several techniques to preserve single-race schools:

> One such technique was the construction of schools in locations which were predicted would become (and did become) racially segregated on the basis of long apparent trends of black population movement. A second technique was the establishment of school attendance zones which assigned black pupils to predominantly minority schools. A third technique was the use of mobile classroom units to increase pupil capacity at predominantly minority schools rather than assigning them to nearby, under-utilised Anglo schools.[10]

In the early and mid-1960s black groups succeeded in preventing the construction of new schools in Park Hill that would have been located in areas which could only have resulted in them becoming all-black. The campaign to reverse this School Board policy of segregated schools reached a climax in 1968 when the Board finally produced a programme that provided for the formation of 'complexes' of schools from existing ones, the sharing of facilities and voluntary busing to achieve racial balance. This programme was agreed to in three Board resolutions in the first four months of 1968, and would have provided for integrated education for about 34 per cent of Denver's schoolchildren. However, in May 1969 two candidates for the Board who favoured school desegregation were defeated for election by two men who identified themselves as 'anti-busing'. Subsequently the resolutions implementing desegregation were reversed. Immediately after this election defeat eight children and their wards brought a law suit against the Denver School Board. The result was a judgment in 1970 in support of a programme of forced busing and other devices for achieving an integrated school system. The judgment in turn spawned a series of appeals to higher courts that ended only at the beginning of 1976. Substantial popular opposition to busing ensued, and this included the blasting of 46 school buses by dynamite and the bombing of several buildings. Yet in comparison with other cities, opposition was restrained. One of the few studies of the conflict has concluded that:

> community reaction in Denver must be characterised as relatively peaceful and mild. The violent hysteria that has gripped other cities confronted with similar problems has not appeared.[11]

Now it might be contended that the relative success of the imposition of busing on Denver is directly related to attempts by the parties to create a consensus on the issue. The argument might be put that the emergence of an ambiguous 'non-position' by the Democrats (to be described below) took the issue out of partisan politics, and thereby made it easier for the citizens to resign themselves to busing. Consensus, and hence political stability, was made possible because the parties did not attempt to educate the electorate directly. Underlying this sort of claim is a view of political leaders as having a role that is merely to do what is possible within the constraints imposed by popular sentiment and opinion. To try to effect changes in opinions directly, it might be argued, is to run the risk of arousing popular demagogues who in turn will try to reinforce existing opinion and enforce these popular sentiments through changes in public policy. Claims of this kind are frequently made by those who see non-programmatic party competition as the most stable form of democratic politics. However with regard to the busing controversy in Denver, this type of argument is founded on a confusion of three different points.

In the first place, it is undoubtedly true that the Democrats could have handled the issue in such a way that social conflict would have been much greater than it actually was. But the ability to induce conflict is related to a particular *style* of politics and not specifically to the clarity or ambiguity of the candidates' attitudes to issues. Secondly, the creation of a consensus is rather different from the refusal to state policy alternatives clearly in the belief that an issue will shortly cease to grip the electorate's imagination. Indeed it can be argued that the former does require candidates to give a higher degree of emphasis to the subject of the conflict, and to attempt to change opinions by virtue of their role as political leaders. On the other hand, the submergence of an issue by according it low emphasis does not lead to changes in the structure of such sentiments in the society; consequently it becomes difficult later to change public policies in areas closely related to the one which was the subject of the earlier intense conflict. Thirdly, low emphasis and vagueness on an issue engenders cynicism about, and alienation from, the political process itself. Most Denver citizens opposed busing and were naturally confused about how and why it had come to be imposed on them.[12] This could only decrease citizens' confidence in the political system and, together with other sources of discontent, lend support to attacks on the institutions of representative government. The first manifestation of this in Colorado was the support for an initiated amendment to the constitution in 1976 that would have required all tax increases in the state to be approved by a referendum. Although this particular initiative was defeated, it is probable that other manifestations of this disenchantment with government will appear in subsequent elections. Continued over a long period this would obviously result in the modification of the state's moralistic political culture, and adversely affect the potential for genuinely democratic government.

How, then, did the Democratic party come to be identified with ambiguity on the busing issue? At the School Board elections in 1969 party divisions were clearly drawn, for at the start of the controversy the Democrats allowed themselves to be seen as the party favouring an integrated school system. Although this sort of election is technically nonpartisan, the Democratic party organisation in the city had increasingly felt under pressure to become more directly involved in them. In particular, they felt that they should respond to what they saw as the Republican party's influence over the Board's policies. For example, one Democratic party officer said that he had personally been told by two Republicans on the board that they met the Republican county party chairman regularly and that he would 'tell them what to do.'[13]

Irrespective of whether these claims about the Republicans' involvement in policy making are correct, they were certainly much better organised in restricting the number of Republicans who sought election to the School Board. Until 1969 the Democrats did not attempt to make a similar effort on behalf of their known party activists who were contesting a Board election. In that year, with the school integration issue paramount and with two well known Democrats running for the two vacant seats, the party's central committee formally endorsed those candidates. Not surprisingly, this resulted in a more extensive election campaign for the Board than any Democrat had been able to mount previously. The candidates, Monte Pascoe and Ed Benton, were both well known integrationists, and they found themselves opposed by two self-identified anti-busers who were endorsed by the county Republican party. In short, the campaign was fought by the two parties on a clearly identified issue division. The anti-busers won a convincing victory (a margin of 2.5:1), defeating the integrationists everywhere except in the black areas, in a city that was heavily Democratic in terms of its voter registration.

The 1969 election was the only one to be contested on an overtly partisan basis, for since then Democratic party support for School Board candidates has become much more discreet. This was not brought about by any change in the party activists' commitment to the racial integration of the schools. They are still pro-integration, and a large majority of the Executive Committee support court-ordered busing in Denver (Table 7.5). But there appeared to many of them to be a conflict between the strategem that would maximise the opportunities for electing candidates sympathetic to busing to the School

TABLE 7.5: *DDPECM: Attitude towards Court-Ordered Busing in Denver*

Will you say whether you strongly agree, mildly agree, are undecided, mildly disagree, or strongly disagree with this statement:

'Judge Doyle was correct to order busing in Denver to achieve equality of educational opportunity.' (N=65)

	Percentage of respondents in each category
Strongly agree	46
Mildly agree	28
Undecided	7
Mildly disagree	11
Strongly disagree	8
TOTAL	100

Board and the desire to educate (and change) public opinion. In the absence of both a party programme that would have committed them more firmly to this education and *de facto* partisan elections for the Board, it was much easier for greater emphasis to be given to the winning of elections. Thus in the School Board elections of 1971, 1973, and 1975 the Denver Democratic party did not formally endorse any candidates. Although the busing issue clearly lies behind this strategy of the party activists becoming only informally involved with Board campaigns, party officers do not directly concede that fear of electoral loss is the prime motive for this. One party officer argued that 'the party has stayed away from School Board elections because the same issue has been the predominant one', whilst another said that the informal approach to party involvement in Board elections will remain 'until we've got busing behind us'. But it is quite obvious that they believe that the best electoral strategy is to make the election as low key as possible and that precludes an obviously partisan approach, and to rely on party workers to help get the vote 'out' on election day. Their most spectacular success in this respect was in 1973, when with no municipal elections to attract the attention of the electorate they reduced the turnout to 10.6 per cent. The result was that at the height of the busing controversy, two pro-busers (including one black) won two of the three seats at stake. In the corresponding election in 1969, again in a year when there were no municipal elections, the turnout had been 55.6 per cent. This overt removal of the party from School Board elections was accompanied by a retreat from clarity on the issue in partisan elections. But to understand how the issue came to affect these campaigns it is first necessary to understand the political implications of what at first sight seems to have been a judicial decision.

As in many other areas of public controversy in America since 1789, the Denver busing dispute began in the political arena (the policy disputes over integration in the School Board up to and including the 1969 election) and ended in the courts. When Judge Doyle had first decided in favour of the busing litigants and the U.S. Supreme Court had finally upheld this, the issue could, and did, enter the political arena again. But apart from the mere slowing down of the court plan by the School Board, the only political remedy for those opposed to busing was to change the laws under which the court had been able to act. At the very least, unless the U.S. Congress specifically passed a law to re-open busing orders, busing would commence in Denver. Moreover, many lawyers argued that an amendment to the U.S. Constitution would be the only way of preventing busing, because the courts might always interpret a law as being unconstitutional by virtue of it being incompatible with the policies required to enforce the 14th Amendment of the Constitution. In other words, the only alternative to an acceptance of busing was a change of policy at a level of government at which those elected by the inhabitants of Colorado would form only a small minority. But if the Congress alone was involved directly, other state office holders, and especially the Governor and the General Assembly, could be concerned indirectly through their rights to memorialise Congress and through informal political contacts. Busing could thus 'spill over' into election arenas other than that of the School Board because these offices could have some effect in determining whether busing did come to Denver. Beginning in 1970 this overspill effect did indeed occur.

Despite the controversy that had surrounded the 1969 election, the Democrats did not immediately attempt to disguise their commitment to integrated schools. At the Colorado State Assembly in 1970, the party resolved that the state law require racial integration to be imposed in public schools.[14] More important than this, though, for the maintenance of both a high emphasis and an unambiguous position on the issue was the designation (and later nomination) of Craig Barnes for Congressional District 1. As one of the lawyers who had drafted the original litigation for the plaintiffs in their suit against the School Board, Barnes's views on busing could scarcely be misrepresented. Even so, he gave little emphasis to the issue in the campaign, and when it was raised by his Republican opponent a week before the election, Barnes himself now admits that he may have equivocated on it then.[15] Indeed, this indicates the pressure from within the electorate felt by many Democrats, for in all other respects the Barnes campaign was acknowledged as being one in which clear alternatives were placed before the electorate. And in contrast with later elections even Barnes's stance on this issue was not obscure – his recent involvement with the litigants meant that he was unable to deny his commitment to busing.

By 1972 busing was even more a subject of concern amongst the citizens than it had been in 1970. The implementation of a busing order was that much closer with appeals against Judge Doyle's plan having been heard in the Court of Appeals and in the Supreme Court. This was reflected in the fact that 84 per cent of the respondents in a survey conducted by the Denver Urban Observatory in 1972 thought that racial integration of schools was either a 'serious problem' or 'some problem'. In 1970 only 74 per cent of the respondents had seen the problem in this way.[16] Furthermore, the immediacy of the problem had also been generated in part by the 1971 mayoralty election in Denver. The incumbent, an old-style Democrat, accused his regular Democratic opponent of being an ally of Craig Barnes and a supporter of busing. This charge, made between the original election and the run-off, seems to have been largely instrumental in Mayor McNichols' overturning the large plurality his opponent obtained at the first election. Naturally many Democrats became worried about the ability of candidates to tag Democratic candidates as busers and gain votes merely by doing so. Although the commitment of the organisation Democrats to integrated schools does not seem to have diminished, many of them were quite content to support two candidates in 1972, one being ambiguous on the issue and the other using it to gather votes in much the same way as Mayor McNichols had. The latter was Floyd Haskell.

The candidate who was able to produce an ambiguous, and winning, campaign strategy in 1972 was Patricia Schroeder. As already noted in the last chapter, she was recruited to run for Congress by a group of liberal Democrats, rather than being self-recruited. But like most Congressional campaigns the candidate had a degree of autonomy with regard to campaign strategy, and most activists were content to let Schroeder show how the electoral liability of busing could be overcome. Her tactics were to be employed by other candidates in 1974. In discussing the Schroeder case a good example is found to illustrate the point made by Benjamin Page that the ambiguous politician is not necessarily one who makes no specific proposals on policies.[17] For Schroeder, a low emphasis on the busing problem was the least important of the three ways in which she could create ambiguity about her position. This is hardly surprising: although candidates can always choose what issues to emphasise, and can usually choose which set of social conflicts to bring to the attention of an electorate, sometimes there are issues which intrude into a candidate's campaign because they are an immediate concern of the citizens. The evidence of the opinion polls already mentioned makes it apparent that busing was one such issue. Thus whilst Schroeder could choose not to give high emphasis to this issue, there was a minimum amount of attention that she had to devote to it. Nevertheless she was able to create some ambiguity by giving it much less attention than she could have. More interesting for this analysis are the ways in which she was able to present to the electorate an unclear image of what the major alternatives were on this matter.

The second aspect of her strategy was to take different stances at different places, in other words, she employed what might be called a dual-market strategy. This is not to say that her claims were directly contradictory to one another. To have done this would have been to have risked a complete loss of credibility. But she was able to make claims that would raise the expectations of both the integrationists and the anti-busers. On one occasion she argued that 'busing was a tool of racial integration', and on another that she did not approve of 'forced massive cross town busing.'[18] Even the party regulars who worked on her campaign seemed to have dissimilar ideas about what her stance was. The first three regulars whom we interviewed gave separate, and mutually exclusive, accounts of her position on busing in the 1972 campaign. Many of her opponents, both in the primary and the general election, believed that she had employed a blatant dual-market strategy. One Democrat state legislator, 'F', put this argument as follows:

> Mrs. Schroeder lied about busing, and did so successfully. In one part of town she would say: 'I'm against busing, I feel the same as Mr. Decker does.' In the part of town that was pro-busing she would say: 'I'm for busing, it's the solution to integration.' There have been other candidates who have succeeded in being able to talk in that manner.[19]

This part of the stratagem was only likely to be convincing if she could show voters that busing was not a real problem. Her line was that busing was being discussed too much, and that the real issue was not busing but the quality of education in Denver.[20] And thus we see the third aspect of the stratagem – an attempt to make busing seem to the voters as an irrelevant problem *per se*. Now at this stage, it might be argued, is this not precisely what has been argued in this book to be the most important form of competition between parties? Was it not claimed that the redefinition of political reality, and the presentation of alternative images of the major lines of division in the society, should be one of the main functions of parties in a democracy? Certainly it is contended that a major part of what was called 'primary' competition by parties or candidates are the efforts at restructuring the voters' issue and policy priorities. The object of this is the maximisation of autonomous choice for the citizens with regard to the sorts of policies they wish to see promoted by government. This is an educative process, making it more possible for the citizen to exercise more autonomous choice than he would otherwise be able to. Of course, this requires that the candidate (or party) explain to the electorate why what seems to be one kind of problem or demand is better seen as an instance of another. What the candidate cannot do, if he or she is to educate the electorate, is to misrepresent the nature of a group's demands or concerns in the attempt to restructure the lines of social cleavage. But it was precisely this last tactic that was employed by Patricia Schroeder in defusing the busing issue.

For although Mrs. Schroeder claimed during the campaign that the real issue was the quality of education in Denver, she did not attempt to explain to the electorate in what respects it was deficient or with what kinds of policies it would be improved. She would have had to have outlined to the voters why it was desirable to abandon busing as a priority and substitute for it the improvement of education quality. But she did not do this – it was a policy that would have undermined her chances of both gaining the nomination and winning the general election. The reason for this being that she would have lost many votes in the Black middle-class communities, particularly Park Hill. Most Blacks were deeply committed to busing as a tool of desegregation, albeit one which would improve the standard of education for Black children at the same time. For Schroeder to have claimed directly that integration was being accorded no priority at all by her, or that she opposed integration, would have been to risk the defection of Black voters. What she did was to present to the Anglo community an appearance of opposition to busing, in the guise of the claim that quality education was the real problem. This claim would be seen by Blacks as evidence of support for integration. For the latter group she did not have to uphold explicitly the policy of busing, and sufficient Anglos saw her stance as anti-busing to allow her to win both primary and general elections by margins of less than 10 per cent.

To represent the busing policy to Anglos as an inadequate solution to low quality education was to misrepresent the nature of the division between Blacks and anti-busers, at least as it was seen by Blacks. Although the demand for integrated schools had been fuelled in Park Hill in 1968 by the revelation of poor achievement records in Black schools, integration was wanted for itself, rather than merely as a means for correcting the bias in school facilities available to the different racial groups.[21] One prominent leader in the Black community (an educationalist) provided a typical account of how busing was strongly felt by Blacks to be a means of integrating them into the wider

community, and not primarily as a device for raising education standards:

> There are folks who say: 'I'm for integration, but I think busing is for
> the birds.' What they're saying really is: 'Let's go slow, let's let the
> neighborhoods integrate themselves.' We'll be 500 years old when
> black people are economically able to live in one hundred thousand
> dollar houses.... Those who say 'I'm for integration but I'm against
> busing', what they're saying is 'We'll take the acceptable black who
> wants to move out', but this doctor is moving to a neighborhood with
> a bunch of shoe salesman. *We* have to send doctors out there.[22]

The Schroeder strategy did not involve the educating of the electorate
to change the attitudes of either Anglos or Blacks to racial integration
in the city. Rather, it was designed to obscure this area of mass conflict
and to draw attention in the campaign to an issue with which it could be
conflated – quality education. In doing this she undoubtedly adopted a
winning stratagem, but it did nothing to ameliorate conflict at the mass
level over the relationship of the minority racial group to the majority.
The lines of conflict had not been redefined, but had been obscured at
the elite level. This tactic thus maximised her chances of election, and it
was acceptable to pro-integrationists who knew that Schroeder was
unlikely to support Congressional action to reverse the court orders.
Yet it did not educate the anti-busing Anglos about the actual alternatives facing them on the 'busing' issue, they were simply left to adapt
themselves to a policy of integration that they had not chosen but
which was being imposed upon them. It was not explained to them
why, in the interest of furthering other objectives, they had to reconcile
themselves to a policy solution they feared.

It would be incorrect, however, to characterise Schroeder's tactics as
completely Machiavellian. She was not an enthusiastic pro-buser who
acted as a political chameleon. The doubts she expressed in the
campaign about busing were undoubtedly sincere. Moreover the
tactics quite obviously reflected her belief that political candidates are
conciliators of conflicting interest, and not educators of the electorate
on the priorities to be accorded the policy alternatives facing the
community:

> It has been [Mrs. Schroeder's] position that people should avoid
> unshakable positions. 'She would prefer', she said, 'that both sides
> on an issue sit down together and work out their differences.'[23]

The price of this approach on an issue about which popular opinions
were strongly felt, and for which a definite policy was being imposed

whether there was agreement or not, was the alienation of many citizens from the political process. However, the party activists, despite their commitment to the education of the electorate remained strongly in support of Patricia Schroeder. On the other hand she proved to be a supporter of busing once in Congress: in 1974 she was one of only 117 Representatives to vote against an amendment to a bill that would have prohibited busing to any school save that closest or next closest to a pupil's home. On the other hand she had provided a winning stratagem for the Democrats, and one which did not seriously split the party organisation. In the absence of a party programme that spelt out policy commitments to the electorate, the party regulars were more than content to go along with tactics that both did not impede directly the introduction of busing and were also electorally successful.

After 1972 several other Democratic candidates seemed to have learnt one lesson from the Schroeder campaign. This was that an election could be won by appearing to oppose busing but at the same time providing indications to the Black community that they would do little that would impede its implementation. Unlike Schroeder in 1972 who posed 'quality education' as being the real problem, Gary Hart in 1974 was to oppose busing for achieving racial integration but argue that the law should be obeyed whilst an alternative to it was found.[24] At no point in the campaign did he outline what such an alternative might be. In 1974, with court ordered busing commencing, Schroeder modified her tactics against a Republican opponent who was running solely on the busing issue. She now stressed her opposition to cross-city busing, but blamed the trouble caused by the court order on the School Board.[25] The three prospective gubernatorial candidates that year also stated opposition to busing, but did little to explain either what policies they favoured in furtherance of their opposition or why they were reconciled to the imposition of busing. Amongst the party candidates for the General Assembly there were vehement pro- and anti-busers as well as those who took more complex and more ambiguous positions. By 1974 there was no visible Democratic party position on the issue. Even for the observant citizen there was no cue as to the view of the Democrats: the 1974 Denver platform made no reference to the realisation of racial integration in the schools. It merely stated that the party was committed to a quality education for children regardless of colour.

The collapse of a coherent Democratic position was largely the product of the desire of individual candidates to maximise their chances of electoral victory and the willingness of the party activists to support them in doing so. But in 1974 there were two additional factors involved. The first was the desire of many of them not to have busing used as a 'scare' issue by one Democrat against another, as it was in the 1971 mayoralty election and the 1972 Senate primary. Fearing an electorally more disastrous consequence to this sort of introduction of the busing issue than had in fact resulted then, many Democrats were quite content for the party not to be overtly committed to a stance on busing. It would be less easy for candidates and factions to engage in a direct conflict on the issue. The second factor was the presence of an anti-busing referendum on the ballot in 1974 – a proposal to amend the state constitution to prohibit busing in the state. To a large extent, it was a device to draw attention to the candidacy of the single-issue Republican candidate, Frank Southworth, in his bid to unseat Patricia Schroeder. But it was quite obvious that it would both pass and would have no effect on the introduction of busing. (It would probably be held by the courts to be incompatible with the U.S. Constitution.) By drawing attention to themselves as the party of busing the Democrats would only be worsening their own election chances with no direct benefit to offset it. No concerted effort was made to defeat the referendum. The result was that five years after presenting a clear alternative to the electorate on the busing question, the party did not seek to clarify the alternatives for the electorate. Busing had arrived in Denver and the citizens would be left to make what they could of it.

Because they were tied to no policy programme, even the pro-busing activists were prepared to see candidates take an unclear and even anti-busing stance in campaigns. Therefore, in this instance, they did not move the candidates towards primary competition and away from secondary kinds of electoral competition. In the language introduced in chapter 3 they allowed the electorate to be 'disinformed'. Had the parties been programmatic ones, then the Democrats would not have been so unaccountable to the citizens on this issue. As it was the actual policy alternatives on busing were not discussed by the major candidates after 1970, and most activists were waiting for the electorate to accept busing so that 'normal' politics could be resumed. It can be seen, then, that a partially-democratised party may not safeguard the citizen from the self-interested behaviour of an oligopolist. When the activists do not control the policies promoted by public office seekers, by means of a party programme, they themselves may collude with the latter to restrict the type of competition employed. Only a more fully democratised party might have prevented this.

8 Party: The 'Non-Displacement' of Conflict

One of the themes of this book is that the cleavages in a western polity exist on two levels; levels which are related to one another but not directly, as populist democratic theory assumes. At one level, there are divisions between political leaders organised, tightly as in Britain or loosely as in the United States, into political parties. It is these leaders seeking public office who are in a position to make sense for the citizens of the divisions at the other level, that of the mass public. They will not always provide this service, and when they do not, the citizens will have no major source from which they can acquire the concepts and consistency of viewpoint with which to comprehend the social and economic divisions of which they are directly aware. The citizens directly understand local manifestations of these cleavages, but it is only by relating them to the divisions to which the elected leaders refer that they can see them as aspects of more general cleavages. Those seeking election as party candidates for public office are not, of course, the only source of political information but they are the only source which, under certain circumstances, has an incentive to supply the electorate with a comprehensive, coherent and simplified model of the political world. Because they are organised into parties, the candidates need not overload the citizens' capacity for understanding by exposing them to too many alternative perspectives. Thus may be seen the unique role parties (particularly 'parties-in-government'), can play in comparison, for example, with interest group leaders, professional public administrators or communicators in the news media.

However, we have also argued that, of itself, electoral competition does not ensure that clear alternative models of the divisions of a society are presented by candidates to their electors. For one thing, as was seen in Chapter 6, the party may not have a programme of policies, and without this there is nothing to encourage candidates to compete with one another in the presentation of a single model to the electorate. In Chapter 3 we further argued that even when parties do

153

act as teams, there are incentives for them to compete in ways other than that of presenting alternative definitions of political reality to the citizens. In particular it was suggested that parties may resist redefining political divisions when new sets of concerns emerge at the mass public level. In this section an examination is made of how the Democratic party interpreted concerns about economic growth in Colorado for the public; the question is considered as to why this partly-democratised party has not placed a straightforward set of growth objectives before the public.

Before the late 1960s there existed a high degree of consensus both at the mass and leadership levels of politics about the desirability of attaining a high economic growth rate in the state.[1] Since then concerns about the extent and nature of economic development in the state have become obvious in a variety of ways. These considerations are at the centre of a complex set of divisions of opinion and interest that are related to the citizen's physical environment. Public opinion surveys provide evidence of the existence of these concerns at the mass level, although they also show that many Coloradans do not have a coherent set of priorities on this issue. This was revealed in one 1976 survey. Nearly two thirds of those interviewed agreed with the statement that 'the protection of the environment should be the state's top priority', whilst only 26 per cent disagreed with it. Yet, later in the survey they were asked whether they agreed that 'economic growth is the state's most important concern', and 57 per cent believed it was, whilst 37 per cent of them that it was not.[2] Another 1976 survey revealed further public disquiet in Denver on growth-environmental problems. Of 24 alleged 'problems' in the Denver metropolitan region, 4 of the 6 environmental problems (air pollution, parking, public transportation and urban planning) were among the 12 issue areas regarded as the most serious. Air pollution was seen by more people as a problem than was any other of the 24 issues, 52 per cent of the sample claiming it was 'very serious' and 29 per cent stating that it was 'fairly serious'.[3] This evidence merely confirms that of earlier surveys conducted by the Denver Urban Observatory in 1972. Apart from the evidence furnished by surveys, there are other indications of mass-level concerns with growth-related problems. For example, much attention was focused in the 1974 elections on the proposal to improve road transportation in the front range area (the plains land immediately to the east of the Rockies) with the construction of an addition to the inter-state highway system, I-470. Again there was considerable publicity for, and interest in, the environmental aspects of several initiative campaigns including that in 1972 on the Olympics issue. Thus, it is pertinent to consider now why concerns related to the economic growth of the state should have become so widespread amongst the Coloradan public in the last few years.

There are two main considerations to be recognised in answering this question. In the first place, the range of alternatives available to the state in respect of the encouragement or the control of growth is very wide. Unlike most western states, theoretically Coloradans could choose to experience either very rapid economic development of the front range area of the state or, at the other extreme, a severe curtailment of the recent expansion of activity in the area. It is the first alternative, in effect the creation of what would become one of America's major metropolitan areas, based on the 'knowledge industries', tourism and most especially minerals, that is not yet available to most other states in the region. Development could be promoted by the provision of tax incentives to companies to base themselves in Colorado, or by the publicising of the state's economic potential to companies in the East. On the other hand, economic growth could be restricted by the kind of land-use laws that are not outside the American free enterprise tradition. An example of such laws are those of Hawaii, where the regulation of land use has been centralised in a Land Use Commission since 1961. Their purpose is to protect the 10 per cent of the land that is cultivatable from other uses, and the Commission has the right to establish zones within which certain uses of the land are permitted and others prohibited.[4] But, secondly, Colorado is unlike some other states, such as Oregon and Vermont, that have also experienced recent mass-level concerns about the effect of development on the 'amenities' within the state. For in Colorado, rapid development of the front range area has already occurred, the quality of some amenities has consequently declined, and voter confusion about the effects of attempting to limit growth has become evident.

Recent growth has given rise to a decline in the standard of a variety of amenities of which it is difficult not to be aware. For example, air pollution has increased; there are traffic jams in the winter between Denver and the ski resorts of Aspen and Vail; and there now has to be a lottery to allocate the restricted number of hunting licences in the elk season. The declining amenities are particularly of concern to immigrants who, having come to Colorado for the combination it provides of big city and wilderness, find that others are doing so and consequently devaluing these amenities. In brief, increasing competition for what Fred Hirsch calls 'positional goods' has not only taken place but has been seen by the citizens to take place.[5] Nevertheless most Coloradans have not acquired a coherent set of values and attitudes to specific growth related issues. Thus a media campaign against the 'nuclear safeguard' referendum in 1976 in which the opponents of control outspent the proponents 6–1 led to a complete change in attitude in a few months towards that particular measure. In July the Amendment to the State Constitution had been favoured 58–32 amongst those surveyed, but at the November election it was defeated 30–70.[6] In short, many voters seem concerned about economic growth and its effects, but, not surprisingly they do not have stable and consistent attitudes towards individual issues and problems. In particular, it would be expected that they would not have firm opinions on policy proposals that are not available to them as small-decision makers.

Now if the populist theories of democracy provided an adequate account of the political process, there would be a coherent set of demands forthcoming from those affected by the loss of amenity. Political leaders would then respond to these demands by balancing them against the demands of others, so that public policy would eventually reflect the wants of all. But the concerns and fears about amenity losses that have emerged in Colorado have not given rise to the politics of coherent mass demands followed by elite responses. Instead, during the last six years, alternative public policies with regard to economic growth have been stated clearly neither by the public nor by candidates for public office organised in political parties. Instead 'environmentalism' has intruded on the political leadership through several initiative campaigns, to which the candidates' main response has, at most, been a campaign style of appealing to environmental *sympathies* in the electorate without educating the public about the major sets of alternative approaches available to the state government. Naturally the initiative campaigns of 1972 (Winter Olympics), 1974 (Nuclear Explosions), and 1976 (Nuclear Safeguard and Container Deposits) have drawn attention to some aspects of growth/ environment issues. But they have not provided the citizens with a framework with which to understand future aspects of a problem area that only briefly becomes politically prominent. In the meantime the suburbanisation of the front range area of the state has continued without the citizens being able to exercise any autonomous choices with regard to the decreasing standard of environmental 'amenities'. It is quite conceivable that they will still not have had an opportunity to exercise such choices at the time when the front range metropolis stretches from the Wyoming border in the north to Pueblo in the south. And this raises the question of why internally democratic party organisations, at least in the case of the Democratic party, have not led to the new concerns about growth being incorporated into the parties' definition of political reality for the electorate.

This question may be approached by first noting that the development of alternative definitions of the nature of the political universe by existing major parties will be resisted by some of the older interests within their organisations. In Colorado, concerns about economic growth cut across one of the traditional lines of division between Republicans and Democrats – that of social class. Indeed it is misleading to suggest, as one recent account does, that the Republican party was inclined to oppose controls of the natural environment because of sympathies for the free enterprise system.[7] There were interests within the Republican party that were opposed to environmentalism, but there were similar tensions also amongst the Democrats. Yet mainly because of its participatory ethic in the 1970s, and because it held few public offices, the Democratic party was a more obvious forum for those concerned about growth-related issues than the Republican party. In fact, Republican identifiers were only marginally less likely to see economic growth as the state's most important concern than were Democrats.[8] Furthermore, amongst that sector of the electorate which traditionally has been most supportive of the Republican approach to free enterprise – the business and professional classes – there is evidence of doubt about the effects of unrestricted economic growth. Unlike the public as a whole, the majority of the business and professional respondents in the Hamilton survey did not believe that economic growth is Colorado's most important concern. And their view of the priority to be accorded to environmental protection was little different from that of the total sample.[9] It is obvious why this sort of person may be sympathetic to governmental controls to protect the environment – he is more able than lower income groups to enjoy the sort of amenities (the positional goods) that are undermined by extensive economic development. (For example, he is more likely to be able to afford skiing at Aspen, a cabin in the mountains, and a house in the previously unpolluted outer suburbs.) Just as the Republican party's electoral base was not likely to be completely antagonistic to all policy initiatives in growth-related issue areas, there was also a group of public office-holders who were the inheritors of the long established 'moderate' tradition in the party. It has been a shrinking element (e.g.

in 1976 the overwhelming majority of National Convention delegates supported Ronald Reagan) but in the early 1970s there were many prominent Republicans, including the Governor, who came within it. In fact, two of the most prominent supporters of land-use legislation in the General Assembly were Republicans John Bermingham and Betty Ann Dittemore. Nevertheless it was the Democrats rather than the Republicans who were generally able to present an image of a party aware of the desirability of some environmental controls, and in certain state elections undoubtedly won votes from traditional Republicans. But this has produced an uneasy marriage in the Democratic party.

In the absence of high-expenditure policies to compensate them for some of the effects of constraints on growth, the interests of many traditional supporters of the Democratic party run counter to those favouring restrictions. To the extent that a high growth rate in metropolitan Denver would maximise employment amongst manual workers, and a low growth rate exacerbate the effects of a national depression, environmental controls and restrictions on growth would adversely affect the poorest groups in the city. Naturally, one industry – building – would be directly affected by many kinds of policy initiative in this area, and not surprisingly the building workers union has been a prominent critic of such policies.[10] The result has been a series of splits amongst organised labour. On the one hand, under the leadership of Herrick Roth the AFL-CIO in Colorado emerged as a champion of policies such as state government control of land-use regulation. On the other hand below the leadership level there was much less support for this policy when it was first discussed in 1973/4, and this was reflected in the attitude of the Denver legislator most closely associated with labour – Charles DeMoulin. Although he is a long-serving Democrat, DeMoulin voted against the 1973 Land Use Bill and abstained on the (Democratic) Lamm amendment to the 1974 bill that would have given stronger controls to the state government (as against the county commissioners) in land-use matters. Similarly leaders in the Black community have criticised environmental policies which they have regarded as incompatible with the maximisation of employment opportunities. In 1976, both the chairman of the *Colorado Black Political Caucus* and the only Black State Senator, took exception to the initiators of the law requiring the regulation (through a two-thirds affirmative vote in the General Assembly) of the construction of nuclear power plants in the state. Moreover the chairman used this issue as a way of broadening the attack on environmental 'elitists' in the party who are not 'sincere when they pillory labor-intensive mining programs and cheap (nuclear) energy sources, while ignoring problems of unemployment.'[11] He argued that Blacks were not opposed to controlling air pollution in Denver, but claimed that the environmental movement was less concerned with this than with priorities that would have adverse effects on the poor. His views were not unusual among traditional economic liberal Democrats, and several prominent activists argued privately that environmentalism was of more interest to traditional Republicans than their own voters. Given this view it was electorally dangerous in the short term for the Democrats to do more than flirt with the issue. In addition to this potential split in the party there was a futher source of antagonism to some varieties of environmentalism. Apart from those in Pitkin County (Aspen), most rural Democrats have not favoured land-use zoning by a state agency, and in 1973–4 a rural/non-rural split was revealed in Democratic voting in the General Assembly on land-use bills.

Nevertheless, despite these problems in the composition of both parties at elite and mass levels, it was the Democrats rather than the Republicans who in several campaigns, particularly that for the Governorship in 1974, were to become partly identified with environmentalism. One reason for this is related to the accepted truth that the Republican commitment to free enterprise made the leaders and activists in that party less responsive to these concerns than the Democrats. For, in a full employment economy there were fewer pressures on Democratic candidates than on Republicans to take account of the potentially conflicting interests in their party's electorate. Again, whilst the poor were under-represented in the Democrats' activist ranks, the libertarian, free-enterprise ethic was increasing in importance in the Republican organisations.

At the same time the Democrats were actively encouraging mass participation in their party by all and sundry, something which the Republicans were not doing. Finally, being the party that had not controlled either the Governorship or the State House from 1966–74, the Democrats became a more obvious focal point for those who wanted to radically change existing policies. But if the Democratic party has more directly appealed to environmental sentiments in the electorate in particular campaigns than the Republicans, there has been no party programme or commitments to specific types of policy. Indeed one aide to the Democratic Governor admitted that the emphasis in any of the latter's future campaigns may switch to the size-of-government issue, since this appeared to be a new mass-level concern.[12] For candidates, the political education of the electorate quite naturally had to take second place to the considerations of electoral success. The problem of the growth related issues for the Democrats is that, without the specific undertakings entailed by a party programme, there is no incentive for candidates to take many stances on specific issues. To do so might be to run the risk of alienating other elements in the coalition – a problem which seemed to be a major one facing Richard Lamm in the 1974 Gubernatorial contest. However, the greater availability of the initiative process since 1972 has meant that the parties have not really had to face up to this problem. The environmentalists themselves have preferred to take issues directly to the electorate rather than get involved in the long term in the parties, something which appears to them less directly productive. The failure of the Democrats to provide a fundamental redefinition of the nature of the cleavages in the state can be comprehended by examining how the party was involved in one issue that at first glance seems to have been about growth – the projected 1976 Winter Olympics.

Commencing in 1964, Colorado bid for the right to hold the 1976 Winter Olympics, and won this right in 1970 from the International Olympics Committee.[13] However, the 'Colorado' that was awarded the Games was neither the Colorado government nor an agency of it. The negotiations were handled by the Colorado (later Denver) Olympic Committee, a body established by Republican Governor Love in 1964 but which was not responsible either to him or to the state legislature. From its inception until the point at which it became obvious that the Games were doomed, the members of this Committee were almost entirely the representatives of those business interests that expected to benefit directly from the Games. Yet the financial commitments of this body were met by appropriations from the state's General Assembly. The Games were to be based in Denver, and the consensus view, that the resulting stimulation to the economy was desirable for Colorado, was endorsed throughout the 1960s by both the Republican administration and the state's then leading Democrat, Mark Hogan. The first controversy to undermine the consensus at both mass and leadership levels was the problem of the siting of the Games. The Olympic rules dictate that the Games must be held in one city rather than in several localities in a region. In Colorado the main sports towns were too small to be developed for competitions in all the winter sports, and it seemed logical therefore that the Olympic village would be in or near Denver. But this created a problem for the Denver Olympic Committee (DOC) because there were no existing facilities in the nearby eastern range of the Rockies. To comply with the rules, therefore, the DOC planned to construct sites at selected places close to Denver. It was this that started a twofold controversy: the residents in areas adjacent to the proposed sites objected to the loss of normal suburban amenities, and on technical grounds the sites proved inadequate for their purpose. These controversies provided an impetus for the small environmental groups that were already opposing the project.

By early 1972 the single Olympic village proposal had to be abandoned, and instead it was planned to have three different villages for each of the major sports, each of the villages being located at existing winter sports centres. Obviously by then the competence of the organisers was more open to public criticism, and already by 1971 a few state legislators had begun to express concern about the more general environmental effects as well as about the specific sites the DOC was proposing at that time. But this criticism was not extensive even among Democrats in the General Assembly, and the legislature never came close to cutting off funds for the Games or referring the issue to the electorate in a referendum. After Common Cause's success in 'opening up' the initiative process in early 1972, it naturally became more attractive to the dissidents to take the issue directly to the voters rather than work for policy change through either of the parties. In response to the possibility of direct action a specially formed group to coordinate opposition to the Games came into being.

This group, The Citizens for Colorado's Future (CCF), filled a gap caused by the absence of cohesion between the existing organised groups. It was a classic piece of political entrepreneurship – a few individuals saw the opportunity for an effective campaign against the Olympics, but an opportunity that was likely to be missed if the disparate efforts were not brought together.[14] Three young (under 30); new immigrants to the state were the mainspring of the CCF's formation and operation; it was they who gave direction to the employment of the group's most important resource, the large number of volunteer workers. In conjunction with the leading legislative opponent of the Games, Richard Lamm, these three (Sam Brown, Margaret Lundstrom and John Parr) arranged the collection of the 76,000 signatures for the initiative in March 1972 and directed the campaign strategy until the November election. Lamm had originally been one of the supporters of the Denver Olympics, but he had come to voice opposition to it in 1971 both on environmental grounds and also in terms of the large cost that would be imposed on the state government. And it is this last point which is the key to understanding the Olympics affair: concern for the environment in the electorate was difficult to translate into a majority position on a specific issue. This is because the citizens would not have an adequate framework for evaluating claims for environmental protection against those put forward by the Olympics' supporters. However widespread sympathies for the former claims might be, it would not have been difficult for the proponents of the Games to win the campaign by drawing attention to the longer-standing individual and group interests of different sectors of the electorate.

In fact, while environment related concerns gave rise to the initial opposition, and a large number of politicians came to see the initiative result as a vote for controlling economic growth, the campaign by the CCF was largely directed towards emphasising the cost of the Games. In interviews, both Sam Brown and John Parr argued that it had been a deliberate tactic to stress the level of expenditure by the state that might be necessary to construct the facilities for the athletes, and more especially the spectators.[15] Indeed, Brown himself believed that costs were the more important consideration. The Olympics, then, were not, as one writer has argued, primarily 'used to dramatise, simplify and produce an interest in environmental action among the electorate'.[16] Undoubtedly the CCF was correct in believing that the stratagem it employed was the one most likely to maximise its chances of victory. For despite the fact that a well-financed campaign was eventually launched by the supporters of the Games, the public image of the DOC was one of incompetence. (In the campaign the organisation The Coloradans for the Winter Games outspent the CCF by more than 5:1.) The DOC members gave a clear impression that they did not know how much it would cost the state to stage the Olympics. What estimates were available in mid 1972 indicated that the cost might be $63.4 million, whereas in 1970 it had been predicted that the total cost would be only $14 million.[17] It was relatively easy for the CCF to suggest that the DOC did not know the probable total cost of the enterprise for it, after all, was the same organisation that had both originally chosen an inappropriate site for the downhill skiing events, and had also failed to include a wide range of interests in its own membership. Without the DOC's obvious mishandling of its affairs it is doubtful whether a serious campaign against the Games could have been raised. The environmental arguments in favour of abandoning the Games were not overwhelmingly strong; the argument that they would stimulate rapid economic growth in the state was especially weak. The tourist industry would have become larger as a result of the publicity and it is possible that some individuals and firms might have decided to move to Colorado after seeing its attractions on television. But it is implausible to suggest that this would have contributed significantly to the state's growth. And it could be contended that the experience of developing facilities for the spectator invasion of the state might have generated ideas for the future control of growth. It might have served as a case study from which both government and public would have learnt of some problems of rapid growth by experiencing them in miniature. The Machiavellian zero-growth proponent could well have taken the position that a disastrous Olympics (traffic jams even on newly-widened roads, ugly Olympic villages etc.) was the best way of educating the public about the consequences of unconstrained growth. However the environmental interest groups, such as the Sierra Club and the Colorado Open Space Council, were not Machiavellians and they became leading opponents of the Games.

From the viewpoint of these interest groups, the Olympic Games provided an attractive issue upon which to focus the problems of the state's growth. It was one likely to gain publicity and there was a fair chance of success on the initiative ballot. But it was not an issue that encapsulated the problems of growth for the electorate – it was not clear that it would have either economic benefits or reduce the amenities of the natural environment. Those who guided the CCF tactics knew this; they wanted to defeat the measure and were prepared to put together any winning coalition. They needed the support of the environmental groups but they were not promoting their causes. Consequently, the campaign was not designed to, and did not, educate the electorate about alternative approaches to growth-related problems. It could not because the Games issue was only indirectly relevant to these problems. The vote to cut off state government funding of the Games (59 per cent–41 per cent) was primarily a vote against the organisers rather than a vote for the kind of environmental protection favoured by the interest groups. As evidence of this there is the results of a private survey commissioned by the Coloradans for the Winter Games towards the end of the campaign. This showed that the voters were evenly split on the question of whether the Games would cause environmental damage. In contrast to this a 53 per cent–33 per cent majority believed that taxes would increase as a result of the Games and, against the view of the DOC, a 56 per cent–33 per cent majority believed that the Games would have few economic benefits.[18]

As with the later initiative campaigns, this one, on the state's funding of the Olympics, provided an opportunity for many politicians not to take a definite stand. There were good reasons for not doing so: it was not apparent how strong environmental sentiments were in the electorate, nor how they would be related by voters to the specific issue. In addition it was unclear what the outcome would be, and, as it was attracting more attention than were most legislative elections, few candidates wanted to be on the losing side. Only the Governor and the Mayor of Denver had to campaign on one side – the one because he had started the project, the other because he was a member of the DOC. The incumbents in the U.S. House and Senate took no chances; they held up hearings in the Congress on a Federal Government contribution to the funding of the Games, so as to guard against the consequences of being associated with an unpopular cause. In the Congressional election in Denver neither Patricia Schroeder nor Mike McKevitt were outspoken on the issue – they preferred not to antagonise any of the interest groups involved. The issue had long been before the General Assembly, but as was mentioned in Chapter 6, Olson found that few legislators were willing to take a public position on it. A few Democratic legislators were active in the CCF campaign, but the issue was not one that divided public office holders on partisan lines. In brief, the political party leaders were waiting to have the issue resolved for them rather than resolve it for the electorate. One paradox of the campaign was that immediately after the Initiative vote many Colorado politicians interpreted the result as a mandate for controlling growth. Moreover, (in the next two years) the Olympics controversy served as a stimulant to the introduction of land-use bills in the state assembly. But such fears about the new concerns of the electorate did not last long. A major land-use bill (SB 337) failed in the 1973 session of the General Assembly, although a much weaker and generally unworkable bill (HB 1041) was passed in 1974.

In 1972, despite its prime objective of mobilising anti-expenditure votes on the Olympics Initiative, the CCF undoubtedly did bring the issue of growth to the public's attention. It did not provide members of the public with a conceptual framework with which to understand the problems, but it did increase their awareness of the immediacy of the problems. In 1974 there was no such immediacy. After the passage of HB 1041 the Colorado Open Space Council did not proceed with an initiative effort, as it had originally intended to, should the General Assembly not pass a major land-use reform bill. Moreover the urban Democratic legislators certainly did not want to confront their rural colleagues who had been the main source of party opposition both to

SB 377 and the Lamm amendment to HB 1041. Many of them wanted to keep the party as a loose coalition even if this meant delaying state involvement in land-use planning. Thus the growth issue was never a party issue in 1974 but one which was centred on Richard Lamm's bid for the Governorship. Indeed, this was the only campaign that year in which the now widespread concerns about growth were directly taken up.

After his overt opposition to the Olympics, Lamm attracted support in both the primary and general elections from those interest groups and individuals most worried about the loss of environmental amenities in Colorado. In 1974 he consistently attempted to explain to the electorate that there were choices about economic development facing the state. He stated that his own position was that of favouring growth in the economy but he wanted growth to be directed to the counties with declining populations.[19] But as a campaign of political education his was deficient, for it gave the electorate no idea of what sorts of policies he favoured and what priority he accorded the different policies. Thus when his administration began in January 1975 there were no specific legislative priorities in this issue area that could be said to be the Governor's. Furthermore, his general theme was at least partly inconsistent with a more specific public theme – that he favoured 95 per cent of the land-use decisions being taken locally with only the remainder, those that required attention at the regional or state level, not being within the province of county government.[20] Whatever the *number* of decisions that could be taken at local level, Lamm knew that growth in the front range could only be controlled when the state, not the counties, could determine the general character of local developments. This was why he had supported SB 377 and put forward a major amendment to HB 1041.

This campaign strategy of ambiguity made sense if the election was close, for then the votes in the rural counties, would be vital to him. (In fact the general election was close – Lamm defeated incumbent John Vanderhoof by only a 54 per cent–46 per cent margin.) Thus he needed to stress to rural voters the role of the counties as the level of government that would be responsible for restricting their freedom to use their land as they saw fit. Had he proposed a more specific set of policies he would have been less able to construct a coalition that included both environmentalists and agricultural interests. Electoral competition thus induced ambiguity on Lamm's part, so that whilst the election was a forum in which concerns about growth were raised it did not enable the electorate to choose between different sets of priorities.

There was no Democratic party programme to prevent Lamm from following the logic of party competition. With no specific commitments, a Democratic Governor and a Democrat-controlled lower chamber introduced no new land-use legislation in the 1975 and 1976 legislative sessions. Despite the belief amongst many Democrats that it was inadequate, HB 1041 remained the legislature's main contribution to the control of economic expansion in the front range area.

The problem for those wanting to give priority to controlling economic growth was that the parties did not bind their candidates to support specific policies. Without this commitment, party activity would always be less attractive than lobbying or other forms of direct approach to public office holders. Even an 'open' nominations process is no substitute for a plank in a party programme as far as individuals and groups wanting specific changes in public policy are concerned. For them the Initiative was a direct and obvious alternative to the party. In 1976, therefore, environmental groups became heavily involved in three Initiative efforts – mineral/food tax, nuclear power safeguards, and the returnable containers proposals. If the parties in office would not address themselves to these problems, then the electorate would be confronted with them directly. 'If the Olympic forces could be beaten, why not the business forces this year?'[21] Yet all three initiatives were heavily defeated. As a guide to the prospects of success by direct action the Olympics initiative was misleading. The issue had been won on the question of cost to the voters, and as always many citizens voted for what they saw as their immediate self-interest. Yet, as with most problems of environmental impact, the policies needed to reduce it (whether it be zero-population growth or banning non-returnable containers) will involve some direct, short-term cost to the voters.

Unless voters can be educated to accept these costs to secure results they prefer, initiative campaigns are never likely to be a means of starting further policy changes as their advocates believe. They are simply the arenas in which some specific proposals are defeated. In Colorado, the business interests that opposed each of these three 1976 initiatives had far greater funds to pay for advertisements than had the environmental groups. It was not too difficult for them to educate (or rather disinform) the voters on why they should vote for their own self interest once they had identified for the electorate what that self-interest was in each of the initiatives. Parties, on the other hand, can more easily serve as educators of the electorate than can under-financed, non-special interest groups. As Schattschneider argued a generation ago, it is the parties which are the best sorts of organisations for countering special interests. In Colorado, though, the Democratic party had not become more coordinated and, as elsewhere in the U.S., the candidates were still not bound by party programmes. The result was that, despite the high degree of internal democracy in the Democratic party, the Democrats were not an effective counter to organised special interests. The democratisation of a party that is only partial has been insufficient therefore to attract public-interest groups to work through them rather than join the pressure-group system. The groups, the parties and the public have consequently all been losers.

9 Conclusion

In some respects the Denver experience does indicate how party democracy, established by amateur activists, may be successful. Between 1966 and 1970 they became a major influence in the nomination process and in the creation of a distinctive, coherent Democratic viewpoint on the Vietnam war issue. Moreover, in its early stages there was a clearly identifiable Democratic party approach to busing. Yet this study has also revealed that office seeker accountability to activists was not merely partial; it was insufficient to provide effective activist control both over nominations and the content of advertising by party candidates to citizens. Although disagreements with state legislators over public policies persisted after 1970, there was no recurrence of the widespread efforts of that year to withhold renomination from incumbents. Equally, after 1970 there was an increasing lack of clarity by party candidates, and some organisation Democrats, on the busing issue. Furthermore, on environment-related issues, of which there was evidence of major concern emerging in the electorate, Democratic office seekers did not attempt to realign political forces in the state: they did not attempt to redefine political reality for the citizens.

Several specific explanations can be given to account for this failure of party democracy, and these are outlined below. All suggest one general conclusion: at the time of the amateur insurgence into the party in the mid 1960s, and independently of this insurgence, it had already begun to decompose, and this decomposition continued.

Intra-party accountability was ineffective both in Denver and statewide because:

i. Activist effort became dispersed. Amateur politics in Denver did not dissolve, as other reform movements have done, through a decline in the number of participants. (Of course, such a decline might now ensue, given the limited influence of amateur politics in recent years.) Rather, even with more party participants after 1970, the movement itself became decentralised. The availability of an exit option – the initiative process – was one cause of this. Moreover, Denver's adop-

168

tion of single-member districts after 1966 had made it more difficult to discipline members of the General Assembly. Finally, the amateurs had been most successful when they had turned their attention to only one or two offices. Just as such activists in New Hampshire could transform Eugene McCarthy's campaign there in 1968, so could amateurs win Colorado for the Kennedy-McCarthy coalition, and so also could they unseat Byron Rogers. This influence was not possible when their efforts were spread between many different offices. They did discipline several assemblymen in 1970, but this was a year in which the Governorship nomination was not contested by the amateurs and there was no U.S. Senate election. This dispersion of the activists' major resource – manpower – among many offices and initiative campaigns was magnified by the second consideration:

    ii. Candidates for public office became increasingly independent of party. At the beginning of the period of the second influx of liberals into the Denver party, 1966–8, parties were an important electoral intermediary in the city. (With multi-member districts, there was little scope for independent campaigns by General Assembly candidates.) However, during the subsequent years, new campaign techniques became increasingly available to candidates for higher levels of office. These made it possible, and indeed optimal, for the candidate to largely by-pass the party organisation. Gary Hart's U.S. Senate campaign in 1974 was the most obvious example of this. Despite their numbers, activists in the party organisation could not deny the party's nomination to some candidates. In effect, the decentralising of campaigning has eroded the important difference between a pre-primary assembly system of nomination and a direct primary system. As a result, activists can probably be most influential in nominations to two kinds of office. One is that of congressman; this is an office that is not so important as to make possible a completely independent campaign, and not so minor that a candidate's friends cannot control the party organisation. The other is the office of delegate to the National Convention, for which there is no opportunity for an appeal directly to the electorate.[1]

    iii. As a result of the decentralising tendencies, the activists have not constituted a cohesive group, and have therefore been unable to commit candidates to a party programme. Only such a commitment by office seekers will provide them with an incentive to act as a cohesive group in office and, in doing so, to discipline mavericks. The activists have had no standard for evaluating the performance of public officials, and thus the members of the General Assembly, for example, have had no incentive to provide party government. Instead, there has developed an institution providing for pseudo-accountability – the issues conference.

The most general conclusion to be drawn is that, from shortly before the period of amateur insurgence, the Democratic party has been decomposing, and this process has not been arrested by amateur participation in the party. This decomposition is not the electoral 'de-alignment' to which attention has been drawn by Burnham and others,[2] though it may have hastened de-alignment; it is organisational de-centralisation. Office seekers have been able to become more independent of party organisations and have thereby freed themselves from some of the demands of purposive benefit-seekers. One manifestation of decentralisation has been the growing importance of the candidate-centred organisation. One result of it is that candidates are ambiguous on issues, when the logic of electoral competition makes this a rational strategy. Thus, on busing and specific environment issues, candidates have, in the one case, tried to take the issue out of partisan politics, and, in the other case they have acquiesced in having the issues resolved for them in referenda. On busing many activists were prepared to be led on electoral strategy by candidates, and they accepted a vote-minimising strategy in school board elections. On growth related issues, office seekers were constrained from redefining the lines of political division, both by the inconsistent nature of mass opinion on the environment, and by the economic liberalism of many organisation Democrats. From their viewpoint, environmentalist 'exit' to the initiative process made it easier to resolve these conflicts. Obviously, these sources of conflict between the older economic liberalism of city-centre Democrats and the newer suburban liberalism (consumerism, environmentalism, the favouring of low public expenditure and open government) form a major area of future research in American party politics.

Party democracy in the Colorado Democratic party was not merely partial, which would have been expected, but has produced only an ineffective system of accountability to activists. It developed when the parties, as organisations, were decomposing; a decomposition that was furthered by the activists themselves. Their willingness to tolerate *all* views within the party, helped to weaken any intra-party accountability. As the party has been taken over by amateurs, so it has declined as an intermediary between rulers and public. The decline of party in this way is an important phenomenon: it suggests that in America the factors supportive of more responsible parties are weaker than those giving rise to parties as merely 'labels', and the associated candidate-centred organisations. Perhaps the most important conclusion to be drawn from the Colorado study was that neither party nominating rules nor amateur activism could prevent Democratic party politics from becoming more like that long-established in California.

We may now turn to more general considerations. It was asserted in chapter 1 that democracy is an essentially contested concept. One aspect of the continuing controversy about the nature of the concept that is in need of revival relates to the role of parties in a democracy. There is a need in that it seems that, if parties continue to be conceived as peculiar kinds of private association, one source of a developing crisis in the western democracies will remain unchecked. In brief, we claim that, unless parties come to be seen more as public utilities rather than competitive voluntary associations, they will be allowed to continue the practices that have contributed to the alienation of mass electorates in the last twenty years. Obviously, it is not being argued that the alleged 'ungovernability' of some polities in the 1970s, or the single-minded pursuit of group interests that emerged after the apparent political stability of the 1950s, is caused solely by the effects of electoral competition. In many respects the arguments of others, such as Fred Hirsch, draw attention to more important sources of social conflict in liberal-capitalist societies. Nevertheless, it is being asserted that the logic of the electoral market can, and does, increase these destabilising tendencies, because the parties lack an incentive to identify clearly for the public the major alternative future states of the society.

The alienation of electorates from their political leaders has taken several forms in recent years. For example, in the United States there has been declining voter turnout and campaigns centred on the style of the candidates. Britain has experienced large anti-government swings in by-elections and substantial, but inconstant, support for minor parties. Even if it is clear that in some countries alienation from leaders has not led to a lack of faith in the institutions of government, though it has in some others, alienation of the first kind seems widespread.[3] One of the dangers of the view we have called 'populism' is that, when acted upon, it contributes to this decline in public confidence in rulers and potential rulers. The populist conceives the political party as a loose coalition of volunteers who, if they fail to provide goods acceptable to a large number of citizens, will be replaced in the political market by other volunteers who do take heed of the laws of the market. This view is dangerous because in the electoral market the volunteers are not perfect competitors: they compete either as cohesive teams in a single oligopolistic market, or as loosely united groups in a large number of oligopolistic markets. In both cases, but particularly in the latter, the consumers (voters) are at a disadvantage. They lack a conceptual framework, obtained from sources other than those connected with the electoral market, with which to competently evaluate the 'product' (i.e. the party in government) of the oligopolist. Of itself, competition cannot counter the politics of alienation, and may indeed exacerbate it.

The populist view of the proper function of parties in a democracy dominates both elite and mass political thought, and this view has to be contested. Until it comes to be widely accepted that voters alone cannot determine the scope of party competition, the point will not have been reached at which reform of the parties is either possible or desirable. (Premature reform would, almost certainly, be partial, being directed toward the alleviation of certain specific problems, such as 'infiltration by extremists'. The American experience of partial reform suggests that it will either weaken the parties, strengthen the position of office seekers, or be ineffective.) Parties can only be reformed if they are treated as oligopolists providing a good needed by all. With this sort of market structure, the desirability of some public regulation has long been recognised. Yet, if this view of the nature of parties is accepted, an important question must be posed. How could party activity be regulated for the public's benefit, without providing a government with the opportunity to undermine democracy by interfering in the activities of its competitors? It is because the question has seemed difficult to answer that the populist conception of party seems so attractive: if party candidates are competing in something akin to a perfect market, the problem of how to regulate them does not arise.

Ironically, in America, where the populist view of democracy is more widely accepted than in Britain, there has been less adherence to the principle of not regulating the parties. Of course, the reason for this is that sectionalising of politics, as occurred in the 1890s, came to be seen as the one factor that could, and did, restrict the operation of a competitive market; once local monopolies were established they were difficult to break down. The public regulation of parties in the Progressive era came about because of a widespread recognition that special circumstances seemed to have been responsible for a monopoly structure. Such monopolies restricted the opportunities for citizens to present themselves as candidates and compete on fair terms with the dominant party's candidates. Although U.S. Supreme Court decisions undermined the control of monopolies established by the Sherman Act of 1890, the courts did not similarly find state regulation of parties unconstitutional. Thus, today, state law normally defines the nomination processes of parties. Moreover, through such Supreme Court decisions as those involving the abolition of 'white primaries' and the upholding of most of the provisions of the 1974 Federal Elections Campaign Act, the courts have further identified a legitimate public interest in the procedures of the parties. In Britain, parties, as legal entities, remain purely private associations although the near-duopoly is maintained principally by an electoral law that is particularly destructive to minor party competition.

Nevertheless, in neither the U.S. nor Britain does a public authority influence directly the supply of the party's product in the way that oligopolistic suppliers of essential goods can be regulated. Indeed, oversight by a public body of a party's equivalent of price, product quality, and future capital investment would seem to involve the negation of democracy. However, it is exactly this sort of control – control over a firm's output – that is accepted as necessary in the case of quasi-competitive public utilities such as the electricity and gas industries. In America, state regulatory commissions are normally responsible for ensuring that the interests of the public are not harmed by the self-interested activity of power and telephone companies. In Britain this conflict between public and private interest has been resolved by placing these essential services in public ownership. Furthermore, British legislation provides for the investigation and regulation of restrictive practices in the supply of products from oligopolies of less essential goods.

It might appear that the democrat faces a dilemma. Either he accepts that, in competing in 'free' markets, parties are private associations whose activities need not be regulated. In consequence he accepts one result of their competition – their contribution to the alienation of mass electorates from political leadership. Or he rejects democracy for the sake of greater political stability or some other goal, and he permits state interference in the activities of the parties. It is this dilemma that we suggest is a false one. Parties can be treated as public utilities, although in a democracy their product, obviously cannot be supervised as that of other utilities can be. The key to the establishment of parties whose product exhibits responsibility to the electorate is, as the APSA Report recognised, a system of responsibility by party leaders to those who would wish to participate in the parties. In other words control of these oligopolists might be achieved through state regulation of their procedures of self-government.

In general, two factors have led to the absence of responsibility by

office seekers to would-be party participants, and both can be coun-
tered through state intervention without the principle of democracy
being undermined. The first is the need for a party, and consequently
its candidates for public office, to have sufficient resources with which
to conduct election campaigns, policy research and related activities.[4]
This need for finance has restricted responsibility to party participants
in two ways. Firstly, in all western democracies, both the formal party
organisations and individual candidates have tended to become finan-
cially dependent on special interests, particularly labour unions and
business. This has resulted in the institutionalisation of these interests
within the party organisations and, hence, undue responsiveness by
public office holders to them. Secondly, in America, the increasing
relative importance of financial resources in campaigns for some
offices, together with the ability of candidates to raise funds independently of party organisations, has further weakened party ties among
public officials. This second consideration has been evident in a new
style of campaigning, especially for U.S. Senate seats, in which many of
the resources of the party organisation are unnecessary.

The second factor that has prevented the growth of intra-party
responsibility is the absence of effective procedures by which party
activists can regularly influence, and possibly discipline, public office
holders. In Britain, continued public adherence to the Burkean stric-
tures about the role of a representative in Parliament, coupled with the
effects of a membership style of nomination, has rendered inoperative
the systems of accountability the parties have in theory. In America,
primaries open to all would-be candidates have minimised the potential for cohesive party teams. Moreover, American reformers have
rarely tried to set up the formal procedures of accountability by office
holders to participants that supposedly characterised the European
socialist parties. Indeed, the tradition of the supremacy of electoral
control over all others in affecting the behaviour of representatives
(the need for only an 'exit' and not a 'voice' mechanism), has been
strong in America, even if not dominant, as in Britain. Furthermore,
party reformers in America have not usually shared the enthusiasm of
Woodrow Wilson or E. E. Schattschneider for 'cabinet government' or
'party government'. They have been hostile to the idea of party as a
cohesive team, because often they have seen this as incompatible with
government open to all, and not just a few, interests. They have wanted
to maximise party responsiveness, and have thereby provided for less
responsibility.

The point that needs to be understood is that a public monopoly in the supply of finance, and a public role in the guaranteeing of internal accountability for the parties, is not incompatible with the maintenance of democracy. Neither freedom of association nor the free expression of ideas are restricted by the enforcement of standards that would ensure access for all interests to the policy-making process. Indeed, in both Britain and America the principle of regulating, at least in part, the *modus operandi* of parties has long been accepted, even though the sorts of measures necessary to maximise accountability have not been implemented. Since 1885, British electoral law has severely restricted the expenditures made by parliamentary candidates such that in real terms election expenditure per elector is now much less than in the 19th century. Furthermore, there are strict guidelines on the availability of television exposure for candidates. The supervision of contributions to party income has not been introduced generally, although there is an obvious exception to this – the law governing the political levy collected by trade unions.

In America public controls on election expenditures have never been effective. In 1974 an indirect approach, public funding, was used in an attempt to limit rapidly increasing expenditures in presidential campaigns. Candidates for their party's nomination had to demonstrate an ability to raise funds from a large number of small contributors before they became eligible to receive a similar amount from the public fund. After nomination, candidates opting to receive public funding could not accept private contributions. No candidate was compelled to finance his campaign from public funds. Moreover, unlike state aid to parties in many of the European countries, for example Norway and Finland, the funds were allocated to candidates rather than the parties and they were provided solely for campaign expenditures. Funds were not provided for permanent policy-research units within the party organisations. Now, it is in the extension of the system of public financing to provide for research facilities that there lies the best opportunity for freeing the parties from the financial support of special interests. Indeed, in West Germany the desire to free the parties from dependence on business interests provided the impetus for the provision of state funding, first introduced in 1968.[5]

The other aspect of public involvement in the parties to make them more accountable is regulation of their internal accountability. In this respect the United States has gone further than other western democracies, at least in regard to nominations to public and party office. The intention of the Progressive reformers was to democratise the parties, although to this end they concerned themselves with the process of nomination, rather than with other forms of internal democracy. In fact, they had the effect in many states of destroying parties, rather than democratising them. When primary laws made it possible for any would-be candidate to compete at a primary, loose legislative coalitions and 'look-alike' parties ensued.

That polities in the past have failed to regulate parties effectively in the interest of the public, is no reason for now ignoring this as a solution to the destabilising effects of party competition. Parties are essential to democracy, in that it is only through their competition that citizens can come to understand the major divisions in the society and the major alternative future conditions of that society. Nevertheless, there is little incentive for party candidates seeking public office to practise this form of competition. To compete in this way would be to choose an unsafe electoral strategy, and thus party competition tends to produce ambiguity on public issues. The result is the increasing disillusionment of an electorate that now cannot comprehend why their ability to satisfy wants seems not to be increased by the activities of those claiming to represent their interests. If the political education of citizens is decreasingly performed by parties in western democracies, then the prospect of creating future political stability is diminished. Yet, in an era in which worker participation in industry has emerged as a subject for public discussion, party democracy has received remarkably little attention. In many countries parties are in need of rejuvenation for, both as educators of the public and as electoral intermediaries, they are in continuing decline. Their atrophy will continue until the perfect competition (private firm in a perfect market) concept of party and party candidacy is widely challenged. Only when parties come to be seen as suppliers of essential commodities, operating in oligopolistic markets, can the process of their rejuvenation begin.

Appendix A: The Conduct of the Research in Denver

The research in Denver was conducted in two stages: the first during March and April 1976 and the second between July and October 1976. The analysis of documents and newspapers, together with some of the personal interviews, was completed during the first stage of the research. The second stage of the research mainly consisted of the interviews with the legislators and interest-group lobbyists, and the administration of a mail survey questionnaire. In all, there were 48 personal interviews with state legislators, party office holders, candidates, district captains, other Democratic activists and interest group lobbyists. Fifteen of the interviews were with state legislators who served in either 1973/4 or 1975/6 sessions of the state General Assembly.

The activists surveyed were the 102 member Executive Committee of the Denver Democratic Party; a questionnaire was mailed to those members serving on the committee in May 1976. The first mailing of the questionnaire was sent in July 1976, and a second copy sent to the committee members in September 1976. The total response rate was 66.7 per cent – 68 of the 102 recipients sending back at least partially completed questionnaires. Allowing for the obvious problems of bias in the response rate to this type of questionnaire, the response seems to represent a cross-section of the whole committee. The response rate was at least 50 per cent for the following types of member: party officers, captains-at-large (those nominated by the county chairman), and the captains, co-captains and finance chairmen in 13 of the 17 districts in the city. Three of the four districts in which the response rate was less than 50 per cent are the source of a slight bias in the sample, for they are all located in the western part of the city, and are areas of generally lower income with a higher than normal proportion of Chicano residents. (As a group, Spanish surnamed members of the committee did provide a response rate of more than 50 per cent.) The response rate in these three districts ranged from 20–33 per cent, and

177

given that they are districts of a distinctive character, any arguments based on the results of the survey are probably liable to a slight bias. With this exception, we believe that the respondents were not unrepresentative of the whole membership of the committee.

In all the tables showing results from the questionnaire we use the expression, N=, to denote the total number of respondents answering the particular question.

Appendix B: Organisation and Nomination Arrangements of Political Parties in Colorado

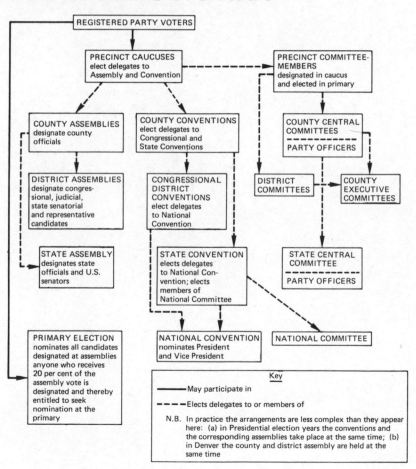

REGISTERED PARTY VOTERS

PRECINCT CAUCUSES
elect delegates to
Assembly and Convention

PRECINCT COMMITTEE-MEMBERS
designated in caucus
and elected in primary

COUNTY ASSEMBLIES
designate county
officials

COUNTY CONVENTIONS
elect delegates to
Congressional and
State Conventions

COUNTY CENTRAL
COMMITTEES
PARTY OFFICERS

DISTRICT ASSEMBLIES
designate congres-
sional, judicial,
state senatorial
and representative
candidates

CONGRESSIONAL
DISTRICT
CONVENTIONS
elect delegates
to National
Convention

DISTRICT
COMMITTEES

COUNTY
EXECUTIVE
COMMITTEES

STATE ASSEMBLY
designates state
officials and U.S.
senators

STATE CONVENTION
elects delegates
to National Con-
vention; elects
members of
National Committee

STATE CENTRAL
COMMITTEE
PARTY OFFICERS

PRIMARY ELECTION
nominates all candidates
designated at assemblies
anyone who receives
20 per cent of the
assembly vote is
designated and thereby
entitled to seek
nomination at the
primary

NATIONAL CONVENTION
nominates President
and Vice President

NATIONAL COMMITTEE

Key

———— May participate in

- - - - Elects delegates to or members of

N.B. In practice the arrangements are less complex than they appear
here: (a) in Presidential election years the conventions and
the corresponding assemblies take place at the same time; (b)
in Denver the county and district assembly are held at the
same time

179

Notes

Chapter 1

1. The term 'party democracy' is, perhaps, ambiguous. Sometimes it is used to refer to democracy *as* party competition. However the application of the term to intra-party democracy is well established; for example, it forms the title of a book by Samuel H. Barnes, *Party Democracy: Politics in an Italian Socialist Federation* (New Haven and London: Yale University Press, 1967).
2. Robert Michels, *Political Parties* (New York: The Free Press, 1962); Moisei I. Ostrogorski, *Democracy and the Organisation of Political Parties* (London: Macmillan, 1902).
3. R. T. McKenzie, 'Policy Decision in Opposition: A Rejoinder', *Political Studies*, V (1957) 180. The assumption that party democracy would weaken the political centre seems to underlie a central argument in David E. Butler, 'The Paradox of Party Difference', in Richard Rose (ed.), *Studies in British Politics* (London: Macmillan, 1969). Objections to party democracy are discussed briefly in A. H. Birch, *Representative and Responsible Government* (London: George Allen and Unwin, 1964) pp. 123–6.
4. Samuel J. Eldersveld, *Political Parties: A Behavioral Analysis* (Chicago: Rand McNally, 1964) pp. 9–10. On industrial democracy see Carole Pateman, *Participation and Democratic Theory* (Cambridge: Cambridge University Press, 1970) and T. E. Cook and P. M. Morgan (eds) *Participatory Democracy* (San Francisco: Canfield Press, 1972) chapter 6.
5. W. B. Gallie, 'Essentially Contested Concepts', *Proceedings of the Aristotelian Society*, LVI (1955–6) 167–98.
6. William E. Connolly, *The Terms of Political Discourse* (Lexington, Mass.: D. C. Heath, 1974) p. 10.
7. The treatment of straightforward majoritarianism as a serious theory of democracy is not confined to self-identified conservatives. Both Dahl and Ranney seem to believe that it is worthwhile to criticise it as a democratic theory. Robert A. Dahl, *A Preface to Democratic Theory* (Chicago: University of Chicago Press, 1956) chapter 2; Austin Ranney, *The Doctrine of Responsible Party Government* (Urbana, Ill.: University of Illinois Press, 1954) p. 11.
8. Brian Barry, *Political Argument* (London: Routledge and Kegan Paul, 1965) chapters 14 and 15; Steven J. Brams, *Paradoxes in Politics* (New York: The Free Press, 1976) chapter 4, and *Game Theory in Politics* (New York: The Free Press, 1975) chapter 4.

9. This criticism of interests is that of J. R. Lucas, *Democracy and Participation* (Harmondsworth: Penguin Books, 1976) p. 106.

10. The traditional equation of democracy with political equality is suggested by Jack Lively, *Democracy* (Oxford: Basil Blackwell, 1975) p. 8. Perhaps the best known defence of democracy as the maximisation of negative freedom is contained in Giovanni Sartori, *Democratic Theory* (Detroit: Wayne State University, 1962).

11. Connolly, *Terms of Political Discourse* (*op. cit.*) chapter 4.

12. L. J. Sharpe, 'American Democracy Reconsidered: Part II and Conclusions', *British Journal of Political Science*, III (1973), 133.

13. By 'pluralism' is meant the analytic pluralism of modern American political science, not the pluralism of, for example, Cole and Laski.

14. The agenda building bias has been analysed by Cobb and Elder, whilst the sources of bias in governmental responsiveness in America have been described in the writing of Schattschneider, Lowi, McConnell and Gamson.

Chapter 2

1. Robert A. Dahl, *A Preface to Democratic Theory* (*op. cit.*); *Who Governs?* (New Haven and London: Yale University Press, 1961); *Modern Political Analysis* (Englewood Cliffs, N.J.: Prentice-Hall, 1963); 'Hierarchy, Democracy and Bargaining in Politics and Economics', in Brookings Lectures 1955, *Research Frontiers in Politics and Government* (Washington D.C.: The Brookings Institution, 1955); Anthony Downs, *An Economic Theory of Democracy* (New York: Harper and Brothers, 1957). Amongst many other works of political science in which a populist conception of democracy is adopted are Robert A. Dahl and Charles E. Lindblom, *Politics, Economics and Welfare* (New York: Harper and Brothers, 1953); Charles E. Lindblom, *The Policy-Making Process* (Englewood Cliffs, N.J.: Prentice-Hall, 1968); Nelson W. Polsby, *Community Power and Political Theory* (New Haven and London: Yale University Press, 1963); David B. Truman, *The Governmental Process* (New York: Alfred E. Knopf, 1951).

2. E. E. Schattschneider, *Party Government* (New York: Holt, Rinehart and Winston, 1942); *The Struggle for Party Government* (College Park, Md.: The University of Maryland Press, 1948); *The Semisovereign People* (New York: Holt, Rinehart and Winston, 1960); Barry, *Political Argument* (*op. cit.*). The American, Schattschneider, like others before him including Woodrow Wilson, regarded the British system of cabinet government within a two party system as the best model of political organisation for providing responsiveness *and* accountability; see also Woodrow Wilson, *Congressional Government* (Boston: Houghton Mifflin, 1885).

3. The intelligibility of statements about wants is questioned in A. J. Watt, 'The Intelligibility of Wants', *Mind*, LXXXI (1972) 553–61.

4. Barry, *Political Argument* (*op. cit.*) p. 80 and pp. 180–2.

5. It is interesting to note that Anthony Downs in a later article drew attention to this point, for it helps to undermine the theoretical founda-

tions of populist democratic theory, of which his *An Economic Theory of Democracy* (*op. cit.*) was an outstanding example. See 'Why the Government Budget in a Democracy is Too Small', *World Politics*, XII (1960) 541–63.

6. For a formal study of the effects of 'sincere' and 'strategic' preferences expressed in voting procedures see Robin Farquharson, *Theory of Voting* (Oxford: Basil Blackwell, 1969).

7. Mancur Olson, *The Logic of Collective Action* (Cambridge, Mass.: Harvard University Press, 1965). A public, or collective, good is a good whose distribution within a group cannot be restricted to those who have contributed towards its provision. An attempt to resolve the 'Olson problem', but one which we believe to be unsuccessful as a general resolution of it, is contained in Norman Frolich, Joe A. Oppenheimer and Oran R. Young, *Political Leadership and Collective Goods* (Princeton, N. J.: Princeton University Press, 1971).

8. Rather different accounts of the features of American politics that exaggerate the effects of governmental responsiveness are provided by William Gamson and Theodore Lowi. Gamson emphasises the power of the status quo in making policy makers more responsive to established, rather than newly formed, interests. Lowi stresses the symbiotic relationship between government and legislators on the one side and interest groups on the other that has developed since the emergence of 'big government' in the New Deal. But both are generally in accord with Schattschneider's conclusion that pressure-group politics is the politics of special interests and not the politics of all interests. William Gamson, 'Stable Unrepresentation in American Society', *American Behavioral Scientist*, XII (1968) 15–21; Theodore Lowi, 'The Public Philosophy: Interest Group Liberalism', *American Political Science Review*, LXI (1967) 5–24, *The End of Liberalism* (New York: W. W. Norton, 1969). Similar themes are developed in Grant McConnell, *Private Power and American Democracy* (New York: Alfred A. Knopf, 1966).

9. Fred Hirsch, *Social Limits to Growth* (London: Routledge and Kegan Paul, 1977).

10. *Ibid.*, p.73.

11. *Ibid.*, p.64.

12. *Ibid.*, p. 52.

13. *Ibid.*, p. 40.

14. Dahl, *A Preface to Democratic Theory* (*op. cit.*) p. 138.

15. This assumption underlies Dahl's discussion of the redevelopment policy in New Haven, *Who Governs*? (*op. cit.*) Chapter 10. In addition, it should be noted that he does not believe that governments should directly reflect public opinion, and this in part constitutes his objection to what he describes as 'Populistic Democracy' (*A Preface to Democratic Theory* (*op. cit.*) chapter 2). Instead, he sees pressure groups as a means by which intensely held opinions can be converted into specific practicable demands on government. Groups not only reveal intensity of preference, but also prevent unrealistic, system-destabilising demands emanating from an ill-formed citizenry from intruding on either the systemic or the institutional agenda of politics.

16. For example, see Isaac Balbus, 'The Concept of Interest in Pluralist and Marxist Analysis', *Politics and Society*, I (1971), 151–77.
17. Connolly, *The Terms of Political Discourse* (*op. cit.*) chapter 2. However, even though Connolly's identification of a person's interests with what he will accept is not the liberal position, we shall see that this consideration of future acceptability of results can be used by a government in a liberal society. For the government must provide for autonomy of choice by the citizens, and it must prevent the oversupply of some policies that would come about if it merely reflected the apparent demand for policies for which strategic intensities of preference had been revealed. To this end the liberal government would have to take account of what citizens will accept as well as what results they want now.
18. In *The Social Contract*, Rousseau argued that participation in what he calls a Republic will result in a natural concern with self-interest developing into a concern for the general welfare. This was made possible because the political institutions of the Republic, together with its socio-economic composition, led citizens to perceive the impossibility of gaining considerable advantage from the pursuit of their own self-interest when others are doing likewise. Because it was in their interest to put the general welfare first, they would do so and would subsequently develop into citizens unconcerned with their own self-interest.
19. Barry, *Political Argument* (*op. cit.*) chapter 10.
20. Barry attributes these conceptions of interest to (i) C. B. Hagan, (ii) S. I. Benn and John Plamenatz and (iii) Bishop Butler respectively.
21. *Ibid.*, p. 176.
22. Connolly, *The Terms of Political Discourse* (*op. cit.*) Steven Lukes, *Power* (London: Macmillan, 1974).
23. Connolly, *The Terms of Political Discourse* (*op. cit.*) p. 64.
24. Barry, *Political Argument* (*op. cit.*) p. 177.
25. Even in America, where in practical politics the identity of a person's wants and interests is most nearly approached by policy makers, evidence of manipulation is accepted as an adequate ground for not taking at face-value someone's wants. For example, in a recent court case a judge granted custody of five adult members of the Reverend Moon's sect to their parents. The parents had requested this so that they could have their offspring 'deprogrammed'. Even though the five members demonstrated in court that their 'creativity had not been impaired by church membership', the judge deemed them to be incompetent and 'at the mercy of artful and designing persons'. *International Herald Tribune*, 26–27 March 1977.
26. Lukes, *Power* (*op. cit.*) p. 34.
27. Theodore M. Benditt, 'The Concept of Interest in Political Theory', *Political Theory*, III (1975) 245–58. In fact, Benditt discusses want *fulfilment* rather than want satisfaction, because he argues that the satisfaction of a want implies a psychological state of pleasure for the beneficiary.
28. Barry, *Political Argument* (*op. cit.*) p. 194.
29. *Ibid.*, p. 179.
30. Frequently 'institutional bias' and 'power' are conflated with one

another. An exception is Steven Lukes who, in *Power* (*op. cit.*) introduces, but does not systematically separate, explanations of the operation of a particular kind of institutional bias from those of certain actors having or exercising power. In part the failure to separate power and institutional bias stems from an ambiguity in the most cited comment on the concept of systemic bias, that of E. E. Schattschneider: 'all forms of political organisation have a bias in favor of the exploitation of some kinds of conflict and the suppression of others because *organisation is the mobilisation of bias*'. (*The Semisovereign People* (*op. cit.*) p. 69.) The ambiguity, which was also embraced in the original analysis of Bachrach and Baratz, hinges on the question of whether organisation enables some actors (those controlling the organisation) to mobilise a bias against others or whether organisation necessarily creates biases irrespective of the intentions of these actors. Schattschneider's arguments about the definition of political cleavages reveal this ambiguity. On the one hand, he argues 'institutions do not treat all forms of conflict impartially, just as football rules do not treat all forms of violence with indiscriminate equality' (p. 70). On the other hand, shortly afterwards, he focusses attention on the *exercising* of the advantages of organisation: 'In politics the most catastrophic force in the world is *the power of irrelevance which transmutes one conflict into another and turns all existing alignments inside out*' (p. 72). In this book the term 'institutional bias' is used to refer to that source of advantage in the distribution of benefits to some political actors that emanates from the rules of social, political and economic institutions and the interaction of these institutions.

31. Barry, *Political Argument* (*op. cit.*) pp. 176–8, and 297–9.
32. Flathman, who correctly argues against the identification of interests with self-interest, incorrectly sees the relationship between 'being interested in' and 'having an interest in' as a necessary one. He makes the point that 'to have an interest in an *x* is to be 'interested' in it – an expression that signals an attitude or feeling on *A*'s part.' Richard E. Flathman, 'Some Familiar but False Dichotomies Concerning "Interests"', *Political Theory*, III (1975), 282.
33. Even with a set of institutions that make radical policy initiatives difficult, the United States adopted by constitutional amendment in 1919 a prohibition of the sale of alcohol.
34. Evidence that middle class citizens are more likely to be public-regarding in politics than members of the working class, and in America this corresponds closely to the suburbanite/city dweller categories of this example, is contained in James Q. Wilson and Edward C. Banfield, 'Public-Regardingness as a Value Premise in Voting Behaviour', *American Political Science Review*, LVIII (1964) 876–87.
35. Barry, *Political Argument* (*op. cit.*) chapters 14 and 15.
36. Brams, *Paradoxes in Politics* (*op. cit.*) p. 108. The study to which Brams refers is E. E. Schattschneider, *Politics, Pressure and the Tariff* (New York: Prentice-Hall, 1935).

Chapter 3

1. An extensive bibliography of the socialisation literature is provided by

Jack Dennis, *Political Socialisation Research: A Bibliography* (Beverly Hills: Sage, 1973).

2. When no clear interpretations of the political universe are forthcoming from leaders then, in times of crisis, the patterns of socialisation will be disrupted. This appears to have occurred in America during 1964–74. See, for example, John F. Manley, *American Government and Public Policy* (New York: Macmillan, 1976), pp. 333–51. It can be further argued that this role of political leadership is particularly important in societies where there is least trust in government itself. Although survey evidence shows high popular support in America for its representative institutions, the U.S. is still a good example of a western democracy in which trust in government is low. Ippolito *et al.* have interpreted this as showing that Americans' primary commitment is to direct democracy, rather than representative democracy. However this view ignores the anti-cooperative ('politics of self interest') element that is central in American political life. Dennis S. Ippolito, Thomas G. Walker, and Kenneth L. Kolson, *Public Opinion and Responsible Democracy* (Englewood Cliffs, N.J.: Prentice-Hall, 1976), p. 110. On the problem of the absence of public trust in government in the U.S. see Sharpe, 'American Democracy Reconsidered: Part II and Conclusions', (*op. cit.*) 129–67.

3. Theodore H. White, *Breach of Faith* (New York: Atheneum, 1975), p. 57. Others, such as Kevin P. Phillips, have argued that the effect of television has been to create an independent source of values and opinions that is a rival to political leaders, particularly the President, and this source comprises those employed in the media. K. P. Phillips *Mediacracy* (New York: Doubleday, 1975). On the role of television in American politics see Marvin Barrett (ed.), *The Politics of Broadcasting* (New York: Thomas Y. Crowell, 1973), and Sig Mickelson, *The Electric Mirror: Politics in the Age of Television* (New York: Dodd, Mead and Co., 1972).

4. In fact, Downs seemed to believe that his theory was derived from Schumpeter's. Anthony Downs, *An Economic Theory of Democracy* (*op. cit.*) p. 29.

5. Joseph A. Schumpeter, *Capitalism, Socialism and Democracy* (London: George Allen and Unwin, 1943) p. 270.

6. The closest approximation to control over '*quality*' is probably that provided by the party list system of voting; a version of this is found in West Germany, where a citizen has two votes, one of which is counted in the election of an individual candidate and the other in determining the distribution of the remaining seats between the parties.

7. The absence of an incentive for the citizen to participate in politics on grounds of self-interest is explained in Brian Barry, *Sociologists, Economists and Democracy* (London: Collier-Macmillan, 1970) Chapter 2.

8. On the problem of volunteerism see K. Prewitt, 'Political Ambitions, Volunteerism and Electoral Accountability', *American Political Science Review*, LXIV (1970) 5–17.

9. K. Prewitt and W. Nowlin, 'Political Ambitions and the Behaviour of Incumbent Politicians', *Western Political Quarterly*, XXII (1969) 298–308.

10. Anthony Downs, *An Economic Theory of Democracy* (*op. cit.*) p. 99.
11. Lewis Froman, *The Congressional Process* (Boston: Little, Brown, 1967) p. 170.
12. With seniority largely determining committee chairmanships in the U.S. Congress, an incumbent may attract financial support from groups who want to prevent another congressman from becoming a chairman. For example, in 1974, J. William Fulbright received considerable contributions from the bank lobby in his primary campaign against Dale Bumpers. The lobby knew that Fulbright's defeat would lead to Alabaman Senator Sparkman giving up the chairmanship of the Banking, Housing and Urban Affairs committee to take over the chairmanship of Foreign Relations from Fulbright. Sparkman would then be replaced by a known opponent of the bank lobby, William Proxmire. In fact, Fulbright lost the Arkansas primary despite these contributions, and Proxmire duly became chairman of the Banking committee. See also David R. Mayhew, *Congress: The Electoral Connection* (New Haven and London: Yale University Press, 1974) pp. 92–4.
13. However, one analysis of parties as oligopolists is provided by Donald A. Wittman, 'Parties as Utility Maximizers', *American Political Science Review*, LXVII (1973) 490–8. J. R. Lucas discusses parties in terms of oligopolistic competition, but he seems to believe that the main danger of oligopoly is that it tends to collapse into monopoly. He provides no evidence for this claim, the validity of which is belied by the experience of many oligopolistic industries in Britain (for example, cars and soap). *Democracy and Participation* (*op. cit.*) pp. 190–3. A call for analysis of oligopoly in this context has also been made by Mayhew, *Congress: The Electoral Connection* (*op. cit.*) p. 175. Some of the 'internal contradictions' of electoral competition are outlined in Samuel Brittan, 'The Economic Contradictions of Democracy', *British Journal of Political Science* V (1975) 137–42.
14. Frank J. Sorauf, *Party Politics in America*, 3rd ed. (Boston and Toronto: Little, Brown, 1976) p. 49. In fact, the Supreme Court rejected this claim, and Ohio was forced to place the American Independent Party's Presidential candidate, George Wallace, on the ballot.
15. Olson, *The Logic of Collective Action* (*op. cit.*).
16. The identification of representative government with government involving freely elected representatives is a common one. A. H. Birch, for example, claims that: 'It is generally agreed that a political system can properly be described as a system of representative government if it is one in which representatives of the people share, to a signigicant degree, in the making of political decisions.' '... it is the manner of choice of members of the legislative assembly, rather than their characteristics or their behaviour, which is generally taken to be the criterion of a representative form of government.' *Representative and Responsible Government* (*op. cit.*) pp. 13 and 17.
17. Albert O. Hirschman, *Exit, Voice and Loyalty* (Cambridge, Mass.: Harvard University Press, 1970); see also Brian Barry, 'Exit, Voice and Loyalty', *British Journal of Political Science*, IV (1974) 79–107.
18. A much more sophisticated analysis of party competition is contained in

David Robertson, *A Theory of Party Competition* (London: John Wiley, 1976).

19. In fact Downs believed that only when there was a 'normal' distribution of electors along the continuum would the parties tend to move towards the centre. When most voters were not located in the political centre but on the left and right flanks of the ideological spectrum, the fear of extremist abstentions would keep the two parties apart, *An Economic Theory of Democracy* (*op. cit.*) pp. 118–19. However, the two cases are not as dissimilar as Downs suggests. Even with a bimodal distribution there may still be an incentive for one party to move 'inwards' if, for example, the other party's extremists have a much higher propensity to abstain when their party becomes more centrist. Furthermore, if we assume, as does Downs, that the extremist believes that there is at least some difference between a slightly left-of-centre party and a slightly right-of-centre party, then a centrist-moving party may eventually out-bluff its extreme voters into supporting it by showing that it will not return to an extreme position. It is difficult to be more specific than this because the strategies adopted by the parties will depend on the assumptions they make about the ability of new parties to form to capture 'abandoned' groups of voters on the ideological continuum. Downs does not resolve the problem because he does not explain why new parties will form: he does not state, for example, what proportion of the electorate must be available to be captured to provide an incentive for the formation of a party. What he does is to assume that certain numbers of parties are simply 'appropriate' for particular kinds of voter configuration, but this does not enable him to predict the movement of parties along the continuum. With certain assumptions about the formation of new parties, any movement by either party towards the centre of the continuum would lead to it being outflanked by a new party even when there is a normal distribution of voters.

20. Two of the most recent analyses of the Liberal voter as protester are Peter H. Lemieux, 'Political Issues and Liberal Support in the February 1974, British General Election', *Political Studies* XXV (1977) 323–42 and James Alt, Ivor Crewe and Bo Sarlvik, 'Angels in Plastic: The Liberal Surge in 1974', *Political Studies*, XXV (1977) 343–68.

21. George Dangerfield, *The Strange Death of Liberal England* (London: Constable and Co., 1936). Downs's argument that, in 1900 the Labour party leaders 'correctly guessed that they could outflank the Liberals by froming a party to the left of the latter because there were now many newly enfranchised voters well to the left of the liberals' (pp. 128–9) is undermined by studies such as that of Adam Przeworski. Przeworski argues that extensions of the franchise in Europe have led to the participation in elections of those 'who are already organised by political parties and have a clear and stable preference' with regard to party. In other words, after 1900 the Liberal and Conservative parties were not faced by an electorate demanding a product they would not supply; rather they had previously socialised the electorate into patterns of voting – they had swayed their beliefs about what products they wanted. Adam Przeworski, 'Institutionalisation of Voting Patterns, or is Mobil-

isation the Source of Decay?', *American Political Science Review*, LXIV (1975) 59.

22. Walter Dean Burnham, *Critical Elections and the Mainsprings of American Politics* (New York: W. W. Norton, 1970). In the U.S. there are pressures on the minority party not to seek a redefinition because this may extend the party's exile in the political wilderness. At the time it was argued that this was one of the effects of the Goldwater Presidential candidacy in 1964. For the argument that party realignment in the U.S. normally results in a majority party ('the sun') and a minority party ('the moon') see Samuel Lubell, *The Future of American Politics* (Garden City, N.Y.: Doubleday, 1956) and E. C. Ladd, *American Political Parties* (New York: W. W. Norton, 1970).

23. On the decline of the Liberal party in Britain see R. Douglas, *The History of the Liberal Party, 1895–1970* (London: Sidgwick and Jackson, 1971).

24. For a variety of reasons it can be argued that the 1964–6 Labour government should not be placed in the category of ministries that attempted a radical change in public policy. An additional factor that discourages a 'progressive' government from implementing radical policies can be derived from Downs, 'Why the Government Budget in a Democracy is too Small' (*op. cit.*). Downs argues that the citizens want the benefits of public goods but are more aware of the cost (higher taxes) than the individual benefits. Thus the government that requires higher taxes for its policies is at a disadvantage.

25. In the 1950s the 'Michigan school' of voting analysis explained that partisan identification, and not policies, was the most powerful determinant of voting behaviour in America. See Angus Campbell, Philip E. Converse, Warren E. Miller and Donald E. Stokes, *The American Voter* (New York: John Wiley, 1960). On the recent breakdown of party loyalty and the rise of issue voting in America see especially Norman H. Nie, Sidney Verba and John Petrocik, *The Changing American Voter* (Cambridge, Mass. and London: Harvard University Press, 1976); David E. Repass, 'Issue Salience and Party Choice', *American Political Science Review*, LXV (1971) 389–400; Richard Boyd, 'Electoral Trends in Postwar Politics', in James David Barber (ed.), The American Assembly, *Choosing the President* (Englewood Cliffs, N.J.: Prentice-Hall, 1975).

26. For example, the *Daily Express* publicised itself for many years as a 'quality' paper in an atttempt to reassure some readers and potential readers that it was a 'respectable' alternative to the *Daily Telegraph*. Declining sales and the consequent adoption of a tabloid layout led to the abandonment of this policy.

27. A theoretical account of the incentives for elected public officials to take ambiguous stances as part of their electoral strategies is Benjamin I. Page, 'The Theory of Political Ambiguity', *American Political Science Review*, LXX (1976) 742–52.

28. Without taking the analogy too seriously, it is akin to car manufacturers continuing to emphasise the maximum speeds of their respective vehicles, when the road casualty rate is high and has been rising for some years. In addition to the British example of obsolete sources of political

division, it should be noted that Herbert Tingsten has made a similar claim about Swedish parties, 'Stability and Vitality in Swedish Democracy', in A. J. Milnor (ed.), *Comparative Political Parties* (New York: Thomas Y. Crowell, 1969).

29. These references are to (i) Hugh Gaitskell's attempt to change the political perspective of the party through the abolition of the public ownership clause (Clause 4) in the party's constitution, and (ii) the Conservative's adoption of policies intended to reduce government intervention in, and responsibility for, the private sector of the economy.

30. Downs, *An Economic Theory of Democracy* (*op. cit.*) p. 96.

31. In Britain party memberships are small and have been declining in size since the 1950s, particularly in the Labour party. Even the party's general secretary was forced to admit in early 1977 that most constituency parties have fewer than the one thousand individual members that supposedly all have (*Guardian* 7 March 1977). Richard Rose points out that even in 1970 there were some safe Labour seats with fewer than 50 members, and that only one sixth of the constituencies had Labour parties with more than one thousand members. The average size of constituency party membership was 500–600. This would suggest that there were then about 350,000 members in Britain. The Conservative party, which has always been more able to recruit a large number of 'social' members who are rarely active on the party's behalf, had about 1½ million members in 1970 – an average of 2700 members per constituency. Richard Rose, *The Problem of Party Government* (Harmondsworth: Penguin Books, 1976) p. 153. See also Colin Martin and Dick Martin, 'The Decline of Labour Party Membership', *Political Quarterly*. XLVIII (1977) 459–71. On the decline in the membership of other European parties see Leon D. Epstein, *Political Parties in Western Democracies* (New York: Praeger, 1968) pp. 164–5 and 251–5.

Chapter 4

1. Joseph A. Schlesinger, 'The Primary Goals of Political Parties: A Clarification of Positive Theory', *American Political Science Review*, LXIX (1975) 840–9.

2. This consideration suggests an important qualification to an argument introduced by Frolich and Oppenheimer. They claim that 'Differences between political and economic competition are critical for the understanding and analysis of the incentive structures facing the political entrepreneur. In economic competition one competes for shares of the market. In politics one competes to drive one's opponent out of business'. Unless there is a tendency for party duopoly to collapse into monopoly, it would be irrational for a party to attempt to drive its competitor out of business. Of course, in attempting to win the next election, the party is *necessarily* trying to remove the opponent temporarily. However, the best strategy for maximising its stay in office in the long term may involve it not presenting issues to the public that would provide it with only a short-term advantage. Norman Frolich and Joe A. Oppenheimer, *Modern Political Economy* (Englewood Cliffs, N.J.: Prentice-Hall, 1978) p. 71.

3. William E. Wright, 'Comparative Party Models: Rational-Efficient and Party Democracy', in Wright (ed.), *A Comparative Study of Party Organisation* (Columbus, Ohio: Charles E. Merrill, 1971).

4. Joseph A. Schlesinger, *Ambition and Politics* (Chicago: Rand McNally, 1966). Examples of research that draws on the conceptualisation in his book are: Joseph A. Schlesinger, 'The Governor's Place in American Politics', *Public Administration Review*. XXX (1970) 2–10; E. N. Swinterton, 'Ambition and American State Executives', *Midwest Journal of Political Science*, XII (1968) 538–49; Prewitt and Nowlin, 'Political Ambitions and the Behaviour of Incumbent Politicians'(*op. cit.*); Prewitt, 'Political Ambitions, Volunteerism and Electoral Accountability,' (*op. cit.*); Gordon S. Black, 'A Theory of Professionalisation in Politics', *American Political Science Review*, LXIV (1970) 865–78; Michael L. Mezey, 'Ambition Theory and the Office of Congressman', *Journal of Politics*, XXXII (1970) 563–79; Gordon S. Black, 'A Theory of Political Incentives: Career Choice and the Role of Structural Incentives', *American Political Science Review*, LXVI (1972) 144–59; Jeff Fishel, *Party and Opposition* (New York: David McKay, 1973); Paul L. Hain, 'Age, Ambitions, and Political Careers: the Middle Age Crisis', *Western Political Quarterly*, XXVII (1974) 265–74.

5. Schlesinger, 'The Primary Goals of Political Parties,' (*op. cit.*); William H. Riker, *The Theory of Political Coalitions* (New Haven: Yale University Press, 1962). The ambition of an individual to have a political career, as someone might simply want to become a stockbroker rather than a civil servant, is actually confused by Schlesinger with two other reasons for seeking office. The first is the desire to acquire the status that accompanies political office (p. 843). The second is the desire to obtain office 'because it is there' and cannot be acquired by all men (p. 843 and 848). But the person who wishes to become a political broker is not logically committed either to the pursuit of status or the challenge ethic.

6. This characterisation of the types of political reward is introduced in Peter B. Clark and James Q. Wilson, 'Incentive Systems: A Theory of Organisation', *Administrative Science Quarterly*, VI (1961) 129–66.

7. In the U.S. some commercial and other organised interests 'hedge their bets' by making financial contributions to candidates of both parties. The main consideration in this strategy seems to be a desire to maintain 'a sympathetic ear' in Washington whoever is in the White House or whichever party controls the Congress.

8. Michels introduced this argument when discussing the ability of strike leaders in Turin in 1907 to operate counter to the decision of the workers. He claimed that the leaders were not removed because of a rank and file desire not to appear weak in the face of the bourgeoisie. Michels, *Political Parties* (*op. cit.*) p. 169.

9. The decline of party, and the growing importance of incumbency, as an influence on re-election to the Senate in the post war years is examined in Warren Lee Kostroski, 'Party and Incumbency in Postwar Senate Elections: Trends, Patterns and Models', *American Political Science Review*, LXVII (1973) 1213–34.

10. For an analysis which is based on the allocation of time by Presidential

candidates to the various American states see Brams, *Game Theory and Politics* (*op. cit.*) chapter 7.

11. Samuel H. Barnes, 'Party Democracy and the Logic of Collective Action', in William J. Crotty (ed.), *Approaches to the Study of Party Organisation* (Boston: Allyn and Bacon, 1968) p. 115.

12. An ideology is a type of promissory symbol, something which is cheap to supply and is a substitute for the delivery of 'material' rewards both now and in the future. For an analysis of promissory and other kinds of symbolic rewards see Robert E. Goodin, 'Symbolic Rewards: Being Bought Off Cheaply', *Political Studies*, XXV (1977) 383–96.

Chapter 5

1. For an analysis of the 'party government' origins of the theory see Austin Ranney, *The Doctrine of Responsible Party Government* (Urbana, Ill.: University of Illinois Press, 1962). The conditions necessary for the practice of party government are outlined in Rose, *The Problem of Party Government* (*op. cit.*) pp. 372–5. There have been few contemporary theoretical defences of party democracy in the socialist tradition, but brief exceptions are Ralph Miliband, 'Party Democracy and Parliamentary Government', *Political Studies*, VI (1958) 170–4 and C. B. Macpherson, *The Real World of Democracy* (Oxford: Oxford University Press, 1966) pp. 20–21.

2. One book in which these arguments reappeared is John S. Saloma III and Frederick H. Sontag, *Parties* (New York and Toronto: Random House, 1972).

3. Committee on Political Parties of the American Political Science Association, 'Toward a More Responsible Two-Party System', *American Political Science Review*, XLIV (1950) Supplement. Its critics have included: Austin Ranney, 'Toward a More Responsible Two-Party System: A Commentary', *American Political Science Review*, XLV (1951) 488–99; T. William Goodman, 'How Much Political Party Centralisation Do We Want?', *Journal of Politics*, XIII (1951) 536–61; Sorauf, *Party Politics in America*, 3rd ed. (*op. cit.*) Chapter 16.

4. Gerald M. Pomper, 'Toward a More Responsible Two-Party System? What Again?', *Journal of Politics*, XXXIII (1971) 916–40.

5. APSA report, 'Toward a More Responsible Two-Party System' (*op. cit.*) p. 23.

6. *Ibid.*, p. 23.

7. This point is not recognised by Ranney who believes that the APSA's Report had been unclear about the nature of the realtionship between intra-party and inter-party democracy, *The Doctrine of Responsible Party Government* (*op. cit.*) pp. 156–7. This stems from his claim that the Committee had adopted a 'ticket-voter', rather than a party activist, conception of party membership (pp. 17–18), which he sees as diametrically opposed to Schattschneider's own views on membership. He believes that Schattschneider, as a 'majoritarian democrat' had gone along with the Committee view after being outvoted. This claim of a split between Schattschneider's views and those of the majority of the Committee is perpetuated in David Adamany, 'The Political Science of E. E.

Schattschneider: A Review Essay', *American Political Science Review*, LXVI (1972) 1322.

8. For a discussion of the difference between instrumental and developmental theories of participation see Geraint Parry, 'The Idea of Political Participation', in Parry (ed.), *Participation in Politics* (Manchester: Manchester University Press, 1972).

9. APSA report, 'Toward a More Responsible Two-Party System' (*op. cit.*) p. 66.

10 Wright, 'Comparative Party Models: Rational-Efficient and Party Democracy' (*op. cit.*) p. 20.

11. APSA report, 'Toward a More Responsible Two-Party System' (*op. cit.*) pp. 65–73.

12. Austin Ranney, *The Doctrine of Responsible Party Government* (*op. cit.*) pp. 17–19.

13. E. E. Schattschneider, *The Semisovereign People* (*op. cit.*) p. 64. The main themes of this book were first developed in 'Intensity, Visibility, Direction and Scope', *American Political Science Review* LI (1957) 933–42.

14. *Ibid.*, p. 66 (italics in original).

15. *Ibid.*, pp. 71–2 (italics in original).

16. *Ibid.*, p. 73 (italics in original).

17. Walter Dean Burnham, 'The Changing Shape of the American Political Universe', *American Political Science Review*, LIX (1965) 7–28; 'Party Systems and the Political Process', in William Nisbet Chambers and Walter Dean Burnham (eds.), *The American Party Systems* (New York: Oxford University Press, 1967); *Critical Elections and the Mainsprings of American Politics*; 'Theory and Voting Research: Some Reflections on Converse's "Change in the American Electorate"' *American Political Science Review*, LXVIII (1974) 1002–23, 'American Politics in the 1970s: Beyond Party?', in Louis Maisel and Paul M. Sacks (eds.), *The Future of Political Parties* (Beverly Hills and London: Sage, 1975). The most direct challenge to Burnham's interpretation of realignment in the 1890s is Jerrold G. Rusk, 'The Effect of the Australian Ballot on Split Ticket Voting: 1876–1908', *American Political Science Review*, LXIV (1970) 1220–38.

18. Burnham characterises the political consequences of the 1896 realignment as follows: 'The alignment pattern was broadly composed of three subsystems: a solidly Democratic South, an almost equally solid Republican bastion in the greater Northeast, and a quasi-colonial West from which protesting political movements were repeatedly launched against the dominants components of the system. The extreme sectionalism of this system can be measured by virtually any yardstick. For example, excluding the special case of 1912, 84.5 per cent of the total electoral vote for Democratic presidential candidates between 1896 and 1928 was cast in the Southern and Border states.' 'Party Systems and the Political Process', in The *American Party Systems* (*op. cit.*) p. 300. His conception of the realignment cycle is outlined on p. 288 of this article.

19. However, in 'Theory and Voting Research' (*op. cit.*) Burnham moves away from a straightforward economic-political analysis of realignment

to take account of the significance of the religious divisions emphasised by Richard Jensen in *The Winning of the Midwest* (Chicago: University of Chicago Press, 1971).

20.   *Ibid.*, p. 1022 and p. 1053.

21.   For a comparative analysis of labour unions in American city party organisations see J. David Greenstone, 'Party Pressures on Organised Labor in Three Cities', in M. Kent Jennings and L. Harmon Zeigler (eds.), *The Electoral Process* (Englewood Cliffs: Prentice Hall, 1966).

22.   Schattschneider, *Party Government* (*op. cit.*) pp. 86–7. Curiously, given his view of parties as protectors of general, rather than special, interests, Schattschneider actually welcomed the increasing identification of national interest groups with particular parties in the 1950s. E. E. Schattschneider, 'United States: The Functional Approach to Party Government', in Sigmund Neumann (ed.), *Modern Political Parties* (Chicago: University of Chicago, 1956) pp. 213–14. Yet, if this tendency does weaken regionalism and 'bossism' in the parties, it is also likely to increase the kind of symbiotic relationships between organised interests and government that have worried writers such as Lowi.

23.   In America the most important debates on this subject were in connection with the Federal Elections Campaign Act of 1974. Although the United States was not the first western democracy to institute some form of public financing of electoral activity, following in the wake of 'Watergate' the Act gained considerable publicity both inside America and elsewhere. For an analysis of the Act see David Adamany and George Agree, 'Election Campaign Financing: the 1974 Reforms', *Political Science Quarterly*, XC (1975), 201–20; see also Frank J. Sorauf, *Party Politics in America* 3rd ed. (*op. cit.*) pp. 327–32. Bibliographies of the research on public financing of campaigns in America are contained in the first three articles in Louis Maisel (ed.), *Changing Campaign Techniques* (Beverly Hills and London: Sage, 1976). In Britain the debate has been stimulated by the report of the 'Houghton Committee': *Report of the Committee on Financial Aid to Political Parties* (Cmnd. 6601).

24.   Birch, *Representative and Responsible Government* (*op. cit.*) pp. 126–30.

25.   Analyses of the precise nature of the 'iron law of oligarchy' are contained in C. W. Cassinelli, 'The Iron Law of Oligarchy', *American Political Science Review*, XLVII (1953), 773–84 and John D. May, 'Democracy, Organisation, Michels', *American Political Science Review*, LIX (1965), 417–29.

26.   Gordon Hands, 'Roberto Michels and the Study of Political Parties', *British Journal of Political Science*, 1 (1971) 160.

27.   It is worth noting that one set of researchers has maintained that this phenomenon has occurred to a lesser degree in the Norwegian Labour Party than in its British counterpart. Contrary to the explanation that is presented here, they argue that this is the result of an indirect party structure in the British Labour Party, which makes it more difficult for the party members to establish effective claims. E. Spencer Wellhofer, Victor J. Hanby and Timothy M. Hennessy, 'Clientele Markets, Organisational Dynamics and Leadership Change: A Longitudinal Comparison of the Norwegian and British Labor Parties', in Maisel and Sacks, *The Future of Political Parties* (*op. cit.*).

28. It is interesting to contrast the problems facing the parties in Britain and America in 1976. In Britain, Labour M.P.s Prentice and Tomney, claimed that the Labour party was in danger of being taken over by small groups of 'extremists' who appear to have denied the party nomination to these two men. Whatever the validity of this argument, it is certainly the case that the decline in party membership in both major parties since the 1950s has been dramatic. And many constituency parties have only a skeleton membership that could be taken over by a small, but determined, minority. On the other hand, in America there is periodically thrown up a 'name' winner in a primary system that makes it easy for a candidate to get on the ballot. In 1976 it was a John Adams, who won the Republican nomination for the Senate in New Hampshire. In 1962, a man named Kennedy (an ultra-conservative) won the Democratic nomination for Congressman at Large in Ohio, and there have been many other instances in elections for lesser offices.

29. Accounts of this diversity are contained in V. O. Key, *Politics, Parties, and Pressure Groups*, 4th ed. (New York: Thomas Y. Crowell, 1958) chapter 14; Frank J. Sorauf, *Party Politics in America*, 3rd ed. (*op. cit.*) chapter 9; Frank B. Feigert and M. Margaret Conway, *Parties and Politics in America* (Boston: Allyn and Bacon, 1976) chapter 6.

30. V. O. Key, 'The Direct Primary and Party Structure: A Study of State Legislative Nominations', *American Political Science Review* XLVIII (1954) 1–26 and *American State Politics* (New York: Knopf, 1956) chapters 5 and 6. The assumption that primaries always weaken parties underlies, for example, Leon D. Epstein's claim that 'it appears illogical to combine primaries, intended to make legislators independent of party, with a parliamentary system that requires cohesive legislative parties in order to provide stable government.' 'A Comparative Study of Canadian Parties', *American Political Science Review*, LVIII (1964) 55.

31. R. John Eyre and Curtis Martin, *The Colorado Preprimary System* (Boulder, Colo.: Bureau of Governmental Research, University of Colorado, 1967) chapter 7.

32. An account of the establishment of the principle of seniority in selecting committee chairmen is Nelson Polsby, Miriam Gallaher and Barry Spencer Rundquist, 'The Growth of the Seniority System in the U.S. House of Representatives', *American Political Science Review*, LXIII (1969) 787–807. On the subject of the unwillingness of congressmen to enforce party discipline Kay Lawson has argued: 'Theoretically the party may withdraw seniority and committee assignments from an uncooperative legislator, but in practice, such sanctions are reserved for only the most serious cases. There is some evidence that party loyalists are more likely to get preferred committee assignments, but consideration is also given to the electoral *need* of the legislator, especially the freshman, for a particular committee assignment'. *The Comparative Study of Political Parties* (New York: St. Martin's Press, 1976) p. 182.

33. Epstein, 'A Comparative Study of Canadian Political Parties' (*op. cit.*) 54–9.

34. Schlesinger, 'The Primary Goals of Political Parties; A Clarification of Positive Theory' (*op. cit.*).

35. In fact, Schlesinger seems to have in mind only those seeking purposive benefits when he outlines this argument. It is not at all obvious that the interests of the seeker of material or solidary rewards are best served by a membership party.
36. *Ibid.*, p. 848.
37. *Ibid.*, p. 849.
38. This was one of the main considerations that led Epstein to argue that the American type of caucus party was the most advanced form of party organisation, *Political Parties in Western Democracies* (*op. cit.*). This contrasts with the view of Maurice Duverger who had earlier argued that 'caucuses are an archaic type of political party structure', *Political Parties*, 3rd ed. (London: Methuen, 1964) p. 20.
39. For an example of central party intervention see Robert J. Jackson, *Rebels and Whips* (London: Macmillan, 1968) 266–7.
40. Jim Bulpitt, 'English Local Politics: The Collapse of the *Ancien Regime?*', paper delivered to the Annual Conference of the *Political Studies Association*, March 1976.
41. Jackson, *Rebels and Whips* (*op. cit.*) pp. 290–1.
42. This was a close contest which was won by 27 votes out of over 54,000 that were cast.
43. APSA report: 'Toward a More Responsible Two-Party System' (*op. cit.*) pp. 65–6.
44. In terms of their numbers this decline has been more obvious in the House than in the Senate. However the problem of career advancement for Senate moderates is revealed by the fact that two of them (Weicker and Mathias) have publicly mentioned the possibility of a Presidential campaign as an Independent. The trend toward the erosion of the Republican's liberal wing was interrupted in 1974 when many conservative, but few liberal, Republicans lost House elections. See Philip M. Williams and Graham K. Wilson, 'The 1976 Election and the American Political System', *Political Studies*, XXV (1977) 192.
45. On the removal of the House committee chairmen and subcommittee chairmen see Barbara Hinckley, 'Seniority 1975: Old Theories Confront New Facts', *British Journal of Political Science*, VI (1976) 383–99.

Chapter 6

1. For both a statement of the conduct of the research in Denver and also an explanation of the table format see Appendix A.
2. Daniel J. Elazar, *American Federalism*, 2nd ed. (New York: Thomas Y. Crowell, 1972) pp. 96–7.
3. Accurate figures for caucus attendance for the whole period of this study are not available for either Denver or most other counties. However one long-standing precinct committeeman provided me with his own records of attendance at precinct caucuses, which he and others argued were an accurate reflection of the change in the city party since 1968.
   Average attendance before 1968: 6–8
   Attendance in 1968: 34
   Attendance in 1970: 40

Attendance in 1972: 21
Attendance in 1974: 38

4. Interviews 30 and 31 March 1976.
5. Interview 1 September 1976.
6. *Denver Post*, 4 October 1970.
7. Donald B. Johnson and James R. Gibson, 'The Divisive Primary Revisited: Party Activists in Iowa', *American Political Science Review*, LXVIII (1974) 67–77.
8. Andrew Hacker, 'Does a "Divisive" Primary Harm a Candidate's Election Chances?', *American Political Science Review*, LIX (1965) 105–110. However, for an opposed view see Robert A. Bernstein, 'Divisive Primaries do Hurt: U.S. Senate Races, 1956–72', *American Political Science Review*, LXXI (1977) 540–5.
9. Eyre and Martin, *The Colorado Preprimary System* (*op. cit.*) p. 39. It might be added that this enthusiasm for the primary was not reflected in the number of primaries for the U.S. House in the period of their study. Between 1928 and 1962, in only one out of every two instances with a Republican incumbent was there a primary; when there was a Democratic incumbent there were no primaries whatsoever.
10. 76 per cent of the 1976 Executive Committee reported having supported her, whilst only 12 per cent claimed to have supported her opponent Arch Decker.
11. In fact this is a good example of how redistricting to maximise party advantage can go badly awry. Not only did the Republicans fail to hold District 1, but they made District 2 unsafe from challengers in a 'Democratic year'. In 1974 an 8 year incumbent was defeated by a Democrat who was able to hold the seat in 1976.
12. Alan Ware, 'The End of Party Politics? Activist-Officeseeker Relationships in the Colorado Democratic Party', publication forthcoming (1979) in the *British Journal of Political Science*.
13. The other states which have a preprimary convention system of nomination, sometimes known as the 'Hughes plan', are Idaho, Massachusetts, New Mexico, Rhode Island and Utah.
14. Eyre and Martin, *The Colorado Preprimary System* (*op. cit.*) p. 48.
15. In a straw-poll of the Denver party's Executive Committee in January 1968, McNichols obtained more first choice votes (30) and more combined first and second choice votes than the other five candidates. From the 78 members voting, Monfort received only 15 combined first and second choice votes, finishing fifth in the balloting. Source: Minutes of the Meeting of the Executive Committee of the Denver Democratic Party, 11 January 1968.
16. As a Republican until 1970 Floyd Haskell was certainly an outsider. But Gary Hart was also one in 1974. Although Hart was McGovern's campaign director in 1972, his previous experience in Colorado politics was limited to 'fringe' organisational work. Until 1974 he was undoubtedly much less well known in the state than his former colleague in a Denver law practice, Craig Barnes.
17. Some of the arguments used in the remainder of this section were first published in Ware, 'The End of Party Politics?' (*op. cit.*).

18. Interview, 11 September 1976.

19. Page, 'The Theory of Political Ambiguity' (*op. cit.*) 744.

20. An account of the Roth-Meany dispute is contained in Herrick S. Roth, *Labor: America's Two-Faced Movement* (New York: Petrocelli/Charter, 1975) chapter 5.

21. Interview with Harold Haddon, 11 September 1976.

22. A substantial difference in philosophy is taken to be the application of different categories of response contained in the survey question to the respondent's own viewpoint and his perceptions of the legislators' viewpoint, e.g. there is a substantial difference if the respondent sees himself as a moderate and the legislators as conservative. An example of a partial difference in philosophy is the activist who sees himself as moderate-to-conservative and the legislators as conservative.

23. Survey conducted by the Vietnam Veterans Against the War, 20 June 1972. 1500 convention delegates replied – a 50 per cent response rate.

24. Laura Katz Olson, 'Power, Public Policy and the Environment: the Defeat of the 1976 Winter Olympics in Colorado', paper delivered at the Annual Meeting of the American Political Science Association, 1974. The CCF was The Citizens for Colorado's Future; we discuss its role in the Olympic Games controversy in chapter 8.

25. *Denver Post*, 18 March 1976.

26. Because of the opinion poll evidence published in the press, the Republicans undoubtedly believed the proposed Democratic initiative would win in November. Indeed after the Democrats finally started their effort in May, the Republicans attempted to get their own initiative proposal on the ballot which would have simply repealed the food tax. They failed to get the necessary number of signatures by the deadline for filing the initiative with the Secretary of State.

27. 'In several test votes, Democrats in the House seemed willing to settle at the compromise level. But the Governor, joined by State Treasurer Sam Brown and State Democratic Party Chairman Monte Pascoe, was under increasing Democratic party pressure and was increasingly tempted to bypass the Assembly for a big rush to the people'. *Denver Post*, 14 May 1976.

28. Interviews with Democratic state legislators from Denver, August and September 1976.

29. Interview, 10 August 1976.

30. Eyre and Martin, *The Colorado Preprimary System* (*op. cit.*) p. 72.

31. Ron Wolf, 'The Benavidez Case', *Straight Creek Journal*, 16–23 July 1974.

32. Rudolph Gomez, 'Colorado: The Colorful State', in Frank H. Jonas (ed.), *Politics in the American West*, Salt Lake City: University of Utah Press, 1969.

33. Between 1948 and 1962 only 6 out of 64 (9.4 per cent) lower-line designated candidates in Denver won the party's nomination at the primary, Eyre and Martin, *The Colorado Preprimary System* (*op. cit.*) p. 55. Between 1968 and 1976, 8 out of 37 (21.6 per cent) of primary contests led to lower-line candidates winning (Table 6.4). As two of these contests involved a three candidate primary, 8 out of 39 (20.5 per cent) of lower-line candidates won.

34. Interview with June Hurst, former county party secretary, 23 August 1976.
35. In fact unlike the avid fund-raisers described by Jim Bulpitt (quoted in the last chapter), many of Colorado's activists do not enjoy this aspect of party activity. Interview with Mrs. Jean Graham, 5 August 1976.
36. In regard to open housing referenda, an issue like busing which affects basic emotions of the electorate, H. D. Hamilton has argued that a referendum campaign does not result in any changes of opinion amongst voters. In brief, these are issues where campaigning can change little, whereas when the issue does not touch on such potent predispositions, extensive advertising campaigns can win a referendum. This is scarcely a surprising conclusion, for political scientists have long recognised that referenda provide a bias in favour of special interests. H. D. Hamilton, 'Direct Legislation: Some Implications of Open Housing Referenda', *American Political Science Review*, LXIV (1970) 124–37. On the special interest bias of referenda see Penelope J. Gazey, 'Direct Democracy – A Study of the American Referendum', *Parliamentary Affairs*, XXIV (1970–1) 123–39 and W. W. Crouch and V. O. Key, *The Initiative and Referendum in California* (Berkeley: University of California Press, 1939).
37. Plan of Organisation and Rules of the Democratic Party of Colorado (as amended 1974), Article 5, Section 5–13 (d).
38. The ability of a speaker to maintain party rule in a non-parliamentary system is best illustrated by the examples of the Speakers in the U.S. House in the period of the 'Reed Rules', 1890–1910.
39. Schlesinger, 'The Primary Goals of Political Parties' (*op. cit.*) 848.
40. *Denver Post*, 21 July 1974.
41. *Denver Post*, 30 November 1975.
42. *Denver Post*, 9 December 1973.
43. *Colorado Democrat*, 13 March 1976.
44. *Ibid.*
45. Interview, 26 August 1976. Naturally, opposition to mid term conferences at the national level was strong amongst congressional incumbents, Mayhew, *Congress: The Electoral Connection*, p. 177.

Chapter 7

1. Leo M. Snowiss, 'Congressional Recruitment and Representation', *American Political Science Review*, LX (1966) 629.
2. *Denver Post*, 2 September 1970. The unsuccessful Hatfield-McGovern amendment would have placed a time limit on American involvement in Vietnam.
3. The survey was organised for the *Vietnam Veterans Against the War* by Gary Mundt whom I wish to thank for making the survey results available to me.
4. *Denver Post* and *Rocky Mountain News* 24 July 1966.
5. *Denver Post* 26 June 1966.
6. *International Herald Tribune*, 13 May 1972. Survey conducted by Sindlinger and Co.
7. Dennis R. Eckart and John C. Ries, 'The American Presidency', in Leroy

N. Rieselbach (ed.), *People versus Government: The Responsiveness of American Institutions* (Bloomington and London: Indiana University Press, 1975) p. 19.

8. John F. Manley, *American Government and Public Policy* (New York: Macmillan, 1976) p. 344.
9. For a comprehensive account of this litigation, from which some of the background material used here is drawn, see Jessica Pearson and Jeff Pearson, *Litigation and Community Change: The Desegregation of the Denver Public Schools* (Staff Paper prepared for the U.S. Commission on Civil Rights, 1976).
10. *Ibid.*, p. 39.
11. *Ibid.*, p. 85.
12. Evidence of the opposition to the principle of busing in Denver is contained in a survey conducted in 1972: 'As you know, in some places they assign children to schools in other neighborhoods to get a more even spread of minority and white children in schools. Do you think this is a good idea, or not?'

	Anglos	Blacks	Spanish-Surname
Good Idea	16% (79)	63% (95)	26% (208)
Not a Good Idea	81% (403)	31% (47)	69% (555)
No Answer/Not Ascertainable	4% (18)	6% (8)	5% (37)

Denver Urban Observatory, *Majority-Minority Citizen-Voter Attitudes in Denver*, Denver, Colo., 1972, p. 47.
13. Interview 5 August 1976.
14. 1970 Democratic Party State Assembly Resolution No. 16.
15. Interview 31 March 1976.
16. Denver Urban Observatory, *Majority-Minority Citizen-Voter Attitudes in Denver*, p. 46.
17. 'A candidate who said nothing at all about policy would likely be punished at the polls. Thus Richard Nixon in 1968, much accused of ambiguity, proudly claimed that he had taken stands on 227 specific issues, and put together a book of quotations to prove the point.' Benjamin I. Page, 'The Theory of Political Ambiguity', *American Political Science Review*, LXX (1976) 750.
18. *Denver Post*, 8 September 1972 and 30 October 1972.
19. Interview, 2 September 1976.
20. *Denver Post*, 15 October 1972.
21. Pearson and Pearson, *Litigation and Community Change*, pp. 45–46.
22. Interview, 27 August 1976.
23. *Denver Post*, 8 November 1972.
24. *Rocky Mountain News*, 15 September 1974.
25. *Cervi's Rocky Mountain Journal*, 15 September 1974.

Chapter 8

1. This consensus even permitted the use of public funds to send members of the business community to other parts of America to 'sell' Colorado, see Olson, 'Power, Public Policy and the Environment: The Defeat of the 1976 Winter Olympics in Colorado' (*op. cit.*).

2. Survey conducted by William Hamilton and associates, July 1976. Inconsistent attitudes to growth related issues is scarcely surprising given that the choices normally facing the citizen on these matters are those in his role as a small-decision maker. (See chapter 2, section A.)

3. Denver Urban Observatory, *Voter Attitudes in Denver*, Colo.: 1976, pp. 17–18.

4. Richard Schneider, 'Land Use: How Colorado stacks up', *Rocky Mountain News*, 19 May 1974.

5. See chapter 2, section A.

6. Ted Carey, 'Polling played crucial role in elections', *Rocky Mountain News*, 27 December 1976.

7. Barone, Ujifusa and Matthews, *The Almanac of American Politics 1976*, p. 127.

8. 'Economic growth is the state's most important concern' – Republicans: 60 per cent agree, 36 per cent disagree; Democrats: 60 per cent agree, 30 per cent disagree. Survey conducted by William Hamilton and associates, July 1976.

9. 'Economic growth is the state's most important concern' – Business and Professional social group: 32 per cent agree, 63 per cent disagree; total sample: 57 per cent agree, 37 per cent disagree. 'The protection of the environment should be the state's top priority' – Business and Professional social group: 66 per cent agree, 32 per cent disagree; total sample: 66 per cent agree, 26 per cent disagree. Survey conducted by William Hamilton and associates, July 1976.

10. At one meeting in March 1976 Joe Donlon, leader of the building workers' union, handed out bumper stickers which stated 'If You're Hungry Eat an Environmentalist'.

11. Clarke R. Watson, 'Elitism and certain racist views are guiding Colorado's environmental movement', *Colorado Democrat*, 28 August 1976.

12. Interview, 26 March 1976.

13. An account of the background to the controversy over the Games is provided in Olson, 'Power, Public Policy and the Environment', (*op. cit.*).

14. The entrepreneurial aspect of the CCF was emphasised in a highly critical account of the organisation by Norman Udevitz in the *Denver Post*, 'Small but artful Activist Group Wielding Rare Power', 11 October 1972. After the 1972 ballot the CCF was disbanded although four fifths of its 3000 volunteers wanted it to continue in existence. The problem was that there was no agreement about the issues to which it should attend: it was not an environmental group, and in any case there was no need for any more of these groups.

15. Interviews, 26 August and 26 March 1976.

16. Olson, 'Power, Public Policy and the Environment' (*op. cit.*).

17. *Denver Post*, 29 September 1972.

18. *Denver Post*, 3 November 1972.

19. *Denver Post*, 22 September 1974.

20. *Denver Post*, 11 October 1974.

21. Ted Carey, 'Does spending "pollute" Colorado politics', *Rocky Mountain News*, 28 December 1976.

Chapter 9

1. For an account of activist influence on delegate selection see A. Ware, 'The End of Party Politics?' (*op. cit.*).
2. Burnham, 'Theory and Voting Research' (*op. cit.*); 'American Politics in the 1970s' (*op. cit.*).
3. Manley argues that alienation in America in the 1970s did not extend to alienation from the institutions of government themselves. In this view he is undoubtedly correct, although, of course, it might be expected that continuous lack of confidence in political leaders would eventually affect attitudes to institutions. Manley, *American Government and Public Policy* (*op. cit.*) pp. 345–6.
4. In fact, in Britain, the self-interest of candidates in securing election has led to only a small amount of the funds that are available being given to research into policy alternatives. The absence of intensively researched *party* policies, together with criticism of a non-socialist approach to policy during the 1964–70 government, led the Labour government in 1974 to introduce political appointees into the major departments as a way of injecting a 'political dimension' into the policy-making process.
5. *Report of the Committee on Financial Aid to Political Parties*, (Cmnd. 6601), p. 48.

Index